# Next

## Co-authored Books by Darrell Bricker

*Empty Planet: The Shock of Global Population Decline* (with John Ibbitson)

*The Big Shift: The Seismic Change in Canadian Politics, Business, and Culture and What It Means for Our Future* (with John Ibbitson)

*Canuckology: From Dollars to Donuts—Canada's Premiere Pollsters Reveal What Canadians Think and Why* (with John Wright)

*We Know What You're Thinking* (with John Wright)

*What Canadians Think About Almost Everything* (with John Wright)

*Searching for Certainty: Inside the New Canadian Mindset* (with Edward Greenspon)

# Next

## Where to Live, What to Buy, and Who Will Lead Canada's Future

**DARRELL BRICKER**

Co-author of *The Big Shift* and *Empty Planet*

HarperCollins*Publishers*Ltd

Published by HarperCollins Publishers Ltd

First edition

HarperCollins books may be purchased for educational, business,
or sales promotional use through our Special Markets Department.

HarperCollins Publishers Ltd
Bay Adelaide Centre, East Tower
22 Adelaide Street West, 41st Floor
Toronto, Ontario, Canada
M5H 4E3

*www.harpercollins.ca*

Library and Archives Canada Cataloguing in Publication

Title: Next : where to live, what to buy, and who will lead Canada's future / Darrell Bricker.
Names: Bricker, Darrell Jay, 1961- author.
Identifiers: Canadiana (print) 20200163434 | Canadiana (ebook) 2020016354X |
ISBN 9781443446525 (hardcover) | ISBN 9781443446549 (ebook)
Subjects: LCSH: Social prediction—Canada. | LCSH: Economic forecasting—Canada. |
LCSH: Political leadership—Canada—Forecasting. | LCSH: Canada—Social conditions—21st
century. | LCSH: Canada—Economic conditions—21st century.
Classification: LCC FC95.5 .B72 2020 | DDC 303.4971—dc23

Printed and bound in the United States of America
LSC/H 1 2 3 4 5 6 7 8 9 10

*To Nina and Emily, my little family.*
*Without you, there is no me.*

# Contents

# Welcome to New Canada

## Shifting Demand

Canada's demography is changing radically and rapidly, opening a gap, which will soon be a gulf, between the new demand and the old supply. Anyone who is in the business of supplying goods and services to Canadians, ranging from the CEOs of our biggest banks to the operators of small-town dollar stores, needs to understand and deal with these changes to be successful in what I refer to as New Canada.

The good news is these changes aren't bolts out of the blue, and they certainly aren't random. They are reasonably predictable. Why? Because as someone once said, two-thirds of everything can be explained by demographics. Sure, this might be a bit of an overstatement. But understanding demographic change is critical to understanding Canada's future. Knowing the basic facts of the Canadian population—our age patterns, how we work and with whom, and where we will live and work, as well as where we're coming from and where we're going to—tells us a lot about the future of Canada. This knowledge won't fill in all the blanks, because demography isn't destiny. But it represents a significant set of facts that any person dealing with Canadians should be well acquainted with.

I'm a big fan of understanding the nature and direction of demographic change. That's why I lean on emerging demographic realities to tell the story about Canada's future. Demographics represent the essence of any population. Before you look at what people think (opinions) or what they might do (behaviours), it's important to understand who they are and who they are becoming.

What's especially useful about demography is that it is precise, objective, and projectable. Demographics are facts, not opinions, and they're not new. In Canada, we can trace our first regular census back to 1871. Depending on how much you want to stretch things, there was a census in New France as far back as 1666. But the twentieth century was truly Canada's first measured period, and we continue to build on the wealth of information collected every day. For the past hundred years, many aspects of Canadian society have been and are being constantly and thoroughly measured. This includes who we are, how we behave, and what we think.

What's especially useful about demographic data is not what they say about our past or even our present, but what they reveal about our future. Like satellite reports showing future weather patterns, data about people show us our future marketplace patterns. Demographic change is observable from a distance. And it is very, very difficult to alter a demographic trend once it gets rolling. Meaningful demographic changes tend to be locked in for a quarter century or more. Opinions and behaviours, on the other hand, can change quickly depending on the course of events. Therefore, **demographics are especially useful when considering medium- to longer-term scenarios such as the ones I'll present in this book.**

## Turning Data into Advice

I always have data—lots of data. Data are facts, and facts have power. *The Economist* magazine has gone so far as to declare that "the world's most valuable resource is no longer oil, but data."

But while data is a great place to start, it doesn't tell the whole story. There's tragedy and romance in the data, and it's my job to find it and relay it. But the narrative can be elusive. And even if I find it, if I don't tell it right, it can devolve into a spray of useless numbers that the audience quickly forgets. You know, just like that high-school math class you might have hated.

Fortunately, after three decades as a pollster, social researcher, strategic advisor, speaker, and writer, I've learned how to tell a pretty effective story with data. That's a bold statement, I know. But as one of my colleagues likes to remind me, the marketplace always decides. You aren't invited into the room if you can't deliver.

I also have the best day job any data geek can have. I'm the Global CEO of Ipsos Public Affairs, the world's leading social and public opinion research company. We have people on the ground in thirty-eight countries and work for clients all over the world. Ipsos Public Affairs is part of Ipsos, the world's third-largest market research company. Ipsos is based in Paris, France. I just happen to be Canadian and choose to live in Canada. Frankly, I can't imagine living anywhere else. Canada will always be my home (but it's great to hang out in Paris too).

Being part of an amazing organization like Ipsos gives me access to an incredible array of data, but also to some of the world's most insightful social scientists. I learn from them every day. While Ipsos is a global research company, it is also the biggest and best-known research company in Canada. For someone with my skills and interests, being at Ipsos is the perfect match.

What do we do at Ipsos? At the most basic level, our clients hire us to tell them data-driven stories that inspire them to change. For private-sector clients, change means expanding their base of loyal customers. For public-sector clients, it means happier citizens. For political clients, it means more supportive voters. In the end, though, it's all about advice. Numbers are just the tool for coming up with the advice. Over the past thirty years, I have had the privilege of advising prime ministers, premiers, mayors, and countless cabinet ministers and other public officials on public issues. I've also advised many corporations and industries confronted with big consumer challenges in Canada and around the world.

## Declining Birth Rates

To prepare for Canada's future, the first bits of data we need to understand concern our national fertility. The average number of children a Canadian woman gives birth to in her lifetime—that is, Canada's birth rate—is currently 1.5. To maintain a steady state population that neither grows nor shrinks, a country needs an overall birth rate of at least 2.1. That's one child born to replace each of their parents, and a little bit extra to compensate for those of us who can't or decide not to have kids. With a birth rate of only 1.5, we will eventually have more people dying in Canada every day than are being born.

**Canada is half a baby short of the number necessary to maintain its population without immigration.** This wasn't always the case. Back in the early 1960s, which corresponds to the end of Canada's Baby Boom, our birth rate was nearly 4.0. We had natural population growth back then, without immigration.

What changed with our national fertility? While the explanation we often jump to is the mainstreaming of the birth control pill, it's more complicated than that. What really happened is a good news story about the empowerment of Canadian women: taking control of their education and workforce participation; deciding to move to the city; deciding to have smaller families and to start them later (a decade later than the Boomers). What has reduced Canada's birth rate is the choices Canadians—especially Canadian women—are now making about the families they want to have and how they want to live their lives. The birth control pill, long heralded as causing the decline of birth rates, just made these choices easier.

You don't have to take my word for it. Look at your own family. How many children did your grandparents have? What about your parents? What about you? And if your children are old enough to start their own families, how many children do you expect them to have? When you look at the overall picture, I expect that your family's generations have gotten smaller over time. If your family's fertility was drawn as a graph, it would likely look like a funnel: wider at the top, narrower at the bottom, as each progressive generation's birth rate decreased in size. Sure, there are always exceptions. But the power of demography is in understanding the bigger trends, not in getting distracted by the small stuff.

Canada's latest census shows that the total number of kids in our population has now been surpassed by the total number of seniors. The number of people 65 or older outnumbers those under 15 for the first time in our history. When you add it up, you can see how demographic trends like low fertility are critically important to shaping a country's future.

**Declining birth rates are a very big deal for the future of the world and not just for the future of Canada.** Although we don't talk about it much, fertility is crashing in just about every country, and has been for years. Here's a wake-up call. If you look at the top ten most populated countries in the world today, their collective birth rate has fallen by over 50% since 1960. That's right: their birth rate has dropped by more than half in less than sixty years. Eight of the top ten most populous countries now have below-replacement-level birth rates. Humans, as a species, just aren't having as many offspring as we used to. And we're having fewer every day.

One country that's being deeply affected by this low fertility trend is Japan. The Japanese population today is about 126 million people—three and a half times larger than Canada's population. Japan's current birth rate is 1.4, which is only 0.1 smaller than Canada's. But that means that Japan is *more* than half a baby short in replacing its population. Because of its low fertility, Japan's population is expected to shrink by about 13% by 2050. As a result, the Japanese population will have more than 16 million fewer people in just over thirty years. To put this into context, that's six times more than the number of Japanese people who died in the Second World War. Below-replacement-level fertility is a calamitous population trend for Japan and will have a huge impact on their future.

Because of Japan's declining fertility, not only is its population shrinking, it's also becoming much older. Japan has the longest average life expectancy of any large-population country in the world. The average Japanese person now lives to 84 years. It's estimated that by 2060, 36% of the Japanese population will be 65 or older. What are the implications of Japan's aging population? Here's one example of consumer demand shifting as a direct result of demographic change: in 2019, there were more adult diapers sold in Japan than children's diapers. I wonder if diaper manufacturers and retailers saw this coming twenty years ago and acted on it in terms of how they planned to serve today's Japanese market.

We should also keep in mind that **an older population is an**

**expensive population in terms of social costs.** Older citizens need costly pensions and health care. And there will be fewer young Japanese people to absorb the growing economic burden of all this spending on seniors. No wonder the Japanese have become obsessed with perfecting and building service robots. They are now also considering creating guest worker programs, like those Dubai and some other countries have. Guest workers are foreigners who are permitted to live in a country only to work. They are not allowed to remain on a permanent basis. Japan must consider such options because they are running out of young people to offset and take care of their aging population.

Japan is not alone in being challenged by low fertility. Germany has a birth rate of 1.6 and, as a result, is projecting a population decline over the next few decades. Germany's current population is about 83 million. By 2050, it is expected to decline by about 5 million people. That's even after inviting in almost a million migrants from the Middle East and Africa over the last few years.

Here are some other countries that have below-replacement-level birth rates.

- Poland: 1.4
- Greece: 1.3
- Italy: 1.3
- China: 1.7
- Ukraine: 1.4
- Brazil: 1.7
- Russia: 1.8
- Australia: 1.8
- United Kingdom: 1.8
- United States: 1.8

What? China has a fertility problem? It does. And it is very likely lower than the 1.7 number reported by the United Nations. Local sources suggest it could be as low as 1.2, and maybe even below that in major urban centres. Although China does have the world's largest population, by the mid 2020s, its growth will slow to the point where India (with a birth rate of 2.2) will surpass them. While China's one-child policy is often cited as the cause of their fertility decline—larger families invited state sanctions against the parents—there are bigger social forces at play. Even with the recent elimination of the one-child policy, China hasn't experienced a significant second child baby boom. Chinese women are now in the habit of making the same decisions about motherhood as Canadian and European women. And once low fertility becomes the social norm in a country, it's almost impossible to reverse it. Demographic experts call this the low-fertility trap.

China's declining birth rate is being driven by the same forces that have decreased Canada's fertility. You can also roll in the impact of nearly a half-million Chinese people emigrating every year, with little offsetting immigration (new people moving to China). The *Shanghai Daily* reports that in 2011 there were fewer than 600,000 foreigners living in China of a total population of nearly 1.4 billion people.

Which country do you think has the highest birth rate in the world? It's Niger, in Western Africa, with a birth rate of 7.0. But even this number is down from 7.9 in 1980. Niger's total population is about half of Canada's, but half of its people are under the age of 15.

Is having a slowing and eventually declining population in Canada and around the globe a good thing or bad thing? It depends who you ask. An environmentalist will tell you it's absolutely a good thing. If most of the bad things happening to our environment are the product of human activity, it must be better to have fewer people adding to the problems. If you are a businessperson, you likely agree that cleaner air and water are good for humanity, but you also worry that fewer people will mean fewer customers. If you are a public servant, you would celebrate a healthier environment, but you worry about how a shrinking base of younger taxpayers will support a growing elderly population.

Population decline is a complicated subject, especially when it is accompanied by declining fertility and increasing longevity. The results will be mixed and the consequences difficult to predict. What I can say for certain, though, is that everybody should be preparing for it now. It's just a matter of time.

## Looking Through the Rear-view Mirror

I was born in 1961. This puts me on the cusp of being a late Boomer or early Gen Xer (see chapter 1 for definitions of the generations). It can be argued that 1961 was one of the worst postwar years to have been born, given the demographic circumstances in Canada at the time. I am, of course, grateful to have been born at all. And anyone complaining about being born in Canada in the early sixties really needs some perspective on what life has been like for people born at the same time in places like Africa, India, or China. Canadians, even those born in 1961, have been very lucky indeed.

Nonetheless, the reason that 1961 was such a challenging birth year in Canada was that it was at the tail end of the Baby Boom. This huge generational cohort was an unprecedented population anomaly for Canada. It was so big that it eclipsed the entire marketplace for the second half of the twentieth century, forcing the rewriting of the marketing rule book for selling to Canadian consumers. Almost overnight, everything switched from delivering what moms and dads wanted to trying to keep up with the exploding demands of their kids. Baby Boomers had the numbers, which meant they also had the most power in the marketplace.

Babies born in 1961 would forever be seated in the caboose of the Boomer train. Most of our competition would always arrive en masse at the station before we ever made it to the train door. Canadian babies born in the late fifties and early sixties would always be at the back end of a very long line for everything in life.

Apart from being overrun with Boomers, Canada in 1961 was a very white nation. We spoke either English or French at home and at work, but rarely both. That doesn't mean there were no visible minorities, bilingual people, or people who spoke non-official languages. Canada was home to an Indigenous population as well as many immigrants from other nations. But most Indigenous Canadians—at least those who were prepared to acknowledge their Indigenous ancestry—lived in out-of-the-way places where the majority white population rarely ventured. And almost all immigrants came from white-majority countries like the United Kingdom, the United States, Italy, and Germany. After a generation, they were easily assimilated into the majority population.

As for bilingualism, it simply wasn't a priority in Canada before 1968, when Pierre Trudeau became prime minister. Unless you grew up in a place outside Quebec where both official languages were in regular household usage, such as Eastern Ontario or New Brunswick, you most likely spoke only one language, usually English, in your day-to-day life. That was all that was expected of you, even if you worked in our national capital for our national government.

The typical Canadian kid born in 1961 lived with two married parents of opposite genders, in a house full of genetically related siblings. That was the case for me. My parents got married in their early 20s and started their family shortly afterwards. They raised a total of four kids: my identical twin brother, Cal; my younger brother, Russ; my sister, Angela; and me. While a single household containing four children might seem excessive by today's standards, it was the national average back in 1961. We were a country of big households with lots of kids.

I lived my early years in a small Nova Scotia town, Greenwood, in the idyllic Annapolis Valley. My father served in the Royal Canadian Air Force, and Greenwood was an RCAF base back then and remains so today. Greenwood and its environs had a population of about 5,000 in the early 1960s, and it has close to the same population today. My mother worked outside the home, which was rare for Canadian women in the early 1960s. Rarer still was that she ran her own business. She owned the local lady's hair salon. One of my earliest memories is of combs arranged in a glass beaker filled with blue Barbicide that sat on the shelf in my mother's salon.

By 1961, Canada had already become a majority urban nation. Even Greenwood qualified as an urban community, according to Statistics Canada's definition (towns of 1,000 or more). But Canadians in 1961 weren't as clustered into major cities as we are now. Growing up in a smaller hometown was a much more common childhood experience for a Canadian Boomer than it is for kids today.

From a political and economic perspective, 1961 Canada was fixated on the Atlantic Ocean, as it had been throughout our history. Anything important that crossed an ocean, whether it was our international relationships or immigrants, tended to come across Atlantic waters. Sure, if you lived in British Columbia, the Pacific was your ocean. But in a country so completely dominated by Ontario and Quebec, what happened on the Pacific coast rarely mattered for Canada. All the decisions that counted were made by white men living and working in the downtowns of Montreal, Ottawa, and Toronto. To underscore and even rub in this point, national elections were mostly decided before voting was even finished in the West.

Of course, Canada has always nervously cast its eyes south; we are obsessed with the United States. Reaction to the threat of American annexation was what initially brought us together as a nation. But Canada also had a strong imperial tinge to it, especially in English Canada. We still valued our relationship with the British Empire as a counterbalance to the American colossus (hence the Atlantic obsession)—at least emotionally and symbolically, if not practically. Even if foreigners often mistook Canadians for Americans, we were *always* certain that we absolutely weren't them. And our link to the "Old Sod" was part of what we saw as our difference, starting with the Queen's face on our currency.

This imperial affection didn't apply to *La Belle Province*, however. Canada overall has changed a lot since 1961, but one would be hard-pressed to find a province that has changed as much as Quebec has. Back then, Quebec was a more rural, traditional, and religious society than it is today. True, so was Canada generally. But Quebec was even more so, especially when compared to its central-Canadian cousin, Ontario. The election of Liberal Premier Jean Lesage in June 1960 changed all that. Lesage's election kicked off a massive process of modernization in Quebec called the *Révolution Tranquille*, or Quiet Revolution. We're still feeling the effects of it today.

Given how feisty, progressive, and modern Quebec (especially urban Quebec) is, it's sometimes hard to believe that from 1936 to 1960 it was ruled almost without interruption by a single conservative, almost authoritarian premier and his political party. Under Maurice Duplessis and the Union Nationale, Quebec was socially and politically stagnant. It featured a high degree of alignment between an especially conservative Roman Catholic church and the Quebec state. The election of Lesage in 1960 began a revolution that broke down the church's domination of Quebec society. It also kicked off the expansion of francophone rights in Quebec and across Canada. The cultural and political effects of Quebec's transformation dominated the formative years of Canada's Boomers.

While anyone with even a passing interest in Canadian history is aware of how change in Quebec has altered Canada's national character and politics, we tend to be much less aware of how it has also affected Quebec's and Canada's demography. This is especially true for family relationships and fertility. Both have gone through a massive transition in Quebec since 1960.

Canada in our rear-view mirror is very different from the one we now see rushing at us through our windshield. What do we see when we look over the hood?

## Looking Through the Windshield

New Canada started coming together through the tail end of the twentieth century, but has really come into its own since the turn of the millennium. New Canada is a more urban—and especially suburban—place than Old Canada was. It is also much more multicultural, especially in and around our largest cities, where our population is growing fastest.

Along with becoming an urbanized, multicultural society, New Canada's population is much older on average than it was. In 1960, the median age of Canadians was 27. Today, it is an astonishing 41 and getting older every day. This means half of Canada's population is now older than 41, and half is younger. We are getting better at keeping people alive. What we aren't so good at now is making new people. That's why our population continues to age. That's what happens when people live longer and fewer babies are born.

Households in New Canada are much smaller on average than they were in Old Canada, not only because we are choosing to have fewer children, but also because we are more often choosing to live alone.

Solo living is most common at the start of our adult lives, but also happens at the end, especially for women.

One emerging theme is the growing importance of women, and their life choices, in defining our overall population structure—and ultimately consumer demand in the New Canadian marketplace.

One thing that hasn't changed is the ongoing domination of the Boomer generation. **Despite endless conversations about the emerging power of Millennial consumers, the truth is that Boomers will continue to dominate the marketplace for the foreseeable future.** This generational divide, and the tension it creates, will be a dominant feature in the emerging Canadian consumer marketplace, as well as in our politics.

There has been a major shift in the distribution of Canada's population from east to west over the last sixty years, making the Pacific Ocean much more important. This shift has been driven by the consistent pattern of economic opportunities emerging in the suburbs of Toronto and increasingly in western Canada. In addition, for the last two decades, most of our immigrants have come from Pacific nations. There is an inexorable rule of people movement: we always move to where the jobs are. By bringing in job-seeking immigrants from Pacific nations, we are creating a Canada that is increasingly brown, religiously diverse, suburban, and Pacific-oriented.

## Forecasting Our Future

Let's consider the Canadians of 2030. Applying the scientific method, along with a sprinkling of intuition and imagination, we have the ability to craft a compelling narrative about what the Canadian consumer will look like in 2030. Why 2030? Because while 2030 may seem like a long way off, it's really only a decade away. A decade is a reasonable time frame for thinking about the medium-term future.

Of course, other forces will have a major impact on Canada's future and will very likely disrupt aspects of whatever I offer here. But barring a catastrophic political, economic, or environmental upheaval like a major war, the collapse of a significant market commodity such as oil and gas, or the more rapid, deeper onset of an environmental transition such as climate change, this demography-based forecast should prove to be reasonably accurate up to 2030.

How might forces other than demography affect Canada over the next decade or so? Let's consider just two: politics and technology. On politics, we don't have to go all the way to millenarian scenarios like a nuclear holocaust (or the emergence of a Canadian Trump) to conjure up a very different Canada in ten years. The collapse of the world order that has supported the expansion of freer trade since the end of the Second World War would shake Canada's economy to its core. Without relatively free international trade, Canada's trade-based economy would be, to paraphrase US media commentator and former presidential candidate Pat Buchanan, in "deep, deep shape."

As for technological forces, there are so many unpredictable ways they could affect our world that they are difficult to incorporate into a forecast in any serious, predictive way. Flying or self-driving cars, Blockchain and Bitcoin, cold fusion nuclear reactors, the internet of things, a cure for cancer—all could have a major impact on Canada's future. But just as extreme political change is difficult to predict, so too is extreme technological change. Don't believe me? Plug "retro futurism" into YouTube and watch the videos that pop up. Or just watch a few episodes of *Star Trek*. These are marvellous worlds to be sure, but they certainly aren't the world we live in today, and they likely won't be the world of the next decade or two.

If video doesn't do it for you, read some of Jules Verne's work from the turn of the last century. Sure, there are glimpses of today's world, especially if you're into steampunk. But much of what he predicted hasn't come to pass, at least not yet. It's better, then, to focus on the impact of demographic change. That is a much surer, more reliable bet about the future than wagering that flying cars will occupy every suburban garage or that Captain Nemo will emerge from the depths to battle the Kraken.

It's also critical to keep in mind that the most important aspect of technological change is rarely the tech itself. What tends to be more important is how people decide to use it—or not use it. Again, this is very hard to predict. For example, the internet was developed by the American government and various academics for a combination of defence and other research purposes. It wasn't developed to stream movies on Netflix or to hook up terrorist networks. That's how everyday people, not the inventors, decided to use it.

Let's focus on people, then. They make for more accurate forecasting. And a good place to start our journey into the future is with Harley-Davidson, a company that knows the shape of Canada's market demand is changing, and is adapting its products and strategy to deal with it.

### Born to Be Wild

I was at the Grand Villa Casino Hotel and Conference Centre in Burnaby, British Columbia, to speak at the annual meeting of Harley-Davidson's Canadian Dealer Network. I do lots of presentations like this for different groups across Canada and around the world. This time, Harley-Davidson asked me to help their dealers understand why the Canadian marketplace for motorcycles is changing, and how they can adapt to succeed in New Canada.

The company is right to be proactive. Canadians are changing far more than most businesses, community organizations, and even governments appreciate. These changes are fundamental and are redefining everything about us, including who we are, how we live, and what we will be buying. Harley-Davidson, like many businesses, is struggling to adjust. Worldwide sales are down by 6%, and their dealers are restless.

Harley-Davidson is the world's most iconic maker of motorcycles. But they are about much more than just making and selling bikes. Harley has evolved into a true lifestyle brand. As the company's ads say, "Fulfilling dreams of personal freedom is more than a phrase. It's our purpose and our passion."

A Harley-Davidson motorcycle is a very personal statement about who the owner is. It's about how they see themselves, but it's also about how they want to be seen by the world. Even wearing a Harley-branded T-shirt communicates something about the person wearing it. You're a rebel. You're committed to living the dream, and only the very best will do it for you. And you might be a little bit of a badass. As Steppenwolf celebrated in "Born to be Wild," Harley-Davidson is the ultimate personal freedom machine.

Prior to travelling to Burnaby, I had scheduled a couple of calls with the folks at Harley-Davidson to find out what they wanted to hear from me. When we spoke, they asked me to focus my presentation on **the topic that's at the centre of this book: how businesses and other organizations need to change to succeed in a changing Canada.** That was fine with me, I said. I'm comfortable with this topic and knew I could pull together something solid that would both resonate with their dealers and get them thinking about their future in the Canadian marketplace.

I told Harley I appreciated the calls because I wanted to work out any logistic problems that might occur at the venue in Burnaby ahead of time. This was a bit of a fib. Sure, logistics are critical to any successful speech or presentation. These are the little tics and bobs in the setup for the talk that can cause even the best speakers to stumble. For example, the selection of the type of mics being used (podium or lapel?). Who will advance the slides? How much time will be allotted for questions and answers? What happens if nobody asks a question? The more presentations I give, the more I focus on checking off these little worries before I get to the venue. I've learned the hard way. So, of course, I'm concerned about logistics. That was at least a bit true.

As I said, though, logistics weren't foremost in my mind on the calls. Truth be told, I was intimidated by the audience and the subject matter. I'm not a Harley guy. I know nothing about motorcycles. I find them scary as hell and have never had a desire to own one. But I have several friends who own Harleys, and I know how passionate they are about their freedom machines. What I anticipated in Burnaby was standing in front of a room full of passionate, expert marketing people who knew everything there is to know about the Harley dreamer. I could very quickly lose them if my ignorance became obvious. Lucky for me, though, the Harley team was very generous with their knowledge and didn't mind educating me. I learned a lot about what their dealers cared about by listening closely on the calls. I also spent time on the Harley website, looking at their products and getting a sense of how they presented themselves to the marketplace. After all of this, I was more confident about being able to deliver in Burnaby.

As for the venue, the Grand Villa Casino comprises a modest complex of buildings, including a casino, a hotel, and convention spaces, located in suburban Vancouver. Nobody would mistake it for the Las Vegas strip. The more I walked around the casino, the more obvious it was that it had been built to serve a very specific market: Asian-Canadian gamblers. The signage was in Chinese and English, the restaurants were Asian-themed, and pai gow and mahjong tables, with Asian-Canadian dealers, were more prominent than the traditional blackjack and poker tables that dominated the other casinos I've been to. I made a mental note to mention all of this in my presentation as an example of a business that was adapting for success in the Canada of the future. I thought the addition of some local perspective that the Harley dealers could see around them would help drive home my message.

The next morning, I arrived about thirty minutes early at the room where I was to present. I wanted to check in with the event planners and make any last-minute logistic adjustments. Experience tells me that even with the best planning, something always gets screwed up. It's always better to catch it early, while there's still time to fix it.

Another speaker was wrapping up at the podium when I arrived, so I searched for an empty chair at the back of the room and sat down. I figured the meeting would take a break and I'd get a chance to do my logistics checks. Instead, the speaker finished and the room went silent. I noticed a man sitting at another table staring directly at me. He then gestured to the empty podium. *Really?* I thought. I wasn't supposed to go on for another half hour. I hadn't even had a chance to check in with the audiovisual staff. But the conference seemed to be running ahead of schedule and needed me to start earlier. I walked up to the podium, accompanied by uncomfortable silence.

I started to speak to the audience as I fumbled with the technology. I introduced myself, cracked a couple of jokes (nobody laughed), and briefly told them what I planned to talk about. Then, for the first time, I lifted my head and looked directly out into the crowd. I was shocked. I was standing in front of 250 people who could have easily passed for extras on *Sons of Anarchy*. The room was packed with big, middle-aged men sporting ponytails, tattoos, and elaborate facial hair, dressed in black leather and denim. Several women were also scattered about the room. They were attired like the men (sans the facial hair), sharing similar tastes in clothing and body art. After my calls with the team at Harley, I was expecting a room full of corporate marketing types: business-casual and sensible hairstyles.

I got over my initial shock and delivered my presentation. It seemed to go well enough. The audience was attentive and even laughed in the right places. When it was time for questions, I was joined on the stage by some Harley-Davidson executives. They looked more like what I expected based on the phone calls. Sure, they were doing their best to fit in with the crowd. They wore Harley bowling shirts and kept mentioning, almost defensively, that they were riders too. But take away the Harley gear and they could have fit in at a marketing meeting for any major packaged goods company.

Then the questions started coming in from the floor. It quickly became clear that the Harley dealers, despite how they might have appeared to me, were sophisticated and observant marketers too. And why not? They work at the front line of the business and see every day who is coming into their dealerships, who is buying a Harley, and how they are different from previous customers. The market for motorcycles is changing, and they wanted to know what Harley was planning to do to help them adjust. They especially wanted to know what was being done to appeal to the **three main groups they saw as transforming their market: aging Boomers, women, and new Canadians.**

Harley's executives proved just how tuned in they are to what is happening with their customers. Harley gets that Canadians are changing. They recognize the need to expand their offer beyond their traditional core audience of middle-aged, reasonably affluent, male Boomers. They also get that meeting changing customer demands requires changing their products. Historically, Harley-Davidsons have been big, expensive bikes. For decades, you had to be strong and reasonably affluent to own a Harley. Just look at two of their popular touring bikes, the Road King and the Road Glide. A Road King weighs about 380 kilograms, and a Road Glide about 390 kilograms. They are beasts. Their sheer size and weight, as well as their cost—the Road King costs $25,000 (all prices before taxes); the Road Glide, $35,000—exclude all but a very select audience from owning one. And these aren't even Harley's biggest, most expensive touring bikes. That honour goes to the Street Glide CVO: weighing in at nearly 400 kilograms, it will set you back a hefty $50,000. You could buy *two* Volkswagen GTI hatchbacks for roughly the same amount.

So, if the big touring bikes aren't as well aligned to Canada's new consumers as Harley would like them to be, how are they adjusting their products to match the emerging marketplace? There are some smart lessons in what Harley is doing that demonstrate how to shift gears to meet shifting consumer demand. Canada's businesses, community organizations, and governments can all learn from Harley.

### Aging Boomers (and Gen Xers)

Everybody gets older. Even a core Harley customer gets to the point where his (it's usually a his) body tells him to say goodbye to what once was. So what's Harley doing for them? How will they keep these core customers on the road? Harley has come up with a potential solution. Some of the fastest-growing segments of Harley's sales today are the Trikes: the Freewheeler and the Tri Glide Ultra. They offer all the freedom of a big touring bike but with fewer physical demands on the rider. Not only are Trikes suitable for aging core customers who want to extend their ride, they also offer an entry point for new customers who lack the physique and experience necessary to handle a big touring machine. For them, a Trike is an ideal entry into the Harley lifestyle.

Trikes are a new and potentially lucrative product line for Harley. According to the Harley website, at the time of writing, the cost for a Freewheeler was around $33,000, while a Tri Glide Ultra would set you back around $43,000. That's even pricier than some of the big road bikes.

But what Trikes really communicate about Harley-Davidson is that the company understands that a lucrative segment of their future marketplace will be aging Boomers. They're right about this. **Canadians are living longer and living healthier, and older Canadians have most of the money.** Millennials are an important market segment too, and the savvy product and marketing group at Harley is thinking about how to get them on bikes, but at the same time, they aren't forgetting about expanding products for older riders. They know aging Boomers are an important power segment in the market.

## Women

While their mothers and grandmothers may have been content to ride on the seat behind their Harley man, women today want to ride their own bikes. Why not? Today's women are quite different from their mothers and grandmothers. They are waiting a decade longer to get married and to start families, if they decide to follow that path at all. They are pursuing higher education in greater numbers than ever, and are building independent, successful careers that give them access to their own financial resources. An increasing number of Canadian women now have the desire, opportunity, and assets to become Harley-Davidson customers.

Like many forward-thinking businesses selling products and services to Canadians, Harley-Davidson is responding to the emerging economic power of independent women. Get ready for it. You will be hearing more and more about how independent women are shaping the marketplace because the role and influence of women in our economy has evolved over the last few decades. While women have always been regarded by marketers as the important decision-makers on day-to-day household purchases in Canada, this position was driven by their roles as wives and mothers. Women will continue to make everyday purchasing decisions on behalf of their families, but the story will increasingly be about how they are using their own resources to act as independent decision-makers when it comes to purchases that used to be shared family decisions. Think real estate, personal investments, and, yes, whether to buy a motorcycle.

Kate Robertson examined the relationship between women riders and motorcycles in *Inspired* magazine. Robertson quotes Greer Stewart, the founder of the Canadian Women's Ride Day, on the growing popularity of motorcycling for women in Canada. According to Stewart, "The rate of women motorcyclists is increasing every year, and based on the current trend, should reach 50% of riders in the next five to ten years." Why are women embracing motorcycling? asks Robertson. "It attracts women of all ages, lifestyles, and riding styles for the camaraderie/sisterhood, the thrill, and the empowerment it brings," says Stewart.

While it's difficult to corroborate Stewart's optimistic claim that gender equity will be achieved in Canadian motorcycle sales within the next decade, there is a lot of evidence to suggest she's right about the number of women riders increasing in general. For example, *Women Riders Now* presents itself as a magazine dedicated to "women, and men who ride with women." *WRN* says about 12% of American motorcycle riders today are women, which is an increase of 35% over the last decade. The Motorcyclists Confederation of Canada has it slightly higher in Canada, with women now buying 18% to 20% of all motorcycles sold. *WRN* also tells us that the most popular bike for women today is the Harley-Davidson Sportster. The Sportster is a budget-priced, entry-level model that is smaller and lighter than a touring machine but still has the style and performance to match Harley's bigger bikes.

According to the Harley executives in Burnaby, the company has a clear strategy for attracting women riders, and it is paying off. Part of the strategy is product, but it also entails community building and outreach to nurture the camaraderie/sisterhood mentioned by Stewart. Harley dealers now offer special riding clinics just for women, and make mentors available for new riders. What's the payoff? Harley claims that 62% of women who ride motorcycles today own a Harley.

## New Canadians

The final group of potential customers the audience asked about at the conference was new Canadians. Given where we were—Burnaby, on the Pacific coast—and that they had just heard from me about the massive growth in immigration from Pacific nations, it's no surprise that the audience asked questions about the market for Asian Canadians. The answers from the Harley executives were both fascinating and reflective of how much they are thinking about their future customers.

The first point they made was that their biggest challenge in attracting new customers is getting *any* Canadian to think about riding a motorcycle. As one Harley executive noted, "Canada is a car culture—when Canadians see a road, they think about cars. Most Asian cultures, however, are more motorcycle cultures. They see a road; they think about motorcycles." The Harley executive wasn't specific about why this was the case, but based on the reaction in the room, this was common knowledge among the dealers. Therefore, Harley believes they are a step ahead selling to Asian immigrants because these customers both think about and already know how to ride motorcycles.

Harley-Davidson is right about the differences between Asian cultures and Canadian culture when it comes to preferred vehicle options. Only about 2% of Canadian households own a motorcycle, while 80% have a car. In the three Pacific countries that represent Canada's top sources of immigrants—India, the Philippines, and China—the vehicle ownership statistics are completely different. In India, 47% of households own a motorcycle, while 6% have a car. In the Philippines, 32% have a motorcycle, while 6% have a car. In China, 60% have a motorcycle, and 17% have a car.

Although selling Asian immigrants on riding motorcycles should be easy, Harley faces a significant challenge when it comes to selling them one of their products. Again, it is the size of those big Harley bikes that's a barrier. As a Harley executive on stage observed, "Men and women of Asian ancestry are smaller in stature and lighter than the average Canadian. Old-school Harleys can be too big for them to comfortably manage."

Is the Harley executive right about this? Are male Asian immigrants smaller in stature than Canadian-born men on average? According to WorldData.info, the statistics on average heights for men by country show that they are, at least for first-generation Asian immigrants. The average Canadian man today is 5'10" and weighs 186 pounds. The average man in India is 5'5" and weighs 132 pounds. The average man in the Philippines is 5'5" and weighs 146 pounds. And the average man in China is 5'6" and weighs 146 pounds. On average, then, a Canadian-born man is 5 inches taller and 45 pounds heavier than an Asian-born male immigrant. This pattern of height and weight differences is comparable for Canadian-born and Asian-born women.

Accommodating the physical needs of willing, motorcycle-acculturated customers from Asian nations is one of the reasons that Harley has expanded its entry-level options to bikes that are smaller and lighter than those in their more traditional lines. Sure, this helps in the Asian markets directly, but it also helps in nations that have experienced significant Asian immigration, like Canada. Yes, the Sportster is popular with women riders, but it isn't designed just for them. A smaller man might also look at the Sportster as his perfect entry-level Harley.

But there's also Harley's line of street bikes, which they describe as "sleek and nimble, with an authentic urban attitude." Since Canadians have overwhelmingly become urban and suburban creatures, especially if they are new Canadians, something designed for the city street, as opposed to the open road, could be just the ticket for them.

## Fixing the Game

In thinking of your own organization, have you mapped out how changes like aging Boomers, different life decisions by women, and escalating immigration from Pacific nations (among many others) will affect you? In my experience, most organizations have not. These changes are now happening so quickly, and are so fundamental, that many of us will not recognize Canada in a few short years. Those businesses and organizations that can figure these changes out and adapt to them will thrive in the future. Those that don't will struggle to stay alive. It's just that simple.

It's not by chance that we began our journey into Canada's future in a casino. Understanding the future of business, politics, and much else about human affairs sometimes seems like gambling. Everybody is desperate to make the right bet about the future. That's how you win, after all. While we can't know everything about what's to come, we'd all like to know what the next turn of the card or spin of the roulette wheel will bring. Is there a way to predict that? I believe there is. It comes down to having superior knowledge about the odds.

We call most gambling "games of chance." What this suggests is that the odds for any particular outcome are completely unpredictable, due to this fickle thing we call chance. Casino operators know this isn't true. That's how they make their money. Their thinking is based on a statistical concept called the law of large numbers. Think about it in terms of flipping a coin. If the coin is fair, when you flip it a hundred times, you should almost always get close to fifty heads and fifty tails. The more times you flip the coin, the closer it will be to the expected fifty-fifty result. That's the law of large numbers at work.

What looks to a casino player like luck, both good and bad, looks to a casino operator like just another flip of the coin in a long game that's yet to play out. They know that the longer you play, the more likely it is that they will win and you will lose. The law of large numbers practically guarantees it. That's where the free drinks and other perks come in. The casino needs you to stay at the table. While the casino may lose a few hands to a lucky player, the more hands that are played, the more likely the expected result will occur. Sure, you may go on a winning streak from time to time, but unless you walk away from the table, the law of large numbers will catch up with you. Kenny Rogers' hit song "The Gambler" is instructive on this point.

This book is about showing you how you to fix the game, tilting the odds in your favour to win in business, politics, and any other activity that involves dealing with Canadians. Think of it as informed gambling. A good card counter, who keeps track of all the cards that are played to exceed the expected outcome (an activity that will get you kicked out of a casino), knows that all versions of the future aren't equally certain. A good businessperson or politician knows this too. Certain outcomes have better or worse odds associated with them. Some things are more likely to happen than others.

How do we decide what's more likely to happen? It's based on what statistics experts call known priors. What we know about what has already happened helps us to better evaluate what will happen next. Some people's known priors are based on previous experience or intuition. In my opinion, these are the gamblers casinos make their money from. We're not them. **We're card counters. That means we use our superior knowledge of data, which are our known priors, to fix the game to our benefit.**

Yes, using data to fix the game might seem like an obvious strategy. But we live in a noisy age that's cluttered with too much data. How do you sort through it all? What matters and what doesn't? Breaking through the clutter and creating understanding is the biggest challenge we face in using data to make better decisions. This book will help you to do that. I will focus on the most essential data: the data about how Canadians are changing.

# PART 1

# WHO WE REALLY ARE

# CHAPTER 1

# *Ready, Fire, Aim*: Why Marketers Miss the Mark

## Defining the Generations

How can we define Canada's generations in a way that best helps us understand the future? It's a challenge, especially when it comes to the post-Boomer period. There is a healthy cottage industry of academics and business experts making careers out of mapping multiple subsegments of the population born after 1965 in exquisite, contradictory, and often confusing detail. Let's keep it simple. We will stick with a slightly modified version of what Statistics Canada uses to define generations. And rather than obsessing over precise birthdates, we'll keep things more general.

Statistics Canada sees five main generations making up Canada's population today:

- **Pre–Baby Boomers:** The first generation, born before 1946, is the pre–Baby Boom generation (the parents of Baby Boomers). Canada's oldest citizens represent about 14% of our population, or about 5 million people alive today.

- **Baby Boomers:** The next oldest generation is the ubiquitous Baby Boomers, born between 1946 and 1965. They remain our largest generation, at 29% of today's total population, or over 10 million people.

- **Generation X:** After the Boomers come their kids, whom Statistics Canada calls the Baby Busters or Generation X (the first of the alphabet generations). Members of Gen X were born between 1966 and 1971 and represent 8% of the population, or about 3 million people.

- **Millennials:** There's some confusion among experts about whether Gen X and the next generation, the Millennials, are part of the same generation or constitute two different cohorts. We'll go with Statistics Canada on this and treat them as separate generations. Statistics Canada defines Millennials (whom they call Generation Y or the Children of Boomers) as those born between 1972 and 1993. Millennials are the second-largest Canadian generation at 27%, or just under 10 million people.

- **Generation Z:** The final generation is those born after 1993, which Statistics Canada pegs as the first year of the internet. Gen Z represents about 8 million Canadians, or just over 20% of our population. These are the kids of Gen Xers and the oldest Millennials.

Another way to break down the generations has been proposed by Pew Research in the United States. It has some different age groupings and names, but is quite similar. Pew sees the following structure of generations:

- The Silent Generation: Born 1928–45
- Baby Boomers: Born 1946–64

- Generation X: Born 1965–80
- Millennials: Born 1981–96
- Post-Millennials: Born 1997–present

Like Statistics Canada, Pew struggles with capturing where the Millennials end and what they call the Post-Millennial generation begins. Their Millennial cutoff date of 1996 is important because it points to a generation that is old enough to have experienced the events of 9/11, as well as the effects of the 2008 recession. While Canadian Millennials were certainly affected by the events of 9/11, the recession of 2008 did not hit them the same way as it hit their equivalent cohort in the United States. The movie *The Wolf of Wall Street* doesn't have the same cultural relevance for Canadian Millennials as it does for their American counterparts.

One interesting point about generations that's emphasized by Pew is the importance of technology in separating them. Generations, says Pew, differ according to technological experience. For example, Baby Boomers saw the domination of TV; Gen X experienced a computer revolution; Millennials grew up with the internet. This is consistent with how we will look at generations. **How generations learn to experience and interact with the world is a big part of how they construct their world view.** But we can take the connection between technologies and generations too far. I've certainly seen it done.

## No Generation Is an Island

I was sitting in the audience, waiting to go on at yet another conference. Like everybody else there, I was focused on the speaker. I've seen versions of the same presentation too many times. I bet you have too. A business consultant sporting a sleek, flesh-coloured head mic confidently stalks the stage. He is dressed in whatever business-casual uniform his ilk favours these days. A hand-steeple comes up to his face as he kicks off an anecdote about his toddler at home. Little Emma is a big fan of the iPad, he says. She has been since before she could walk or talk, so much so that the other day, when she swiped her tiny hand across a blank TV screen, she experienced her first existential trauma when *nothing happened*. Total confusion and frustrated tears ensued. The moral of the story is then delivered from the quivering lips of the tiny prophet: "Daddy, why is our TV broken?"

Yes, Emma's generation will have a different relationship with technology than those before her. Every generation does. The truth, though, is that touchscreens and swiping will be but a brief interlude in humanity's relationship with accessing and communicating information. Touchscreens are hardly generation-defining on their own terms. Unless, of course, you also consider eight-track tape players to be generation-defining for Boomers.

A decade from now, we will remember touchscreens with no more wonder than we do the stylus or the PalmPilot—remember those? That's because we are now living in the world of "the internet of things," a marvellous term attributed to British scientist Kevin Ashton. The internet of things is the network in our world that is embedded with electronics, software, sensors, and connectivity. These connections allow any object we carry or interact with, knowingly or unknowingly, to collect and exchange data. The internet of things allows objects to be sensed and controlled remotely, creating opportunities for direct interaction between the physical world and computers without humans ever having to intervene with a screen or any other interface.

Imagine buildings that sense whether you are cold or hot and automatically adjust the room climate to make you more comfortable. Imagine household appliances that sense when you are hungry and automatically prepare a meal based on your physical and even emotional needs. Refrigerators already exist that can communicate directly with grocery stores to replenish themselves.

Still, you can't walk through a bookstore, visit a news site, or attend a business conference without being pummelled by a gaggle of experts emotionally relating tales about their own touchscreening toddlers and how their experiences will change everything. Okay, perhaps I'm being a bit harsh, but there's a kernel of truth here. Focusing on the demands of a specific generation can be important, especially if it is the generation representing the most people. It is also correct to observe that, as generations work their way through the various stages of life—childhood, adolescence, work–family balance, retirement— **the needs of the biggest generation will always wield the greatest power in the market.** Think of how the tsunami of kids born in the Baby Boom defined that generation.

But no generation is an island. While the overall tone is set by the generation with the most people, the overall structure of the population and how it is moving or changing through time is more important than what's happening within one cohort. Is the overall population getting younger or older? Which is growing, our cities or our rural areas? Is our population growth coming from domestic childbirth or from new immigrants? Where will new immigrants be coming from? Where will they be moving to? What is the prevalent family structure? This more holistic view of the population is the right one to focus on.

## Generational Emblems

Although it's important to understand which generation is numerically dominant, as well as the overall structure and movement of the population, we also need to avoid falling for easy, breezy stereotypes about generations. We love these stereotypes: they make for great headlines. But experts who look at a lot of data know generations are a complicated topic, especially when you consider that there can sometimes be bigger differences *within* a generation than there are *between* generations. For example, Millennial men and women have more divergent views on the benefits of technology than Boomer and Millennial men do.

Nonetheless, saying that generations are complicated doesn't mean we can't summarize the dominant traits that make up their personalities. By treating these traits as heuristics, or rules of thumb, we can focus our analysis so that it doesn't become all trees and no forest. While I don't want to be overly simplistic, it's possible to say that within each generation there are defining personality tendencies or traits constructed from the specific cultural emblems that its members accumulate, especially during their formative years, and that add up to a generational world view. What are cultural emblems? Think big news events, the state of the economy when one is entering the job market, cultural practices, technology, fashion, movies, music, and the like. These experiences tend to affect a generation for life.

An emblem marks what a person has lived through for others to see. It's part of who they are to themselves and to the rest of the world. If you ever watch two old soldiers greeting each other, you may notice how they subtly look above each other's right pocket to inspect the ribbons or medals. These emblems communicate, without the need to ask, what each has been through in their respective military careers. Generational emblems serve a similar function in the civilian world. If you are a certain age, there is an assumption that you wear the emblems of your generation, for both good and bad, and that they define who you are, what you value, and how you will react to what happens around you.

A good example of a generational emblem in action is music: the soundtrack of our lives. There's some solid evidence, based on analyzing music-streaming data, that your life's playlist is mostly filled in by the time you reach the age of 30. While there's room for a spectrum of individual tastes, when it comes to song selection, you are likely to have more in common with members of your own generation than with the generation that preceded you or the one that follows you. It's a good bet that if you end up in a retirement home with an enlightened staff, you and your neighbours will be happiest if the sound system plays songs that were popular during the thirty formative years most of you shared. Think about it. Fifty years from now, the halls of Canada's retirement homes will be filled with the autotuned melodies of Drake. Talk about dystopia.

Yes, there are exceptions to every rule. Not every kid who reached adolescence during the sixties bought into the counterculture. Not everyone followed Timothy Leary's advice to "tune in, turn on, and drop out" on their way to the Haight, Yasgur's farm, Yorkville, or Gastown. The truth is that many, many more did just what their parents did: they went to school and work. But it's also a safe bet that whether they were a flower child or a factory worker, they did what they did while listening to the Beatles and the Stones, or other acts that dominated the music charts of their thirty formative years. That's how generational emblems are forged.

## The Mainstream Wins

While I like the idea of emblems and the generational world views they help to define, I don't want to leave the impression that these world views are impervious to change. They are more like tendencies than iron-clad rules. There will always be exceptions. My caution to you is not to be overly distracted by these exceptions. **The mainstream will always have more influence on creating the structure of consumer demand.** The mainstream wins because they are the dominant trend;

they have the numbers. And market success is ultimately a game of numbers.

Let's take the second half of the 1970s. This was an important time for both late Boomers and early Gen Xers. Whenever I see retrospectives on the late seventies, the narrator inevitably states that punk rock was a cultural phenomenon that cast a very long shadow over the entire era. The year that was especially important for punk was 1977, when the most influential punk band, the Sex Pistols, released what was to be their only original album, *Never Mind the Bollocks, Here's the Sex Pistols*. (A strong case can also be made for the Ramones' self-titled album, released in 1976, or the Clash's *London Calling*, released in 1979.)

But 1977 wasn't just a big year for punk rock, it was a big year for pop music overall, maybe its biggest ever. Three of the top-selling albums of all time were released in 1977: *Bat Out of Hell* by Meatloaf; *Rumours* by Fleetwood Mac; and the *Saturday Night Fever* soundtrack. All three have sold north of forty million units worldwide to date. Add in *Hotel California* by the Eagles and you see how big 1977 was for music. (Okay, I'm cheating, as *Hotel California* was released in December 1976, but that's just a rounding error. It doesn't detract from what I'm saying about the times.)

*Never Mind the Bollocks* has sold around three million units since it was first released. So while punks get an awful lot of attention from pop culture experts when they talk about what was important in the late seventies (and maybe they might be forced to give an embarrassed nod to disco), most people younger than 30 at the time were grooving to "Rhiannon," "Paradise by the Dashboard Light," "Night Fever," and "Life in the Fast Lane." These songs dominated the mainstream soundtrack of that period, not "Anarchy in the UK," "Clampdown," or "Blitzkrieg Bop."

## How Emblems Influence World View

The consequences of world views and emblems shared by the parents of today's Boomers were well described by the American sociologist William Whyte in his seminal study of American society, *The Organization Man*. Whyte's key point about those whom journalist Tom Brokaw called the "Greatest Generation" was that they have a generational world view that is strongly influenced by the deprivations of the Great Depression and the sacrifices of the Second World War. These events conditioned them to believe that organizations and groups can make better decisions than individuals, and that serving an organization made more sense than advancing their individual careers. Whyte argued that this created a generation of risk-averse executives and workers who faced few consequences because of their loyalty and could expect to stay in a job for life if they toed the company line. They were committed and loyal to their employers, their spouses, their political parties, and other public institutions, as well as to specific products and brands.

The public opinion and population statistics in Canada align with Whyte's description, although he was writing about the United States. The parents of Canadian Boomers, along with older Boomers, were and are like Whyte's Organization Man. They valued loyalty, including to their employers. Statistics Canada says two-thirds of Boomers entered their 50s (in the eighties and nineties) in long-term employment, in jobs they had held for at least twelve years with the same employer. More than half had worked for the same firm or organization for far longer, often twenty years or more. Therefore, loyalty is an important generational emblem for the Greatest Generation and for the tip of the Baby Boom.

Which emblems will make up the generational world view for today's kids, Generation Z? Some possibilities include the fight against climate change, the rise of e-commerce, the mainstreaming of gender flexibility, and terrorism inspired by radical Islam or the alt-right. And yes, touchscreens just might be part of the mix. Whichever emblems prove to have mainstream influence will define how this generation can be expected to respond to the world and will ultimately define the marketplace they will lead.

## What This Means for Your Business

There's lots of contradictory information out there about the generations. These contradictions create noise that causes marketers to miss their mark. My advice? Keep it simple. Block out the noise by focusing your attention on the big targets. The biggest target is always the mainstream. The mainstream, not the exceptions, defines the marketplace. **In Canada, the emerging mainstream is older than most of us think and is getting older every day.**

The same goes for politics. There's lots of talk about emerging voter segments, especially young voters. Again, keep it simple. To win, you need to appeal to the mainstream. Older voters may not be the sexiest or noisiest voting block, but they pick the winner. It's the same for governing: upset the mainstream, and they will return the favour at the next election.

## What This Means for You

Don't listen to the media, marketers, or pundits on what's happening with generations and the marketplace. They dole out too many buzzwords and too much short-term, contradictory advice. Instead, just look at the numbers. It's all there. The power in the market is older, not younger. **An older mainstream will cause marketplace demand to shift to accommodate older consumers.** Knowing this, should you invest in makers of adult diapers or kids' diapers? Early-childhood education or continuing education for older students? Companies that build theme parks for kids or those that offer adults-only vacations? Now that you understand how our generations are changing, the choices should be obvious.

You also need to understand the new generation gap. It's back, but this time, it's the older generations who are creating it. Back in the 1960s and 1970s, the generation gap was driven by youthful Boomers who had the numbers to demand that the marketplace change to meet their needs. Today, the aging Boomers still have the numbers, and they are still demanding that the marketplace adapt to suit them.

Which side of the generation gap you fall on will affect your opportunities and decisions. For example, our aging population is creating significant labour shortages in Canada, especially for skilled workers. If you're younger and have the right skills, you should see your opportunities grow as the population ages and retirements increase. If you're older, you will be in a good position to negotiate staying in your job longer, if you want to.

# CHAPTER 2

# *Late Bloomers*: Why Business
# Is Blind to the Obvious

## Perennials Have the Money

Look around. Are you seeing more silver hair and wrinkles than you used to? You should be. **Canadians are getting older—much older.** This is because of the Perennials. The Perennial Generation consists of Canadians who have reached or are about to reach the magic retirement age of 65. This covers all of one generation (the Pre-Boomers, or Pew's Silent Generation) and an increasing number of another generation (the Boomers). The Perennial Generation is a silver tsunami that is crashing into all aspects of Canadian life. They have the numbers and wealth to define the marketplace.

Perennial Canadians carry with them a wide range of emblems created by the calamitous twentieth century. The oldest Perennials experienced the deprivations of the Great Depression, as well as the sacrifices of the Second World War. Along with their kids, they lived through the Cold War, Quebec's Quiet Revolution, the October Crisis, and two votes on Quebec's future in Canada. They remember the Kennedy assassination in 1963, saw the Beatles on Ed Sullivan in 1964, and celebrated Canada's hundredth birthday in 1967 (the last time the Toronto Maple Leafs won the Stanley Cup).

They also experienced the first version of Trudeaumania in 1968 and have lived to see the second. They saw the Vietnam War fought on TV, witnessed America's painful struggle with civil rights, and lived through Watergate (the first of the now ubiquitous "gates"). All this cultural, political, and economic upheaval led the Perennials to embrace stability as an important generational emblem.

This brings me to my first important point for people wanting to know where the money will be: **Perennials, not Millennials, have the big money, and will for years to come.**

The Perennials are and will remain the dominant generation of our age. The implications of this are huge for every aspect of consumer and citizen demand in our country, from where and how we'll live to what products and services we'll buy to what policies we'll be demanding from our governments. Any business or organization that wants to be successful must understand how to talk to, sell to, and service the Perennial market. It is and will continue to be the mainstream market for Canada. That's right: not a specialty market, the mainstream market. Yet the tendency is to ignore the Perennials and focus almost exclusively on the tastes of younger generations.

## Our Increasing Lifespan

The average Canadian now has a lifespan of 82 years. That's either ninth or eleventh longest of any country in the world, depending on whether you prefer the World Health Organization or the United Nations Population Division as your data source. And that number keeps climbing. By 2036, it's projected to be 87. That's an increase of roughly 30 years in the lifespan of Canadians since the 1920s. Think about what this means in everyday life. In 1925, if you made it to your mid-50s, you were considered old. It was the equivalent of someone who is 82 today.

Another way of looking at lifespan is by tracking the median average age of our population. That's the age that divides Canada's population into equal parts: half of us are older than this number, and half of us are younger. In 2019, the median age of Canadians was 41. In 2036, it will be around 43. By 2061, it will be around 45. This is compared to a median age of just 27 in 1960.

Sorry, guys, even with these improvements, you will still live about four and half years less than the average Canadian woman who shares your birthday. But this gap is closing. Life expectancy has been increasing more rapidly for men during the past three decades than it has been for women. But for the foreseeable future, women will still outlive men.

Increased longevity is acutely important in determining the shape of Canada's future population. I would argue that our population might age even more quickly than demographers are currently predicting. If immigration slows or fertility doesn't pick up as expected, more rapid aging of the overall population is sure to follow. Migration and fertility offset aging. If either of these factors stumble, we will get older faster.

Why are Canadians aging? It seems trite to say it, but it's mostly because we aren't dying as fast. Our increasing lifespan is due to a combination of factors: better lifestyle choices (exercising more, healthier diets, smoking less), ongoing improvements in medical science (especially in infant and maternity care and treatments for circulatory diseases), and the things governments do to us and for us (fewer armed conflicts, more regulations to reduce accidental deaths, expanded public health care).

What does the Perennial Generation look like in absolute numbers? In 2016, there were close to 6 million seniors, accounting for 17% of the Canadian population. This is twice as many seniors as there were in 1981. In 2015, the number of seniors surpassed the number of children 14 years old and under for the first time in Canadian history. So, we now have more oldsters than youngsters. This trend will continue to accelerate between now and 2031, when all Baby Boomers will have reached the ripe old age of 65.

Apart from appreciating the quantitative magnitude of the Perennial Generation, we also need to understand its geographic distribution, because that will have a big impact on Canada's future marketplace. This silver tsunami is not going to be the same everywhere. If you live in Halifax or St. John's, you will see a greater share of silver more quickly than if you live in Calgary or Toronto. That's because the four most rapidly aging provinces in Canada all share Atlantic waters. But British Columbia isn't far behind.

## Living to 100 Is No Longer Extraordinary

One of the best examples to illustrate the dramatic impact of population aging in Canada relates to centenarians—people who live to 100 or older. Remember when someone hitting the century mark was treated as a rare and special event that even merited a media interview? The usually overwhelmed elderly woman (because the ratio of centenarian women to men in Canada is about 5:1) would be asked by a community reporter to share the secret to her longevity, as well as some stories about how her world had changed over the last hundred years.

Sure, everybody wanted to hear her secret to a long life. But I was more interested in her stories about the past, because she had such compelling material (her generational emblems) to work with. She was a child at the time of the First World War. She started her family during the Great Depression. She became an older adult during the Baby Boom and retired in the 1970s. Think of her life experience as it relates to the evolution of human flight. In her lifetime, she may have seen Canadian air aces Billy Bishop and Billy Barker buzz the audience in their Great War–era biplanes at the Canadian National Exhibition. On TV, she saw Neil Armstrong walk on the moon. And she experienced the growth of consumer air travel, which is now so ubiquitous, we take it for granted.

Interviews with centenarians seem to be less frequent these days. Why? Because making it to your hundredth birthday is a less extraordinary accomplishment than it once was. Centenarians are the fastest-growing population cohort in Canada today. In 2016, there were 7,900 Canadian centenarians. By 2061, that number is projected to climb to 78,300. That's a city the size of Victoria! **Some demographers even predict that children born today can expect to live an average of 100 years.**

## Perennial Relationships

The Perennials aren't into drama. They would make poor reality show contestants. As already noted, one of their most important generational emblems is stability. They have been stable in their work lives (remember the Organization Man) and in their personal relationships. Most seniors (2.8 million) live in "traditional" opposite-gendered married couples, although 8,000 seniors say they live in same-sex relationships. Canadian seniors also stick with the partner they first brought to the dance. Three-quarters of them have had only one union in their life. Only 12% of today's seniors are separated or divorced, although this is still three times more than there were in 1981. But the incidence of divorce will be much more pronounced in the next group of seniors— those who are 55 to 64 years old today—who have had more varied family lives than their parents and older generational peers did.

Stability of relationships is an additional explanation for why Canadian seniors are living so much longer than their parents did. This is especially the case for married men, who tend to live longer than single, divorced, or widowed men. And since men are now catching up to women in terms of longevity, senior women today are more likely to live longer as part of a couple than their mothers did. Because their husband is living longer, and divorce is uncommon in this cohort, they are less likely to be living alone.

What happens when married seniors become single again through death or divorce? That depends on their gender and the reason they became single. Here's one urban legend that's statistically true: senior men are much more likely to remarry than senior women. Seventy-six percent of senior men have a second union after divorce, compared to only 55% of senior women. Also, another marriage is more likely to occur sooner after the breakup of a previous marriage than after the death of a spouse. Widows and widowers may believe they will have a hard time finding a union that stacks up to what they already had, while divorced people appear to be anxious to see if they can get it right with their next partner.

Here's another popular belief about seniors that's supported by data: while most senior second marriages involve couples who are close in age, older men are more likely than older women to marry a younger partner.

## Retirement and Real Estate

What does the dominance of the Perennial Generation portend for shifting demand in Canada? Let's start with the most basic need we all have: a place to live. Can we use what we now know about the Perennials to better understand future housing demand in Canada? I believe we can. But first we need to shelve the idea that what seniors want in terms of housing is based solely on what's economically rational for them. Yes, economics will always play a role in housing decisions—you can only have what you can afford. But the heart is also important in this equation. There is more heart and less head in real estate decisions than many economists and real estate experts would have us believe. Where you choose to live is ultimately about *how* you want to live, not just about monetizing real estate assets. And how you want to live is largely driven by your generational mindset.

Here's an example of what I mean by the heart overruling the head (although a bit of both is always involved). You've likely heard of empty nest syndrome. Empty nesters are older parents whose children have grown up and left home. In this situation, logic (the head) says that these seniors, or soon-to-be seniors, will want to downsize from their family home and move to a more communal living arrangement, perhaps a condo or a seniors' community outside the city. And when the time comes, they will eventually be off to a retirement home.

We all know Perennials who have done this, even in our own families. And we've certainly seen media reports about it, and ads encouraging it. After all, it's economically logical. With real estate markets as robust as they are in our major urban and suburban centres, it's time to cash in on the family home. Why pay for a big house in the city or suburbs, with its extraneous empty rooms and maintenance costs, if you no longer need to? The kids have left, so it's time to convert your home equity into the retirement lifestyle you've always dreamt of. At least, that's what the ads tell us.

Except that's not what most Perennials are doing. Although 65 is the standard retirement age in Canada, being forced by law to retire is rare now. So, if retirement is defined as the complete end of paid work, it is becoming less clear when it begins. The tail end of your working life can now vary a lot and may involve many different types of ongoing work: part-time work, seasonal work, consulting: Perennials are doing it all. This type of work, called "bridge employment," refers to any paid work one does after "retiring." A quarter of Canadians even say they want to start a business when they retire. A quarter are very stubborn and say they will never retire. These decisions about retirement and work have a big impact on what Perennials will eventually do with their real estate.

Many Perennials are healthy enough and motivated enough to embrace bridge employment. They want to keep working to stay busy and fulfilled, or because they can't afford to retire. But continuing to work is less about the paycheque for most Perennials and more about socializing and interacting with colleagues, staying mentally busy, getting out of the house, and having personal goals. There's a lot of motivation to stay close to work-related networks. About 25% of men and 15% of women age 65 to 74 are already bridge employed. Looking at retirees overall, nearly one in five reported working at some point in the last year. This number has doubled since 1995, and we can expect it to keep growing over time.

While many older Canadians want to keep working in some capacity, they can sometimes run into employers who no longer want them because of their age. In a world that's fixated on youth, older workers can face ageist prejudice in the workplace. Some employers believe older employees don't have the stamina of younger workers and are overly averse to change. Even if this is true, older workers also have the experience and institutional memory that many organizations lack and need, and since they are likely to be looking for bridge employment, as opposed to a full-time job, their flexibility makes them a good option in the expanding gig economy.

Of course, not all Perennials want to remain in the workforce. About 1,000 Boomers retire every day. It tends to be the more highly educated Perennials who continue to work. One reason may be that jobs requiring higher levels of education are less physically demanding, so physical limitations associated with aging are less likely to trigger retirement. Another reason may be that many of the jobs done by well-educated workers tend to have more flexible working arrangements, such as working from home or working less than full time. Jobs like this are just easier to fit into a bridge employment and gig economy lifestyle.

The bottom line in all of this is that the decision to keep working affects housing choices. Perennials who are still working will want to live within commuting distance of their place of employment. That's a reason for not being attracted to more remote locations specifically marketed to retirees, and it keeps them living in their family home. Why move if they don't have to? Remember their generation's mindset: stability is important.

If you can retire and choose not to, that's an argument of the heart. So is hanging on to the family home, another emblem of stability. That's what most seniors are doing these days. In 2011, 92% of seniors still lived in a private household, especially if they were in a couple. The number of seniors living on their own instead of collectively is on the rise as well, especially among senior women, even as the overall number of both senior men and women is increasing. Owing to their greater longevity, a higher proportion of women (10%) than men (5%) get to the point in their lives when they do decide to live in a collective environment. Of the almost 400,000 older Canadians living in a collective environment in 2011, 70% were women. What about choosing to live with the kids or another family member? Only 5% of seniors live with relatives—7% of women and 3% of men.

It shouldn't be a surprise, then, that in a recent Ipsos survey, 93% of older homeowners reported that they want to stay in their family home through retirement, or at least until health or financial circumstances force them to leave. Why are they staying put? They say it's to maintain their independence and attachment to their community. The evidence suggests they are right to do so. The same Ipsos survey looked at older homeowners who had downsized. Only 20% said it had been worth it, and only 20% said they were using the proceeds from downsizing to finance their retirement. Maybe the heart and head are better aligned than real estate experts understand.

## Staying Active

How do Canada's retired Perennials spend their days? Statistics Canada says that's mostly dependent on their age and related health status. The older you get, and the less healthy you are, the more passive your activities become. An impressive 75% of seniors say they engage in what Statistics Canada calls "active activities" every day. These include exercising, socializing, and using technology.

Volunteering and community service are an important part of staying active. Seniors, especially senior women, give more time to others than any other group in Canadian society. It's a reciprocal relationship, though. To maintain good physical and mental health, Perennials need to remain engaged in the world as they get older, so volunteering is of equal benefit to them as to the people they help.

How important to the health of Perennials is remaining active and connected? An Ipsos survey for the benefits company Cigna estimated that **loneliness has a similar impact on mortality as smoking fifteen cigarettes a day, and a bigger impact than obesity!** And the health impacts of loneliness are not mitigated by connecting through social media. Heavy and light social media users score about the same on loneliness. Perennials seem to get this. That's why the need for community connection is such a big factor in keeping them in their suburban and urban family homes.

While we tend to think travel will be a big part of our retirement, it turns out seniors care more about taking time for themselves than they do about bouncing around the world. For example, 27% of pre-retired Canadians expect to be snowbirds in retirement, but only 16% of today's retirees actually go south for the winter. Yes, there will still likely be growth in the retiree travel market, but that's more because there will be more retirees around than because they are especially inclined to travel.

## Aging in Place

By 2016, most Perennials were already homeowners and no longer driving increases in home ownership. Home ownership does vary by province and community, though. For example, Quebec tends to have lower home ownership (61%) than other provinces. And, when it comes to our biggest cities, Calgary (73%) leads Toronto (67%), Vancouver (64%), and Montreal (56%). Home ownership rates are much higher outside of metropolitan areas.

If aging in place is what Perennials really want, this upends a lot of theories about the future of real estate in Canada. Instead of our countryside being dotted with purpose-built retiree complexes and acres of abandoned family homes in the suburbs, **we will see growing demand for supports and housing options that allow seniors to live independently in their own homes for as long as they want to**, especially in established urban and suburban communities.

Technology companies that are sensitive to Perennials see their future growth market as being more than just creating new entertainment options for bored Millennials and Gen Zers. Growth can also come from meeting the Perennials' desire for independent living. There's a big opportunity here for monitoring technology, especially when it comes to helping older Canadians manage their health. Many Perennials with health concerns, when faced with the choice of going to assisted care or using monitoring technology, will opt for monitoring options. Imagine technologies that will do everything from keeping an eye on them to coaching them through their day (with medication reminders, for example) to accessing medical care and all the delivery services necessary to keep them healthy and happy at home. Monitoring technologies could allow anxious children to check in on their aging parents and even monitor their key health signs, household entry and exit, bank accounts, and deliveries. The list of possibilities is limited only by the imagination. We will need all of this technology, because Canadians might continue to age in place for a very long time.

Among the countries in the Organisation for Economic Co-operation and Development, Canada has relatively low rates of senior poverty because seniors receive a high proportion of their retirement income from private pensions and other financial assets—a good thing, since only about a fifth of us believe public pensions will be adequate for our retirement. According to Boomerwatch.ca, Boomers, who make up a greater share of our senior population every day, hold 80% of Canada's financial wealth. Perennials are financially secure, with predictable incomes and money in the bank, and are also mortgage-free if they own their home.

For many Perennials, then, there are a lot of good reasons to keep their family home and stay right where they are. Aging in place, together with independent living and bridge employment, is the future for Canada's Perennials.

Keep in mind that one of the most dramatic consequences of age-related deterioration is loss of independence. That is more feared by older Canadians than almost any other outcome. But staying indefinitely within one's own familiar four walls requires an ability to move around safely in a neighbourhood, as well as having access to vital resources such as food outlets, public transportation, day-to-day services, and places of entertainment. A lot of older Canadians live in the suburbs. Our suburbs weren't designed for older people, who, as they age, are less likely to drive. They were built for families who don't mind being car-dependent. Therefore, one of the big opportunities going forward will be for companies that have creative solutions for making our growing suburbs more age-friendly and less car-dependent. This means expanding transportation options beyond the personal automobile.

Are you looking for a great business opportunity? How about solving this problem for Canada's Perennials? Beyond transportation, making urban and suburban amenities more Perennial-focused is an underserved opportunity that will have vast and growing demand. Think homemaker services, grocery and meal delivery, lawn and home maintenance services, and home health services. Not to mention all the technological and service upgrades that will be required to make family homes for aging Perennials suitable for bridge employment.

So, sorry, Gen Xers and Millennials: that house you've been eyeing in Vancouver or Toronto will likely be staying off the market for some time to come. Mom and Dad aren't going anywhere. And where they are living is just going to keep getting better—they will use their political and market power to demand it.

## Unlocking the Perennials' Wealth

The lifestyle that Perennials desire won't come for free. It will require that they spend some of their personal wealth, especially the equity they have tied up in real estate. Perennials don't believe they are wealthy and are deeply worried about being able to afford a comfortable retirement. This is a tough nut to crack. But the anticipation appears to be worse than the reality for most. Nearly half of those considering retirement say they will miss a regular paycheque when they retire, but of those who are retired today, only about a quarter say they miss their paycheque. That doesn't apply to everyone equally, though. Research shows that the pressure to cash out is stronger for older women because they feel less confident about paying for their retirement than men. And it's obviously a different world for less-affluent Perennials facing retirement.

While the anticipation and actual experience of affording retirement may differ for many Canadians, most of us are also aware that our retirement will likely last longer than it did for Canadians in previous generations. Several different studies by Ipsos show that around 60% of us now worry that we will outlive our savings. Only about half of us are confident that we will have enough money to retire comfortably. Still, only about half of us are doing anything about it: 60% of working Canadians say they don't contribute annually to their retirement savings, while 30% say they haven't started saving for retirement at all.

Will our kids be there to help us if we can't afford retirement? While the spirit is willing—72% of younger Canadians say they owe it to their parents to keep them comfortable in retirement—older parents know their children's financial capacity to help them is limited. Three-quarters of Canadian parents don't want their kids to contribute financially to their retirement.

What about help going the other way? In the end, Perennials should just spend their money on themselves. Your kids don't expect or want your help if it means a poorer retirement for you. Only 35% of Canadians expect to inherit from their parents, and over 90% of those who expect an inheritance would give it up to improve their parents' retirement lifestyle.

The financial realities of retirement represent a big challenge for both governments and financial institutions, especially when we consider the rapid aging of Canada's population. To begin with, we need to put to rest the big myth that most retirees are destitute and must make ongoing demands of governments (really, younger working Canadians) to subsidize their retirement. The truth is that the financial position of most Canadian retirees is solid—even more solid than they themselves believe it to be.

Next, we need to encourage Perennials to unlock the considerable wealth they are sitting on. This is important not only for governments and financial institutions, but for any company that wants to sell products and services to Canadians. It will require a message of reassurance. Many Perennials are wealthier than they know. As research from the insurance company Sun Life has found, retirement is less costly and precarious than many Canadians fear it to be. For example, retirees today say they live on about 62% of the income level they earned immediately before leaving the workforce.

**Perennials need to be encouraged to responsibly liquidate their assets and to spend more aggressively during their retirement** than they are planning to right now, especially if they are bridge employed. Financial institutions must get more creative with their retirement products, but governments also need to amend our tax laws so that liquidating assets in retirement is easier and more attractive. Because a quarter of Canadian homeowners expect their home to be their primary source of retirement income, Perennial homeowners should look at their home equity to unlock their wealth while continuing to live comfortably within the asset.

The final part of meeting this challenge will be focusing public funds on those Perennials who need help with their retirement. That means breaking down the universality of retiree benefits to concentrate on those who are struggling. The survey data show that women are disproportionately (but not exclusively) less-affluent retirees. We will likely need to bring in some form of means testing in the not-too-distant future.

## What This Means for Your Business

What are you creating for Perennials? They dominate the Canadian and global marketplace, and will for the foreseeable future. **This silver tsunami of seniors not only has the numbers, they also have the money.** If you're ignoring them, or treating them as a subsidiary market, you're missing the biggest opportunity available to most businesses today.

The Perennials want stability and independence, which means staying in their homes and neighbourhoods as long as possible. Any services that can help them do this represent business opportunities. These could include retrofitting family homes to ease mobility for older owners, maintenance services for everything from light repairs to snow removal, and delivery services to reduce the need to drive.

Employment is part of stability and independence too. Older workers represent the greatest untapped human resource available in Canada today. Unfortunately, the one prejudice that remains acceptable in too many workplaces is ageism. Given the need for skilled workers, employers will need to figure out how to deal with ageist behaviour. Younger employees will have to get used to seeing more grey hair around the workplace, and older workers must find a way to fit in successfully with bosses and teammates who might be considerably younger. Consultants who specialize in helping intergenerational workplaces to function better will be looking at an expanding market.

## What This Means for You

Which companies have figured out how to successfully market to the Perennials? These companies will make great investments. You will still be ahead of the curve on this because investors, like marketers, are obsessed with youth.

Something you will hear a lot about is the pending massive generational wealth transfer from Boomers to their kids. If you're counting on it, don't. It will happen eventually, but it is likely to be slower and smaller than analysts suggest. Boomers are living longer than anticipated and are likely to use their assets to pay for a more comfortable later life, including additional health-care services. **Companies in the business of helping aging Boomers enjoy their expanding golden years will have a growing market.** If you are looking for a solid career with a huge potential upside, work in this area is worth considering.

CHAPTER 3

# *Generation Xtra-Small*: How a Tiny Segment of the Population Can Rule the Country

## The Baby Busters

If the Perennial Generation is composed of Canada's seniors and soon-to-be seniors, what about their kids? Let's start with the generation that immediately follows them, Gen X, also known as the Baby Busters. Why the Baby Busters? The combination of changing choices made by women about their education, careers, marriage, and children (now, now, later, later) and easy access to safe medical technology and legal remedies that enabled those choices (the birth control pill and easier divorce) contributed to the collapse of Canadian fertility rates through the 1960s.

How bad was the collapse? In 1959, the fertility rate for Canada was around 4.0 births per woman. By 1970, it had dropped to 2.3, and it has continued to slide to 1.5 today. In terms of households, this means that families with three or more children have declined from 42% in 1961 to 16% in 2016. One-child families have gone in the other direction. Today, they represent almost half of all Canadian families with kids.

Apart from the absolute decline in the ratio of children being born in the 1960s, and its impact on family and household size,

Gen Xers also experienced the first significant move to the outsourcing of parenting, driven by two-income families becoming more the norm as Mom and Dad both pursued personal fulfillment, financial reward, and independence by being employed outside of the home. Since Mom was now less likely to be at home with the kids than in previous generations, and Dad wasn't inclined to step up to fill in the child-care gap, we saw the creation of the first generation of latchkey kids—children who came home from school to an empty house, a generational emblem if there ever was one.

All of this was part of a major transformation of the Canadian family that we're still experiencing today.

## The Evolution of the Canadian Family

To appreciate the magnitude of this change, consider what the Canadian family used to be like. Believe it or not, family structures at the turn of the last century were in many ways more complicated than they are today, and they were certainly shaped by different forces. Going back to 1901, for example, 31% of census family households contained non-family members, compared to only 9% in 2011. Other household members back then largely comprised additions due to death or employment situations. Farmhands lived with families, or cousins were forced to move in with aunts or uncles because of the death of a parent.

While personal choice, urbanization, medical science, common law marriages, and no-fault divorce are the biggest shapers of household and family structures these days, the Grim Reaper was the biggest shaper of households a century ago. In the early twentieth century, widowhood of parents with children at home was much more common than it is today. Back then, almost one in ten children under the age of 15 experienced the death of at least one parent. Today, it's only about one in a hundred. Unlike today, the proportion of single-parent families headed by men was higher because a significant cause of death among maternal-aged women was health complications due to child-birth. With improvements in maternity care over the last hundred years, the ratio of female to male lone-parent families has surged and is now 4:1, mainly driven by divorce.

While the Baby Boom gets a lot of attention from analysts because of its size, we rarely hear about how unique it was in terms of the families it created. The assumption is that Boomers simply replicated the families that came before them. Not true. For some reason, perhaps pent-up frustration due to the sacrifices of the Great Depression and the Second World War, beginning in 1946, men and women began marrying at a younger age than their parents had, and women started having children earlier and in greater numbers than their mothers did. These demographic shifts, together with reductions in childhood and maternal mortality, contributed to a different family experience for Boomers: two married parents with lots of biological siblings living under a single roof. The irony is that this Boomer model family—which some still uphold today as the "traditional" family—is an outlier in Canadian history.

Boomer families were all about married male and female couples producing their own biological offspring. In 1961, married couples accounted for 92% of census families, while only 8% were lone-parent families. These rare lone-parent families were still mostly created by the death of a parent. About 62% were widowed, 3% were never married, and 36% were divorced or separated. By 2011, the numbers had flipped: 51% of single-parent families were produced by divorce or separation, 32% were never married, and only 18% were widowed. We are much better now at keeping parents with young children alive, but we're a lot poorer at keeping them together in the same household.

The other big change we've experienced in terms of family structure since the Baby Boom has been the growth of common-law families. As recently as 1981, only 6% of us lived in common-law arrangements; that number has now nearly tripled to 17%.

With fewer of us getting married right away, the delay in family formation, the increase in common-law families and urbanization, and the ascent of single-parent families, household sizes have declined in Canada while the total number of households has increased. Relatively high rates of separation and divorce in Canada add to the growth of smaller households. Marital breakdowns produce two smaller households after the dissolution of a previously larger one. But even in traditional families, kids don't live at home forever. When they finally leave Mom and Dad's house for good (provided they don't boomerang back), they also reduce the size of their own household and, if they don't create their own family right away, end up becoming "Singletons" à la Bridget Jones.

## Solo Living and Multigenerational Households

This perfect storm of demographic and cultural forces has created a new and growing trend in household formation in which people, to quote Greta Garbo, "want to be alone." Why are more and more Canadians living alone? Many factors are contributing to this growing phenomenon: more generous income support programs, more and better pensions, and more women in the workforce have created greater economic independence at the individual level, which allows for more choice about personal living arrangements. When we can choose to, a lot of us prefer our own space. Higher rates of marriage breakdown and population aging are also contributors to this trend, especially among women, and particularly older women.

How big is solo living in Canada? **One-person households are**

**now the most common household category in Canada, having surpassed the previously most common category: couples living with kids.** How big a change is this? In 1951, only 7% of Canadian households were occupied by those flying solo; now, it's 28%. Like many of the big demographic trends I've touched on, this is another first in Canadian history. And this trend is not unique to Canada. Single-person households are becoming more the rule than the exception in many developed, low-fertility countries with aging populations, including the United States (28%), the United Kingdom (29%), France (34%), Japan (35%), Sweden (36%), Norway (40%), and Germany (41%).

For anyone interested in housing, this trend towards single-person households isn't a blip or a transitional phase that will create short-term pressure for the rental real estate market alone. Solo home ownership is on the rise as single seniors become wealthier and young people delay (or eschew) marriage and having children. Both groups, when they want to buy rather than rent, are moving into one-bedroom condos. Women, who make up 54% of solo households, are now over-represented in the singles condo market, according to Canada Mortgage and Housing Corporation. Women represent 65% of condo owner-occupants living alone, with that number rising to 76% for those 55 and older.

While solo living is becoming the most common living arrangement in Canada, it's not our fastest-growing household category. That prize goes to multigenerational households, where three or more generations of the same family live in the same home. Although this is still a small category—3% of all households—it has grown by 38% since 2001. And while 3% might not seem like a lot, it represents 2.2 million Canadians.

Why have we seen this increase in multigenerational living? Statistics

Canada suggests it may be partly due to our changing ethnocultural composition. Multigenerational living arrangements are more common among Canada's fastest-growing population segments, Indigenous people and immigrants. But Statistics Canada also gives a nod to pricey real estate in Canada's biggest cities as a potential driver. (For more on multicultural families, see "*McFuture*: Why Suburbia Will Beat Out Downtown, Every Time," page 131.)

## Understanding Gen Xers

Now that we understand how families and households in Canada have transformed over the last hundred years, and what this transformation means for the typical Canadian household (which is no longer so typical), what does this tell us about Generation X, those born between 1966 and 1971? They are the first generation to have experienced this upheaval in their households, and they wear these formative experiences as a generational emblem.

While Gen X is our smallest generation—about 8% of the Canadian population—**they are and will be very important for the short- to medium-term for all aspects of Canadian life because they are the generation of consumers, workers, and leaders who will immediately follow the rapidly retiring Baby Boom.** That is, if the Boomers retire, which they seem less inclined to do these days, at least in the time frame they were originally expected to. Nonetheless, Gen Xers have grown up and started their careers in a job market and workplace dominated by Boomers. They understand the values legacy of that generation, but they have also seen the technological revolution unfold, and they understand the power of the digital world.

Gen Xers are also the first Canadians to represent a more heterogeneous generation that is comfortable with and celebrates social diversity in race, class, religion, ethnicity, culture, language, gender identity, and sexual orientation. All things diversity is a significant Gen X emblem. Just ask our first Gen X prime minister, Justin Trudeau.

Another important Gen X touchstone was the fall of the Berlin Wall and the corresponding end of the Cold War. Thus, the thought of dying in a nuclear holocaust, which had so dominated the formative years of the Boomers, was less of a preoccupation for Gen Xers. Gen Xers did live through the first Gulf War, but as with so many other things in the Gen X world, that looked more like a video game than the real thing. The daily media briefings US General Norman Schwarzkopf gave from the Iraq front featured antiseptic videos of precision-guided smart bombs that always hit their targets. The people those bombs hit were never shown and rarely discussed.

Economically, Gen Xers entered the workforce during the dot-com bubble and bust. They also lived through two big events that raised questions about civilization's ability to control and benefit from technology: the Challenger and Chernobyl disasters. Canadian Gen Xers saw the rise of MuchMusic (the Canadian equivalent of MTV) and the near miss for Quebec separatism in 1995. And Gen Xers everywhere in the developed world experienced the popularization of the personal computer.

Gen X is, like the late Boomers, a "sandwich" generation. They are squeezed between raising their kids (even though they are having fewer of them) and caring for aging parents. They are also working harder to compensate for stalled incomes that must now cover skyrocketing big-city housing prices. (They most likely bought their homes during bubble periods, if at all.) But unlike many Boomers who benefitted from cheap post-secondary education, they are also burdened with paying off significant student debt at the same time as their work and social benefits have likely declined.

All of this makes Gen Xers pessimistic about being able to afford retirement. For Gen Xers, retiring at age 65 and doing exactly what they want to in their golden years seems an unrealistic, romantic notion. An Allianz Life study on retirement in the United States found that 67% of Gen Xers agreed that the supposed "targets" for how much financial capacity one needs to retire are way out of reach for them. Moreover, 68% of Gen Xers believe they will never have enough money to retire. How will they deal with this dilemma? Half of Gen Xers have decided not to worry about it.

While the numbers in Canada are better on this, the trend is basically the same: Gen Xers' heads are firmly entrenched in the sand. With the overall aging of Canada's population, this is a financial disaster just waiting to happen.

## The Myth of the Slacker

The reversal in social and economic progress that marks Gen X has given them the reputation of being a "lost generation" or "slackers." This reputation is based on the belief that the Gen X animating myth isn't Horatio Alger and his rags-to-riches stories about how hard work and exemplary moral character will lead to good life outcomes; instead, it's American actress Janeane Garofalo pointing out in the classic Gen X movie *Reality Bites* that Evian is "naive" spelled backwards. Everything is a con, and we're all being had by the system. Only Garofalo and the more enlightened members of her Gen X cohort see this reality and are doing what's rational in response: living the life of the Gen X slacker stereotype.

Yes, there are likely some Gen X slackers out there. You know, that group of flannel-wearing, alienated, overeducated, overcaffeinated, underachieving and now aging malcontents who are doomed to work forever at McJobs. But that's mostly a convenient pop culture trope that hasn't aged very well.

The truth about Gen X in Canada is that they (and their parents) are the first generation to significantly invest in higher education. They did this at the same time as government investment in both universities and community colleges exploded. Yes, Gen Xers may have started adult life with higher student debt than their parents did, but they also gave themselves advanced degrees and levels of professional accreditation that their parents never dreamt of for themselves. The numbers tell the story. Today, 54% of Canadians between the ages 25 and 64 have a university or college qualification. This is the highest percentage in the Organisation for Economic Co-operation and Development. The question is whether this investment in time and money will pay off for Gen X and the generations that follow them.

The results of investing big time in education have been mixed for Gen Xers. Timing has had a big impact on this. Many Gen Xers, especially men, had trouble entering the labour market in the 1980s and 1990s due to both economic recessions and the misfortune of following the ubiquitous Boomer generation who dominated the workplace. In addition, studies show that people who began their careers when times were tough may never fully catch up to those who started during more prosperous times. But if a Gen Xer got a break, they took advantage of it and then emulated the employee loyalty exhibited by their Boomer predecessors.

A very interesting Workopolis study shows that Gen X employees tend to spend more time in each job they hold than Gen Y employees do. Gen X university grads had an average of 3.2 jobs in the first 12 years of their career. They stayed an average of 41 months, or 3.4 years, in each job. Just 10 years later, Gen Y held 3.9 jobs over their first 12 years in the job market, with a shorter 32.5 months, or 2.7 years, in each job, on average. Gen Y changed jobs 22% more often over a 12-year period than Gen X did. If this Gen Y trend continues, these Canadians can expect to hold roughly fifteen jobs in their careers. This study suggests that **neither Gen X nor Gen Y are really "slackers"—they just hustle in a way that Baby Boomers simply never had to.**

## Workplace Personality Profiles

Just because Gen Xers tend to become loyal employees once they settle down in a career, that doesn't mean they are identical to Boomers in the workplace. A study by Personnel Decisions International surveyed 24,000 mid-level managers and showed that Gen Xers tend to be more independent, self-motivated, and self-sufficient than Boomers, who are more diligent in doing their assigned jobs and tend to prefer more stable working environments (like Whyte's Organization Man). Boomers also tend to work harder and are generally more loyal to their employer than Gen Xers are; this is confirmed by both Statistics Canada and Workopolis.

In an Ernst and Young study, 1,200 professionals across generations and industries were asked their perceptions of generations in the workplace. These professionals saw Millennials as tech-savvy but not great team players; Gen Xers as entrepreneurial-thinking but lacking executive presence; and Boomers as loyal team players who don't necessarily adapt well to change.

Boomers tend to accept the chain of command and expect their managers to give them direction and lead them towards organizational goals. But Boomers are not as technologically savvy as Gen Xers. Gen Xers are also more likely to emphasize personal satisfaction with work as being important to them. They look for opportunities to improve their work skills, rather than just doing the work assigned to them. They are more loyal to their profession than to their specific employer, and are more individualistic, with a higher need for autonomy and flexibility in their careers.

Want to be a good employer who gets the most out of Gen X and Gen Y? Understand that their biggest assets are adaptability, technological literacy, independence, perseverance, and creativity. Also understand that, along with job autonomy, Gen X and Gen Y place a high value on participating in decision-making. They prefer relationship-oriented leadership styles, while Boomers tend to prefer teamwork directed by leaders in positional authority and a task-oriented leadership style. You will do better with Gen X and Millennials if you show them your destination but let them decide how to get there and the role they will play in the journey. And let them pick the tunes and play with the GPS—they like technology. With Boomers, you'll do better if you set the destination and the route and tell them how they can personally help the team get to where you are all headed. Go ahead and pick the music. They are fine with that.

These workplace studies suggest that Gen X (and Gen Y) have created a new profile of needs when it comes to fulfillment in the workplace. What's a profile of needs? Abraham Maslow developed the hierarchy of needs, which was all about trying to understand what motivates people. Maslow believed we are all motivated to meet certain needs. When one need is fulfilled, we seek to fulfill the next one, and so on. At the top of the hierarchy of needs is self-actualization, which involves realizing personal potential and achieving self-fulfillment, seeking personal growth, and enjoying peak experiences. That all sounds very Gen X.

Some analysts go a step further and argue that Gen X has broken the rules of the traditional Maslow hierarchy of needs. Whereas Boomers tended to follow a career path of education, career, marriage, and promotion up the ladder to a final mid-life self-realization, Gen Xers short-circuit this process. They require self-realization from their job and personal life at the same time, and do not want work to negatively affect their quality of life. For Gen Xers, then, job satisfaction is more important than it was for Boomers, and it needs to be balanced with a satisfying life outside their job. They are not prepared to make sacrifices demanded by their organizations if it means becoming a workaholic. They certainly aren't slackers. Far from it. But neither are they the Organization Man of the Boomer generation.

## Tomorrow's Leaders

**Understand Gen X's needs and you will understand an important segment of the consumer and political marketplace for the next couple of decades.** Gen Xers faced several daunting challenges in their lives that have had a huge impact on their prevailing world view. Most obviously, they had the unenviable task of immediately following the generation that still dominates today's world: the inescapable Boomers. To Gen Xers, Boomers had everything so much easier. They got to the good jobs with the best benefits first; they bought the best houses in the best neighbourhoods when they were cheap and abundant; they had the benefit of living in incredibly stable family situations; and the world they lived in was more trusting and predictable.

Yes, some Gen Xers responded to their lousy hand by becoming the cynical slackers that pop sociologists and Hollywood claim they are. However, most have done the opposite of expectations, becoming toughened by the stiff competition that is a product of their unfortunate life timing. They represent the struggling middle class that everybody keeps talking about. And they are an important transitional generation. As Boomers gradually retire, Gen Xers will be the group of leaders who are first poised to take over. Given what they've been through, they have the potential to be a very strong leadership group indeed.

## What This Means for Your Business

**Gen Xers are the next group of leaders for your business.** They have the same aspirations as the employees they will replace, but how they work will be different. What do you know about Gen X work and leadership styles? What changes should you make in your work environment to take advantage of their considerable experience and build loyalty with them? One specific workplace consideration for Gen Xers, especially Gen X women, will be making it possible for them to handle the needs of their aging parents.

What are Gen Xers like as customers? They been through tough times. Their optimism about generational progress—that the current generation will do better than the last—has been shaken in a way the Boomers didn't experience. To help Gen Xers feel like they are making the progress they were told to expect, facilitate their realization of important life markers: real estate and other assets, retirement savings, and those special purchases that say "I've made it." The catch is, you're dealing with customers who also have a lot of expenses. Put simply, the key words are "success on a budget."

## What This Means for You

**If you're a member of Gen X, you are about to have your moment.** Not only are you first up to replace those Perennials who decide to retire, but you are the core of the much-talked-about middle class every political leader in Canada is laser-focused on. Understanding the wants and needs of Gen Xers—especially those who live in Canada's biggest suburbs—is critically important to Canada's political leaders. Sure, they are still most interested in winning the votes of Perennials, but you will be next on their hit parade. Don't sell your vote cheap!

What are Gen Xers looking for? Like their parents, they want stability and independence, but they are also confronted with the challenges of being a true sandwich generation. They worry about their aging parents, and they also had their kids later in life and are now on the hook for their expensive education. **The big Gen X issue is staying ahead of the affordability curve.**

CHAPTER 4

# *Millennial Mystique*: Making the Most of Our Most Misunderstood Demographic

## Dismantling the Stereotypes

The Millennials. Always the Millennials. We're obsessed with what we're told is today's transformational generation. Every day it seems we hear more about them than any other generation. They certainly are a favourite topic for today's marketing consultants, pop sociologists, human resources experts, and journalists, who never seem to tire of telling us about Gen Y's independence, sophistication, confidence, cynicism, impatience, and narcissism—and even their avocado toast!

It's the same with the marketplace impact of Millennials. We are told that Millennials are breaking all the old commercial rules and are immune to conventional marketing channels and sales pitches. They say it's because Millennials are uniquely obsessed with technology, which moves them to a new plane of communication.

Is this the truth about Millennials? Not really. Older and younger generations are coming together on technology, not pulling apart. Millennials may have engaged with the digital world earlier in their lives than previous generations, but access is basically the same now across all age groups. Yes, intensity of engagement varies by generation, but that's changing too. It's the same for Millennial leadership in research and purchasing online, and in abandoning conventional TV and landline telephones. Again, Mom and Dad (and even Grandma and Grandpa) are catching up to their kids very quickly.

We're also told that Millennials reject every chief marketing officer's obsession: brand loyalty. Gen Y is supposed to be uniquely picky, hard to reach, and ultimately fickle and disloyal. All true, according to the data. But the other generations have also followed Gen Y down this path. The more you look at Gen Y, the more it turns out that many of the claims about their unique personality and marketplace characteristics are simplified, misinterpreted, or just plain wrong. What we are told about Millennials misses their fundamental, defining emblem.

## Generation Anxious

What really marks Millennials as unique from other generations is their diminished expectations about achieving important life goals. It's their level of disappointment and frustration, not their self-satisfaction, that stands out. **Gen Y, even more than Gen X, believes they will *not* have a better life than their parents did, in nearly all respects.** That's why they are Generation Anxious.

Why are Millennials so anxious? Because progress, as it used to be understood by their parents and grandparents, seems out of reach for them. Gen Y struggles to get launched. The challenging entry-level job market forces them to accept positions below their post-secondary qualifications and aspirations. They also carry lots of student debt—nearly $30,000 worth, on average. And it can take them until their mid-30s to pay it off. This level of debt delays significant life decisions like finding a fulfilling career, buying a home, forming a committed relationship, and starting a family. You know, those key markers of adult independence and maturity that we've been told are our birthright.

It is these diminished life expectations, and what they mean for all aspects of market demand, that should be foremost in our minds when considering Canada's Millennials. That's because, as with Boomers, **the marketplace will increasingly be shaped by the life stages of Gen Y.** Yes, Gen X will get there first, but Gen Y will eventually overtake them, due to their weight of numbers.

Gen Y is Canada's second-largest generation, at just over a quarter of our population. They are already a big force in the Canadian marketplace and will remain so for the long term as well. While they are a significant force, they are not the dominant force for the time being. That title still goes to the Perennials, because of their relative size and wealth. So the Millennial impact on the marketplace could be less and slower than we are told it will be. This could be a very big problem. Remember those mangled expectations and crushed dreams? The potential for intergenerational envy and anger is staring us in the face.

## What the World Looks Like for Perennials and Millennials

Ultimately, generational influence is about the lives of real people, not statistics. What does the world look like for the people who dominate Canada's population today and for the foreseeable future, the Perennials and Millennials? Which life events are they about to experience, and what issues will they be challenged by?

The oldest members of the Perennial Generation (born in the mid- to late 1940s or earlier) are now pushing into their early 70s and are experiencing all the changes that go along with that stage of life. Older Perennials are wondering where to live and whether to sell the family home (although they're not as set on this as we think); how much to help their struggling kids and maybe even their grandkids; whether they should still be working, at least a bit; and how to make their golden years count. Health is moving higher up their list of priorities with each passing year, and so is paying for a lengthier retirement that few had planned for.

If all has gone well for the younger Perennials (born in the 1950s and early 1960s), they are now enjoying their peak earning years in steady jobs, paying off their mortgages, and attending university graduations (more than their parents did) and weddings (fewer than their parents did) as they contemplate winding down the jobs they've held for twenty years or more. All is not rosy, though. They are living with the issues of being the first true sandwich generation. They are sandwiched between caring for parents living longer than expected and helping their children (and grandchildren), who are having a tough time getting on track with their adult lives.

What about Millennials? The oldest ones (born in the mid-1970s) have just reached their 40s. If they've been lucky, they are now established in the workplace, are on the property ladder (but saddled with a weighty mortgage), are celebrating their first decade of marriage (or other relationship arrangement), and are the proud parents of one or two tweens or young teenagers but don't want more kids. What hasn't changed, though, is that, just like older Canadians, these **Millennials say their top three financial priorities are buying a home, saving for their children's education, and preparing for retirement.** An Ipsos survey showed that 86% of Gen Yers believe that owning a house or condo is a very good investment and an important life goal. So, yes, we all still want to own our homes, regardless of which generation we are in.

The youngest Millennials have just reached their mid-20s and are now confronting all of life's big decisions: where to live, who to love, how to build a career and an income, and when or if they should start a family. When thinking of young Millennials, the HBO series *Girls*, created by and starring Lena Dunham, comes to mind. Yes,

*Girls* reflects a unique American experience, and Canadian Millennials differ from Hannah and her friends in important ways. Yes, as with the Gen X slacker stereotype, *Girls* is an extreme representation of a very narrow slice of this generation. But the issues that the show's characters confront in each episode are all too real for most Canadian late-Millennials. How do I start a career commensurate with my high sense of self-worth and the investment I (and my parents) have made in my education when all that's available are service jobs, internships, and contract gigs? How do I do this while simultaneously managing a crushing level of student debt? How do I live in this city (substitute Toronto or Vancouver for Manhattan) that's *so* expensive? How do I find love and a meaningful relationship in a world of fluid genders and sexual identities, as well as complicated family possibilities?

## Millennial Strengths and Challenges

If Millennials seem complicated, that's because they are. Like Gen X before them, they are the product of huge cultural and demographic changes all around them. They are more likely to have older parents, fewer siblings, and more complicated families than Perennials or even Gen Xers. They are less likely to be in an adult partnership, and more likely to be living alone or at home with their parents.

Millennials gravitate to urban and suburban communities with diverse populations in terms of ethnicity, race, and religious backgrounds. They also have a smaller geographic footprint, since most are avoiding small-town and rural life. At the same time, they are intensely plugged into the bigger world through technology and the internet. Gen Y is the first generation in Canadian history to have the entire history of human knowledge easily available to them online. They also have the skills to use it: **they are the most literate and educated generation in Canadian history, in any way this can be measured.**

Nonetheless, Millennials, on average, do have a harder time in many important areas of life than their parents and grandparents did. Two good examples are buying homes and building careers. It is more expensive for Canadians today in urban and suburban markets (where over 80% of us live) to get on the real estate ladder than it has ever been. And stable careers are also much harder to come by. To get ahead in today's job market, ambitious Millennials need to hustle even more than the pseudo-slacker Gen Xers did.

## Home Ownership in Canada

Let's start with owning a home. Canada is a nation of homeowners and those who want to be homeowners. In 2016, the home ownership rate in Canada was 68%. But it varies greatly by age:

| Age | Home Ownership Rate |
|---|---|
| 20–34 | 44% |
| 35–54 | 70% |
| 55–64 | 76% |
| 65+ | 75% |

Seniors today are more likely to own their homes than they were over a decade ago, an increase of 3%, from 72% in 2006. Conversely, people younger than 65 are less likely to own their homes today than in 2006. Most importantly, though, comparing Millennials and Boomers at the same stage of life, Boomers at 30 had a 56% rate of home ownership, compared to only 50% of 30-year-old Millennials today.

Home ownership is driven by costs. While in the mid-1980s a home would have cost a Canadian family around 1.6 times its annual income, the multiple today is closer to 8 times the average pre-tax family income. In prime urban and suburban locations, average home prices have shot up past that. It is vastly more difficult for Gen Y to hop onto the real estate ladder now than it ever was for their moms and dads.

Analysts at Bank of Montreal describe the situation succinctly: average house prices have increased more than 100% over the last two decades, while income has gone up by only 50%. This makes home ownership much harder for both Gen X and Gen Y. Along with student debt, the inability to buy a home is one of the reasons both generations have fewer kids and have them later in life. And a delay in buying homes and starting families also makes paying for their children's education and saving for retirement (two of Gen Y's other big priorities) more difficult to balance.

When Millennials finally do become homeowners, there's a difference in the type of dwellings they buy. In 1981, 44% of Boomers lived in a single detached home, compared to only 35% of Millennials today. **Young adults are now more likely to live in apartments or condos**, especially when they live in Vancouver or Toronto, Canada's two most expensive real estate markets. This trend is just one example of how the housing landscape has changed across generations because of housing trends such as urbanization and increased condo construction.

## Living at Home

In addition to the huge jump in real estate prices, as well as changing tastes in dwellings, the workplace for Millennials has become a more complicated maze with smaller and fewer pieces of cheese. No wonder Statistics Canada has found that **half of Canada's 20-somethings in the Greater Toronto Area are still living with their parents.** That's right, half. In the country overall, 35% live at home with at least one parent. And this isn't just a Canadian thing. A third of young Americans are in the same situation. This living arrangement is even more prevalent in Europe, where almost half of young adults live with at least one parent. Staying at home is slightly more of a male trend, with a male-female ratio of 5:4.

It is worth emphasizing again that the shift towards remaining single is significant. It has an impact not only on family formation and fertility, but also on our social support structures. More young people are moving into adulthood without the support of an adult partnership or a family they have formed. If your initial work experience is a short-term contract with indefinite earnings, you are really on your own and exposed just when you are trying to manage significant educational debt. No wonder young people are staying at home with their parents longer.

The issue here isn't that young people never leave home. A lot of rebounding goes on. For example, while about 70% of Canadians age 20 to 24 have never left home, the percentage for those age 25 to 29 is much lower, at 27%. Of Canadians who are 30 to 34, only 9% have never left home. And we shouldn't make the mistake of believing this is all about a failure to launch. Almost 10% of young Canadians stay home to take care of one or more of their parents.

As more young adults are living with their parents (for whatever reason), a smaller percentage are living within a family they have started for themselves. The share of young adults living within their own family, without their parents, dropped from 49% in 2001 to 42% in 2016. This also means that a smaller proportion of young adults are living with children, either as part of a couple or in a lone-parent family. The number of younger-parent families has dropped from 33% in 2001 to 26% today.

## Settling for Less

According to the Conference Board of Canada, limited career choices and cost-of-living pressures have caused members of Gen Y to become "hopeless Millennials." They've developed a lower desired job ceiling than even Gen X. Gen Xers are closer to the peak of their careers than Millennials and can therefore see their preferred retirement date more clearly. But the Conference Board also suggests that some of the difference can be explained by lower ambitions. That's right, Millennials may already be giving up the quest and starting to settle for less.

Millennials are setting lower, more realistic career goals for themselves. This also fits with data that show that they are more likely to work part-time and at minimum wage than older generations, making sticking at a company and moving up through the ranks more difficult for them. If they manage to get themselves on a desirable career path, Millennials do expect to be rewarded for their persistence and accomplishment. But as the Conference Board opines, they aren't necessarily defined by the entitlement for which this generation has become notorious. Members of Gen Y (and also Gen X) believe promotions should be tied to an employee's skills and job performance at an almost equal rate. The lesson, according to the Conference Board, is that **young employees expect a meritocratic system, where competence trumps seniority or experience.**

Even after they've landed a job, many Millennials feel their position is too precarious to make the big life decisions that previous generations made more easily. An Ipsos survey showed that about a quarter of working Canadians today don't feel secure in their job. This rate goes up for Canadians under 35: about a third feel insecure. A third of working Canadians say they are considering a career change in the next year, and about half of those are under 35. Again, all of this works against forming life relationships, creating a stable home, and starting a family. You need stability to do all these things.

## Building a Career—or Careers

How are Millennials working their way through the workplace maze? If one strategy is investing in education, another is flexibility and mobility. A lot of Millennials are moving from one employer to another, or from one city to another, to find a job or advance their careers. A Workopolis study shows that Canadians are increasingly changing jobs, and even completely changing careers, to confront the challenges of today's employment market. Survey results reveal that the most common reasons people cite for changing jobs are discovering a new field they are passionate about, becoming disillusioned with their original career field, and career setbacks (cutbacks, layoffs, and limited upward mobility).

Workopolis's research also shows that three-quarters of Canadians won't stay in the same career for life, and that 88% of the time, people need to change employers to advance their careers. Canadians are remarkably aware of the realities of today's job market, and Millennials more so than anyone else. It's a simple rule: you must move on to move up. The new norm is for people to stay in one job for two to three years and then move on.

It's ironic that employers spend so much time, money, and rhetoric on building what they call employee loyalty when employers themselves aren't loyal to their employees. As the Workopolis study points out, employers prefer to hire from outside over internal promotion because they judge those who work for them more harshly than they do outsiders. But employees who do manage to overcome their employer's bias for the new, and are promoted from within an organization, tend to achieve the greatest levels of overall success. Their careers advance further and faster than those who choose to job-hop to move up. Promotions also lead to *real* employee loyalty. Those who are promoted from within stay longer. **If you want a**

**loyal, high-performance staff, give them a chance to build their careers within your organization.** This will be especially effective with members of Gen Y, who are desperate for job stability so they can get on with their lives.

So Millennials can expect to move more for work, as well as change jobs and career paths more frequently than previous generations did. When thinking about future careers, they should look to fields with a healthy demand for talent, a growing workforce, and a generous salary with room to move up. Surprisingly, these mostly include careers in the public sector and many of the traditional industries, including natural resources. What? Video game design doesn't top the list? As with so many other things, this would be a narrow and misplaced view of careers for Millennials. Sure, there will be lots of Millennials who find themselves in technology careers. But what do Millennials want most? In the end, they are not that different from the rest of the generations when it comes to what they expect from a career. Rather than being a revolutionary generation, set to change everything that came before them, they are behaving just as earlier generations did at the same stage of life. Millennials and older generations have the same expectations of their employer: to be rewarded for the work they do and to have the opportunity to grow and work for someone who cares about them. A bit of stability and certainty in their lives, as opposed to being stuck in the gig economy, is what they really want.

If Millennials can game the system by focusing on career fields that are in demand while remaining mobile and flexible, employers (especially those with a need for talent) can break the rules too. Employers should follow Wayne Gretzky's advice on how he became the greatest hockey scorer of all time: he skates to where the puck is going to be, not where it has been (yes, a cliché, but it is a cliché for good reason). If two-way disloyalty defines today's workplace, offer the opposite to your most talented staff members. Retain them by providing opportunities for them to grow and expand their roles within your organization instead of forcing them to hop somewhere else and wasting the investment you've made in building their experience. This all seems so obvious. It's too bad Canada's employers are missing out on the huge asset that's sitting right under their collective noses.

## The Light at the End of the Career Tunnel

Given the grinding existence of Gen Y, is it any wonder that a Pew Research study of generational identity in the United States showed that Millennials have far more negative views of their generation than Gen Xers, Boomers, or other generations? Fifty-nine percent of Millennials described their generation as self-absorbed, 49% say they are wasteful, and 43% say they are greedy. This compares to 30% of Gen Xers who say they are self-absorbed and wasteful, and 20% of Boomers who see themselves that way. Gen Yers are not just anxious, they may also be developing some serious self-loathing.

If Millennials are potentially self-loathing, they are also bitter about being denied their birthright of stimulating careers commensurate with their sense of personal value and extraordinary educational achievement. While they've experienced a lot of hurt in the workplace, there's some light at the end of their career tunnel that might not be a train. Despite any difficulties Millennials might be having these days, they stand to rise through the employment ranks faster than Gen Xers did as Perennial retirements accelerate and create labour shortages.

Keep in mind that Canada's workforce is shrinking overall. This means there will be a struggle among employers to hire and retain good employees. **Employers will need to flatten hierarchies, increase autonomy, and create the flexible structures that both Gen X and Y employees say they want.** Companies and organizations across all sectors will need to decide how they are going to recruit, train, retain, and advance Millennial employees as Perennial retirements accelerate. Yes, those same people who weren't promoted and were underpaid and undervalued. It will be interesting to see what loyalty Millennials show when it becomes a sellers' market. Or will all this pass Millennials by and work to the advantage of the youngest population cohort, Generation Z?

## What This Means for Your Business

Gen Y is the generation that business pundits are most wrong about. Millennials aren't all about technology or being insouciant. What they *are* is saddled with big debts (related to either education or real estate), trapped in insecure careers, and unable to create the stability most of us crave.

What can your business do? The first opportunities relate to helping Millennials better manage their debt. **It's difficult to be a consumer if all you can look forward to is paying monthly interest on debts accumulated as a student.** The next opportunity is helping them buy a home, especially in our most expensive real estate markets. We can debate whether this makes economic sense, but so long as Canadians of all ages continue to believe that buying a home is a primary life goal, solving this problem represents a business opportunity. Solutions could include everything from new ideas about how to buy real estate to new types of real estate to buy. Whoever figures this out will have a big win. Governments that want to attract Millennial votes should make addressing this issue a priority.

## What This Means for You

The discontinuity is real. Millennials aren't the capricious techno-brats that popular culture portrays them as. They really are Generation

Anxious, and anxiety leads to action. **Unless we can find a way to get Millennials on track, the potential for political backlash is real, especially against the privilege of older generations.** Want to avert the conflict? Start by rewarding politicians who are prepared to offer real solutions to the issues confronting Millennials. Some of these are symbolic issues to do with cultural change, but an awful lot more are about managing debt, finding an affordable home in a desirable location, and creating a stable family life.

# CHAPTER 5

# *Virtually There*: Appealing to the First Digital Generation

## The First Global Generation

There's lots of confusion about Gens Y and Z. They are often treated as interchangeable. It's true, when compared to Perennials and Gen X, that Gen Y and Gen Z are more similar than they are different. Both are more ethnoculturally diverse, are more urban, come from smaller and more complicated families, and are heavy users of online social media and portable technologies. Where Gen Z is different, though, is that they are the first true digital natives. They have never known a world without smartphones. They multitask, know all the shortcuts, speak with emojis, and learn with video. They are very visual. The idea that a picture is worth a thousand words really describes how they think.

What truly makes Gen Z different from all previous generations, including Gen Y, is the vastness of their mental space. For previous generations, their mental space was narrowly defined by the geography of where they lived. Their hometown contained almost all of their most important connections to the world: where they worked, where their immediate family lived, and where they created most of the key relationships in their lives. Sure, people moved around. They went away to school, they travelled for vacations and work, but they usually either came back home or settled into a new hometown, where they created new connections as they left their old ones behind.

For Generation Z, their mental space is dramatically different. Globalization isn't an intellectual concept for them; it is their reality. Their world is truly *the world*. They are the first global generation of Canadians whose ideas about community, culture, and identity are developing across time zones and borders. They are exposed to distant issues, niche subcultures, and far-flung celebrities and influencers. They create their own sense of belonging, apart from traditional symbols of unity, like nation states and big brands. Their global mindset and complicated sense of identity compel them to communicate who they are in a very sophisticated, nuanced way. For Gen Z, their lives are less about mastery and more about discovery. It's about what's new, this instant. It's about serendipity and mash-ups. It's about curation rather than creation, then sharing their discoveries with their widely dispersed networks. Regardless of how obscure your passion is, there's probably someone in Osaka, Mumbai, or Berlin who is way more into it than you are. And if they're also part of Gen Z, they already have a fan base others can tap into.

**Gen Z has never known a time in which there wasn't an internet and they weren't instantly connected to everyone, everything, everywhere, for good, bad, and worse.** This generation has all the world's history, knowledge, products, and services, as well as every technology-enabled human being, at their fingertips (as opposed to on their desk or on their lap). And the technology they use to access it all is as intuitive and logical to them as reading and writing were to previous generations.

Here's the new world of Gen Z. In the past, for someone to be classified as your friend, you had to have at least shared physical time and space with them to create a "connection." Not for Gen Z. They have friends all over the world who may be closer to them in their minds than the people sitting in the next room. Gen Zers are true shape- and time-shifters. They live outside of their physical bodies and outside the limitations of time and space as members of previous generations (including Newton and Einstein) understood them. Like Dr. Who, they are present and they are not. Everywhere. Always.

It is true that this new world isn't exclusively the domain of Gen Z. The wonder and possibilities of the internet have struck all generations. Grandparents Skype or FaceTime their grandkids at Christmastime. Aunt Marge pokes her nieces and nephews on Facebook. Your brother bought and sent your birthday gift this year through Amazon. Thirty years ago, none of this would have been possible; today, most of us have incorporated some aspect of these digital miracles into our day-to-day lives. But Gen Z has taken the possibilities to a completely different level. They have seamlessly combined the digital world with mobility and constancy. Gen Z is always online, wherever they are. If they have a fear, it is FOMO, or fear of missing out. This keeps them connected. **Their smartphone is their world. It is their fully converged tool. It is their fully converged self. It is their defining emblem.** And there's probably an emoji for that.

To be clear, this isn't really about smartphones and tablets. The emblem is the thinking enabled by these devices and what they are connected to. For Gen Z, they have created the possibility for a new sense of self as a consumer and a new mental map of the marketplace. Calling Gen Zers "screenagers" somewhat misses the point. Two decades from now we will regard the smartphone as no more than a technological pit stop on the journey to the fully integrated internet of things. But the new commercial thinking the smartphone first enabled will stay with us for much longer.

For Gen Z there are no geographical boundaries restricting where they can shop. Their options are limited only by their imagination, their data plan, and the associated shipping costs. **For businesses, all Gen Zers, regardless of where they live, are your potential customers.** If you build it, and the online reviews are good, Gen Z will buy it from you. You can't hide from them, even if you wanted to.

## Defining Gen Z

Analysts generally regard Gen Zers as a hopeful generation. The advertising firm sparks & honey describes them as connected, educated, sophisticated, industrious, collaborative, and eager to build a better planet. They are also seen by many as a welcome foil to the Millennials, who, as we've discussed, have been stereotyped as tolerant but also overconfident, narcissistic, and entitled (not to mention incredibly frustrated).

But all is not easy for Gen Z. They've been raised amid institutional and economic instability, and they live with the looming shadow of depleting resources and climate change. Their generational emblems include 9/11 and viewing acts of unspeakable depravity posted online. Gen Zers have also watched their older siblings (the few that they have) and their parents struggle with large student debts and precarious employment.

It's generally true that what makes you strong can also make you weak. While many analysts admire Gen Z for their worldliness and ability to multitask over multiple screens, others are wringing their hands over what they see as Gen Z's declining attention span, eroding social skills, and online bullying and sexting. Critics also warn us that Gen Z's preference for communicating in short bursts and emojis (a difference from Millennials) deadens their ability to think in complex ways. Some go so far as to argue that Gen Z is harming the biology of human thinking with their "digital infection."

What's the truth about Gen Z Canadians? We're just starting to figure that out. Contrary to the happy talk from advertisers, a survey of 2,400 young people by Ipsos for Royal Bank of Canada showed that while Gen Z may start off happy, at age 18 they hit a wall. In comparison to their 10- to 17-year-old peers, those who are 18 to 21 are less happy, less optimistic, and less excited about their future, smile less often, and are less likely to say their life has meaning and that they can achieve anything they want. Adult male Gen Zers are especially pessimistic. Their entry into adulthood seems to be more of a shock to their systems than it is for female Gen Zers.

The truth, though, is that a lot of the commentary about Gen Z, is just that: commentary. We really don't know what's going to happen with them. **A lot of what we hear about Gen Z just reads into them what other generations hope or fear they might be; it's projective rather than based on any real proof.** It's too early to know yet. Gen Z will only start to enter the workforce in this decade. While we know they have grown up with Gen X and Millennial parenting styles, and with previously undreamt-of technology and gadgets, we still don't know how they will impact the world.

In the end, it is too early to define this growing generation in anything other than the most general terms. We know some basic things about Gen Z, like their preference for texting, as opposed to sending an email, leaving a voicemail, or talking live to someone. We know they prefer to get their news from social media and prefer to research and shop online. We know about their obsession with speed—they want everything, everywhere, immediately. But as for their true commercial impact, Gen Z is young and has limited spending power.

However, as an Ipsos survey showed, 86% of young Canadians (age 25 to 34) believe owning a house or condo is a very good idea. So while some things can change across generations, on the big things, an awful lot remains the same, regardless of generation.

## What This Means for Your Business

**Gen Z consumers are truly global. You are competing with the world for their business.** This presents a challenge as well as an opportunity. Just as Gen Z Canadians are purchasing from businesses around the world, so Canadian companies should see Gen Zers around the world as potential customers. While a business's online presence and reputation is important to all consumers, it's especially important to Gen Z consumers. You are just one of their global options.

Many Canadian companies highlight their Canadian identity as a part of their marketing campaign. What does your Canadian identity mean to Canadian and worldwide customers who see their shopping options as global? Is it an asset or a liability? You need to know. It matters.

## What This Means for You

What is Canadian culture for someone with a global identity? What do Canadian literature, music, and art mean to someone who has a hyper-curated sense of self that connects better to anime aficionados in Tokyo than to whatever the CBC has on offer? **The consumer habits and lifestyle of Gen Z represent the biggest challenge to Canadian culture we have ever faced.** In the past, we stood up to challenges like this by using government regulations and subsidies. Mostly, we were keeping out American influence by creating barriers to their culture and nurturing our own domestic talent. For Gen Z, Canadian culture isn't just competing with Hollywood, it's vying with K-pop from Korea and the latest meme from France. We weren't very successful at holding back America, and I expect we will be even less successful at holding back the world.

Gen Zers are the most diverse generation, in every possible way: ethnocultural identity, gender identity, sexual orientation, family composition, cultural tastes, and so on. It will be interesting to see the effects of these changes on the tastes and beliefs of older generations. Will diversity be embraced or rejected? Only time will tell.

PART 2

# WHERE WE LIVE

CHAPTER 6

# *The Great White Myth*: Why We Are Handcuffed to Our Past and Missing Our Future

## We the North

There's a persistent and popular myth that we Canadians are defined by our cold, inhospitable, vast environment. We are the Great White North. Ask any card-carrying member of the Laurentian elite—those elites living in downtown Montreal, Ottawa, and Toronto who believe their vision of Canada is the only one worth having—and they'll tell you their myth is our reality. That's because they've been indoctrinated by their fellow Laurentian forebears in a high-school or undergrad Canadian literature course about our garrison mentality. Literary critic Northrop Frye, the inventor of the term "garrison mentality," argued that Canadians have an inborn fear of our vast, empty, and downright dangerous natural environment. In response to what we fear, opined Frye, we have built up garrison walls to defend ourselves. These aren't physical walls; they are psychological walls.

Like so much that defines what too many believe about Canada, this idea is out of date. While fear of the natural environment certainly influenced how our ancestors used to think, that was then, this is now. The average contemporary Canadian may have to deal with an occasional nasty winter day, but that's about the extent of their danger. They may visit our wilderness, but they certainly don't live in it. And it doesn't define what they think about being Canadian. How could it, when **over 80% of us now live in a town, suburb, or city, and 90% of us live within 160 kilometres of the US border?** The last decade in Canadian history when we were even half rural and half urban was the 1920s.

Do you still think our relationship with nature defines us? When was the last time you visited a true wilderness area in Canada and attempted to live there without modern conveniences? I don't mean you went all Leonardo DiCaprio in *The Revenant*, but when was the last time you were in a place where the thought that nature could threaten your physical well-being crossed your mind? For most of us, I bet that's never happened. Canada is now a nation of "townies" (a wonderful Newfoundland term) and is becoming more so every day.

Rather than continuing to pretend that Canada and Canadians are defined by our hostile, defensive relationship with the Great White North, I like the spin created by the marketing people from the Toronto Raptors, Canada's only NBA team. Their slogan is "We the North." Take a second and think about what "We the North" communicates. It is multicultural, youthful, hip hop, contemporary, unambiguously urban, and bold. The slogan reflects Drake, the hugely successful Toronto-based international hip hop star and global ambassador for the Raptors. It is about embracing a positive northern identity, regardless of where you or your parents were born. Sure, we live in the North. But we aren't afraid of it, and we certainly aren't building garrison walls because of it. Instead, we're proudly bringing the North to the world. As the slogan implies, you should envy us because *We* the North (don't you wish you were too?).

## Leafs Fans Versus Raptors Fans

One way to see the contrast between this New Canada and Old Canada is to attend a major sporting event in Toronto. Why Toronto? Because Toronto is Canada's largest city and the only one that has both an NHL team and an NBA team. It'll cost you some money, but if you really want to see what I'm talking about in action, it's worth the investment.

If you can find the hundreds of dollars this requires, try attending a Leafs game, and the next night attend a Raptors game. Given the wonders of modern ice-making technology, you can do this in the same building, the Scotiabank Arena. Now, ignore the games and focus on the crowds. What quickly becomes obvious is that, while the two crowds occupy the same seats in the same building, they couldn't be more different.

Fans who attend Leafs games tend to be white, as are almost all the players suited up for both teams. While half of today's NHL players are Canadian-born, they certainly don't reflect our growing racial diversity. The same can be said of the quarter of NHL players who were born in the United States. The rest of the NHL team rosters are filled by players mainly from Northern and Eastern Europe, which are less racially diverse than Canada and the United States.

For contrast, back in the 1971–72 NHL season (just before the legendary Canada–USSR Summit Series), 94% of the NHL players who played were Canadian-born. But even the big move of imports into the Canadian game hasn't changed its complexion. Today's NHL players remain overwhelmingly white. You will see this the minute they introduce the starting lineups and the players' faces flash across the Jumbotron.

Leafs fans are financially well off. You can't be at a Leafs game unless you've got some serious scratch. Team Marketing Report's last available Fan Cost Index says the aggregate price for a family of four to attend a Leafs game during the 2015–16 season was $628.29. That's the most expensive family night out in the league (the next highest, the Boston Bruins, is 11% cheaper). Keep in mind that Leafs fans are prepared to pay this much to see a team that hasn't hoisted a Stanley Cup since 1967 and hasn't made the finals or had a player lead the league in scoring since then either.

Apart from being white, affluent, and patient, the Leafs crowd is also knowledgeable, subdued, and skewed old. Sure, there are kids in the building. Someone may have scored the company tickets, or maybe they've splurged with an online ticket scalper and are taking the family out as a special treat. You will also see some out-of-towners who've made the trip to the city to see a big-league hockey game in the building they see on TV and have paid handsomely for the privilege. The energy in the building could best be described as modest and appropriate. Sure, the crowd can get gunned up for a fight, a goal, or some good play from the Boys in Blue, but it doesn't last long.

You will also notice that the Leafs now play taped rock music during TV timeouts and other stoppages in play. Former Leafs owner Harold Ballard and his sidekick King Clancy must be rolling over in their graves. When the Leafs really want to bring the crowd into the game, they do still break out the live organ music, or at least a tape of the late Canadian troubadour Stompin' Tom Connors singing and stomping his way through "The Hockey Song."

Stompin' Tom, the writer of such good old Canadian classics as "Sudbury Saturday Night," "Bud the Spud," and "Big Joe Mufferaw," is a favourite of hockey fans across the country. "The Hockey Song" always gets a big reaction in any arena where we gather to enjoy our national pastime. It has become the hockey equivalent of baseball's

"Take Me Out to the Ball Game." However, "The Hockey Song" is more about stomping and clapping than it is about singing and stretching.

Contrast this the next night with a Toronto Raptors game in the same building. To take a family of four to the game in 2015–16 (the last season Team Marketing Report published data) would cost you about $320, about half what it costs the same family to see the Leafs. The Raptors experience is marked by non-stop action from the second you sit in your seat. The crowd is young and multicultural, as are the players for both teams. The atmosphere is *loud*. The hip hop and R & B music is going even when the game is being actively played (the "Rap" in Raptors doesn't seem to be coincidental or ironic). There's even a special soundtrack for the point guard when he's advancing the ball (the opening bars of Missy Elliott's "Get Ur Freak On" is a biggie). Sure, you might get the occasional stadium rock shaker, like the White Stripes' "Seven Nation Army," Guns N' Roses' "Welcome to the Jungle," or AC/DC's "Thunderstruck," but it's almost always urban music blasting from the sound system.

There's a DJ (4Korners, and sometimes Drake himself) and a dance troop (the Raptors Dance Pak) and even a junior version of the dance troop (the Lil Ballas). The dancers aren't doing your standard pom-pom cheerleading either. They engage in full-on hip hop gyrating and move-busting. Cheerleaders with cannons fire T-shirts into the crowd, audience participation is constant and vigorous, and the energy must be experienced to be believed.

Of course, nowhere was the energy and excitement surrounding the Raptors more pronounced than when the team took down the reigning NBA champs, San Francisco's Golden State Warriors, in June 2019 after an epic playoff run. More than a million people flowed into Toronto's streets for the championship parade, a sea of people from all creeds and cultures, ecstatic that a team of players representative of several ethnicities had made Toronto proud. No one was happier than Mississauga car dealer Nav Bhatia, known to all Raptors fans as Superfan, who moved to Canada in 1984 from Delhi and has never missed a Raptors home game in the team's twenty-four-year history. He faced open discrimination and racism when he started working in Canada, but as the result of hard work in the community and his love for the Raptors, he has embedded himself as a pillar of Canadian culture. "Through this game of basketball, I have been bringing [together people] of all faith, culture, religions, gender." Bhatia was the grand marshal of the victory parade and the team gave him his own championship ring. Truly, the Raptors are a global team that represents the changing face of Canada.

Sure, there's some exaggeration and a margin of error in both descriptions. People of colour attend Leafs games, and not all hockey players are white (ask the ultimate modern hockey dad, Jamaican-born Karl Subban). There are also older white basketball fans at Raptors games. Some of them might even know who Drake is. As far as audience participation at the games, it isn't fair to compare what happens at a Raptors game to what happens at a Leafs game. The Leafs play on ice. That would make it too dangerous for many of the stunts the Raptors pull off to excite the crowd. But I have a feeling that even if safety wasn't an issue, Leafs fans would still be uncomfortable with the hyperactive action at a Raptors game.

## Hometown Hockey

Still, when Canadian rocker Tom Cochrane sings "Big League," he can only be referring to one sport if you're a Canadian. Hockey is so much a part of us that Rogers Communications, which won the exclusive broadcast rights for the NHL a few years ago, decided to run a special segment in its Sunday hockey broadcasts, called *Rogers Hometown Hockey*. Ron MacLean and Tara Slone travel across the country to profile our hockey communities. As MacLean put it, "The passion for hockey in this country is unrivalled. Every Canadian has a connection to the game—it is part of our DNA."

Where did Rogers go to showcase Canada's hockey communities and to bring great hockey stories to life? What follows is a list of their twenty-five stops for the inaugural 2014 season. Beside each community I've listed their percentage of foreign-born residents. Keep in mind that Toronto, Canada's biggest census metropolitan area (a city plus its adjacent suburbs), has a foreign-born population of around 50%. Vancouver's is 40%, followed by Montreal at 23% and Calgary at 26%. Compare these numbers to the *Hometown Hockey* stops and their associated foreign-born populations:

- London, Ontario: 19%
- Selkirk, Manitoba: 4%
- Saskatoon, Saskatchewan: 12%
- Red Deer, Alberta: 7%
- Burnaby, British Columbia: 51%
- Kelowna, British Columbia: 14%
- Fort McMurray, Alberta: 15% (this is the percentage for Wood Buffalo)
- Brandon, Manitoba: 12%
- Sudbury, Ontario: 6%
- St. Catharines, Ontario: 21%
- Kingston, Ontario: 13%
- Peterborough, Ontario: 8%
- Owen Sound, Ontario: 7%
- Moncton, New Brunswick: 4%

- Charlottetown, Prince Edward Island: 10%
- Dollard-des-Ormeaux, Quebec: 40%
- St. John's, Newfoundland: 3%
- Cole Harbour, Nova Scotia: 8% (this is the percentage for Halifax)
- Boischatel, Quebec: 3%
- Sault Ste. Marie, Ontario: 9%
- Thompson, Manitoba: 7%
- Regina, Saskatchewan: 11%
- Prince George, British Columbia: 10%
- Lethbridge, Alberta: 12%
- Kanata, Ontario: 23% (this is the percentage for Ottawa)

If this is Canada's DNA, it is a very white, old, shrinking strand. Of the twenty-five hockey hometowns Rogers visited, only four had a foreign-born population of more than 20%, the Canadian national figure. Eleven had foreign-born populations of less than 10%. If, as MacLean said, the motivation behind the *Hometown Hockey* tour was to grow support for the game, their targeting missed the mark. Rather than bringing new converts to the game, they spent most of their time cavorting with their shrinking group of core supporters.

If Rogers really wants to grow the game, they should spend a lot more time in places where more new Canadians live, like Brampton or Markham, Ontario. **New Canadians are the fastest-growing part of our population and represent the future of hockey and any other sport.** Sure, these places might have delivered fewer of the small-town hockey heroes we all love, but those stories are fast becoming quaint nostalgia. If hockey is to have a viable future as our national sport, it needs to change as Canada changes. This means new Canadians must be introduced to hockey. Being able to watch NHL broadcasts in Punjabi in markets like Vancouver and Toronto will help, as will role models like Nazem Kadri, the first Muslim player ever drafted by the Toronto Maple Leafs. New Canadians need to see themselves in the game. What hockey really needs, though, is a rethink of what they see as their future market. One thing is for sure: it should be suburban and multicultural.

This point was never proven in a more accurate or unfortunate way than on November 9, 2019, when Don Cherry, who had been hosting his "Coach's Corner" segment on Sportsnet's Hockey Night in Canada for almost four decades and who is a long-time supporter of Canada's veterans, ranted against people whom he believes don't wear poppies for Remembrance Day. "You people [that] come here . . . you love our way of life, you love our milk and honey, at least you can pay a couple bucks for a poppy or something like that. . . . These guys paid for your way of life that you enjoy in Canada, these guys paid the biggest price." Many interpreted Cherry's comments as targeting new Canadians ("you people") and the outcry that ensued resulted in Cherry's removal from the network—on Remembrance Day. Ron MacLean, who did not push back on Cherry during the segment and was roundly criticized on social media, would apologize soon after for Cherry's words and for his own silence during the rant. In the aftermath Cherry tried to clarify his remarks to suggest he was talking about new Canadians from all over the world, but the public backlash proved far too strong to ignore. Lakhbir Singh, for one, tweeted, "As a Sikh veteran I proudly served 9 years in the Royal Canadian Navy. I have been watching Don Cherry my whole life but his 'you people' comment is personally very hurtful." Harnarayan Singh, co-host of Hockey Night in Canada: Punjabi Edition, said, "It wasn't the hockey that divided people; it was a political statement on a hockey show that caused the issue." He echoed what others have said about waning interest in hockey, especially on the part of new Canadians, often because the sport is too expensive for many families to afford, but also because new immigrants see few representative faces from their communities on the ice.

Clearly, the NBA's effort to bring international appeal to budding basketball fans in North America is working, and the NHL's tired marketing of hockey to diminishing Old Canada is not.

## What This Means for Your Business

If we are no longer the Great White North, who are we becoming? It depends on where you go. Different parts of the country are changing at different speeds and in different ways. These differences are so big, **the idea of having a one-size-fits-all strategy for Canada no longer makes sense**, if it ever did. To understand the differences, we need to go where Canadians live and look at how they are adapting to the changes sweeping our country.

Are you the Maple Leafs or the Raptors? If your business is focused on customers in rural and small-town Canada, you're likely the Maple Leafs. That can still be a lucrative market for a time, but it will shrink— it's inevitable given the demographic changes occurring all around us. To survive, you must break into the cities and suburbs. My advice: learn from the Raptors. Embrace "We the North." It's Canada's future.

## What This Means for You

Get your head out of the snow and cast off the old stereotypes of who Canadians are and what Canada is. Tune out the antiquated cultural message curated by the Laurentian elite; instead, **take a drive through the suburbs and open your eyes.** You'll see what I mean. These changes are too big to stop, and they are here to stay. The logical choice, then, is to embrace and revel in them. Doing so will ultimately give you more success in your career and make you a better citizen and neighbour.

# CHAPTER 7

# *How the East Was Lost*: Why Western Canada Is Our Future

## A National Population Shift

Canada has always been dominated by the centre of the country's geography. If we thought of a coast, it was usually our east coast, not our west coast. This was to be expected. Our country's first European settlers started in the east. It's where most of the people and the power resided, which is why most things that mattered in Canada since 1883 happened during Eastern Standard Time. No longer. Not only is Canada becoming less northern and more urban and suburban as a nation, but we are also reorienting ourselves to the west. We are becoming a Pacific nation. A massive shift of population from our east to our west has played a big role in the emerging New Canada. This shift is so significant that in 2011 the population of those living in the stretch from Manitoba to British Columbia was larger than the population from Quebec to Newfoundland—the first time in our history this has been the case. And the gap keeps growing.

The national population shift has continued unabated through the second decade of this century. It has been well catalogued in a variety of excellent analytical reports and projections produced by Statistics Canada. The reports show that Alberta, Saskatchewan, and Manitoba all had faster-growing populations than any other province in our country, and were also faster-growing than the national average.

Headed in the other direction is Atlantic Canada. Just how challenging are the population trends in our easternmost provinces? Three of the four Atlantic provinces—Newfoundland, New Brunswick, and Nova Scotia—are now recording more deaths every year than births, and overall population growth for the region has been stuck at around zero since the late 1990s. **If things continue as they are in eastern Canada, the population share of the four Atlantic provinces could shrink to less than 5% of the Canadian total by 2063.** That's right: by mid-century, their population could be almost a rounding error in our national population figures. At that point, the idea that Nova Scotia, Prince Edward Island, Newfoundland, and New Brunswick could all maintain their own individual and independent provincial governments, with all the resources this requires and the political authority it entails, will be difficult to sustain. And they are unlikely to get much understanding from the other 95% of Canadians, especially in any jurisdictional or constitutional disputes.

To demonstrate the ground truth of the population situation in Atlantic Canada, let's look at one province, Newfoundland and Labrador. Canada's newest province (it joined Confederation in 1949) provides a window into what is happening in all of our eastern provinces due to population stagnation. By the mid-2030s, seniors will make up almost a third of Newfoundland's total population. In contrast, by the mid-2030s, seniors will be only about 20% of Alberta's total population.

This east-west age imbalance will not be fixed by bringing in a sprinkling of immigrants to St. John's, as some of the more fanciful Atlantic Canada boosters have suggested. Even among those immigrants who do choose to move to the east coast, many likely won't stay. If the past is any indication, at least half are likely to leave within a decade. This pattern could change if we start requiring immigrants to settle in specific parts of the country, as our ancestors did at the turn of the last century, but this strategy isn't being seriously contemplated for the moment. And even if they are required to settle in the east to come to Canada, there's no guarantee they will stay there.

Atlantic Canada's population is expected to fall below 5% of the total population by 2063. Over the same time frame, Canada's other regions are projected to have the following population shares: Ontario 30%, the West 24%, and Quebec 21%. **The West could have a greater share of the Canadian population than Quebec by the second half of this century and will be second only to Ontario in the size of its population.**

## Population Growth

While the Canadian population is shifting west, it is still managing to grow at a steady clip of about 1% every year overall. For much of this century, Canada has led the G7 countries (including the United States) in population growth. But as noted already, this growth hasn't been equally distributed across the country. Alberta leads the pack, with Saskatchewan and Manitoba close on its heels. Of the western provinces, only British Columbia has yet to catch the prairie fire; its growth remains close to the national average. This could change, though, as people potentially fleeing the economic instability in Alberta's oil patch look for greener pastures a bit farther west or in Ontario. But those who choose to migrate from Alberta for better economic prospects are unlikely to be chasing them in Atlantic Canada or Quebec, at least not in big numbers. So we should continue to expect the West overall (as opposed to Alberta specifically) to lead in population growth for the foreseeable future, regardless of the short-term employment prospects in the oil and gas sector.

Canada's perennial population growth leader, Ontario, is now below the national average, while Quebec has almost caught up with Ontario. We already know what's happening in the east. Going forward, unless there is some massive, long-term economic disruption or an unpredictable calamity (or, conversely, a specific regional economic boom, like a nineteenth-century-style gold rush), these regional trends will roll on into our future. Interprovincial migration is driven mostly by perceived economic opportunity. As a result, since the turn of the century, Alberta has picked up about half a million interprovincial migrants, lured mostly from Quebec and Atlantic Canada. **Simply put, people move for work.**

## The Small-Town Fantasy

Perhaps there's another way forward, especially as the Canadian population ages. I have a fantasy I suspect most Canadians in their 50s and 60s share. It's what my ideal retirement will be like. Like a growing number of us, when the time comes, I don't plan to fully retire, at least not in the way we used to think about retirement. I'm hoping to spend more time doing what I like to do—being with family, thinking, and writing, maybe taking on some teaching and consulting—and less time dealing with the drudgery of making a living. Part of my fantasy involves selling our family home in Toronto and moving with my wife and daughter to a small town I used to frequent as a boy. My fantasy small town is Annapolis Royal, Nova Scotia.

Why does Annapolis Royal appeal to me so much? I love its sea air, its down-home friendliness, its beautiful vistas, and its rich history. Even getting there is a treat. Annapolis Royal is a lovely, lazy two-hour drive on a good highway from Halifax to the Annapolis Valley on the southwest shore of Nova Scotia. One side of town rises into the beautiful green rolling hills of the valley; the other borders the Annapolis

Basin, swimming in deep blues and greens. That's what Annapolis Royal looks like to me, especially on a sunny summer day. It's my version of heaven.

Annapolis Royal is Nova Scotia's smallest official town, population 491, and vies for the honour of being its oldest too. It was originally inhabited by the Mi'kmaq and was settled by Europeans as far back as the early 1600s. It also served as the original capital of Acadia, and then Nova Scotia, until Halifax became the capital of the province.

As for its history, Annapolis Royal is one of the most fought-over pieces of land in North America, having been attacked by the British or French at least thirteen times. Fort Anne, one of Canada's oldest historical sites, guards the Annapolis Basin side of town. It was a playground for my brothers and me when we were growing up in nearby Greenwood. This is where my love of history began. Our mom and dad would take us to Fort Anne on weekends to tour the museum and play on its grass ramparts. While history records how often Annapolis Royal changed hands between the British and French, I can't accurately report how many times it changed hands during the War of the Bricker Brothers.

While Annapolis Royal isn't smack on the Bay of Fundy, it might as well be. Like all waterfront towns on the west side of Nova Scotia, it experiences the huge Fundy tides that tourists flock to see. That, plus its history, drives the local economy. It's a summer tourist town, with the requisite attractions. There's a beautiful ornamental garden, several nice bed and breakfasts in historic homes, and arts-and-crafts shops scattered along the high street. Of course, in a town with the oldest formal cemetery in Canada, it is purpose-built for ghost tours.

The Annapolis Royal town website declares that it also has a wharf that supports a scallop-fishing industry. Yes, there is a wharf in town, but the census doesn't record anyone living in Annapolis Royal being employed as a fisher. Maybe fishing is a part-time job, or maybe the fishers don't live in town. It's clear, however, when you visit Annapolis Royal that the main economic activity is tourism. Sure, the wharf exists, but it seems more like a static tourist display than the headquarters of an active fishing fleet.

Appealing as Annapolis Royal is to me personally, it is also a microcosm of the struggles facing small-town and rural Canada. It's all in the demographic data. Like most of non-urban Canada, Annapolis Royal has a shrinking and aging population that isn't being offset by either fertility or immigration. According to the 2016 census, the population of Annapolis Royal has declined by more than 20% over the last thirty-five years. While it has experienced a slight uptick more recently, it has a long way to go to get back to its 1981 level of 631 people.

To the extent that Annapolis Royal has been able to attract new residents, they have been almost exclusively older migrants who have moved from other places in Canada to live out their version of my retirement fantasy. While Annapolis Royal does have foreign immigrants, almost all came to Canada many years ago, most before 1981. The census records that no young foreign immigrants settled in Annapolis Royal between 2011 and 2016. Yes, the actual number the census reports is a zero.

What does this mean for Annapolis Royal's population? It means it is a town made up mostly of Old Canada retirees, with a few immigrant retirees mixed in. There are few people of working age to sustain the economic life of the community. This is borne out by the data. The median age of Annapolis Royal is 63 (compared to Canada's median age of 41), with nearly half being 65 or older. The population 15 or younger is just 7%, which is less than half of the Canadian average.

It makes sense, then, that the labour force participation rate of

Annapolis Royal is only 36%, compared to the Canadian average of 65%. It's also why over 70% of residents receive some form of government transfer, usually a pension. And as we are increasingly seeing among small towns with aging populations, over half of the private households in Annapolis Royal are made up of single people living on their own. This compares to 28% for Canada overall. It's tough to have a vibrant economy with a population like this.

Moving beyond the economic impacts, an older population also changes the demand structure for social services and infrastructure. Since Annapolis Royal isn't attracting or keeping enough working-age people to offset the growing costs of building and supporting the physical and social infrastructure needed by their older residents, it will be forced to look at new approaches to delivering community services. Making these changes won't be cheap. And every dollar Annapolis Royal spends to accommodate the needs of its older residents will be a dollar taken away from the services, like local schools, needed to attract and keep a younger population. Most of rural and small-town Canada is caught up in this vicious circle, and it only spirals in one direction.

Another way you can learn about what's going on in a town is to walk around it. So I did. I had a recent speaking engagement in another beautiful Nova Scotia town, Digby. Annapolis Royal is on the way to Digby from Halifax. I decided to drop in. When you leave the highway to get into Annapolis Royal, you drive along St. George Street. This is also the town's high street. It is dominated on both sides by impressive Victorian-era ramblers, set back from the road on large treed lots. These are the houses that any Canadian city dweller salivates over. Character, space, land—they have it all.

Many of the impressive houses on St. George Street are so big and attractive that they have been converted into bed and breakfasts. But when I was there, many were also for sale. A recent scan of the local real estate listings shows that many still are. And most can be had for $350K or less. Houses like this in Toronto, Vancouver, or Calgary would cost in the millions and would be out of reach for all but the most affluent. Annapolis Royal is an unbelievable real estate bargain compared to urban Canada. But even this isn't enough to attract young families to move there. Instead, two hours away, the jobs and life of Halifax beckon. More likely still, it's the opportunities offered by the suburbs of Ontario or western Canada that pull the young folks away. It's a similar story for small towns and rural communities all over Canada.

Something occurred to me as I walked around town, enjoying my fantasy: when the time comes for me to retire, the last family Annapolis Royal needs is the Brickers.

## Resolving Atlantic Canada's Sustainability Issues

The shift from east to west will continue. The weight of Canada's population will keep moving to Toronto's suburbs and the bigger cities of the West. By 2030, a growing question on the public agenda might be whether any public officials from Atlantic Canada are willing to confront the economic and population realities facing their region. Will they propose a serious debate about reconstituting government structures and public service delivery in Atlantic Canada to a model that can sustain itself without ongoing support from the rest of the country? The heroes here will be those politicians who are prepared to have a serious conversation about this, and the villains will be those who pretend that business as usual is sustainable. It isn't.

**Resolving the sustainability issues of Atlantic Canada could lead to our next big national unity confrontation.** Voters in communities outside of Atlantic Canada, especially our big cities in central Canada and the West, will want a say about how this issue plays out.

They have their own issues to deal with when it comes to major public investments, mostly related to paying for the public transportation and community infrastructure needed to accommodate their ongoing population growth. At the same time, whether they know it or not, they are being asked to pay a big chunk of Atlantic Canada's bills, with no end in sight. Those bills will just keep getting bigger as Atlantic Canada's population keeps getting older, smaller, and more dependent. They who pay the piper will eventually want to call the tune.

## What This Means for Your Business

It's simple. **Follow the people.** People move for work, which means they are moving to the suburbs of the major cities from Toronto to the west (less so to Montreal). The populations of these areas are also younger and will be a source of growth for your business. Residents will need homes, furnishings, and all the consumer goods that younger families require. Need employees? This is where you will find them too.

It's the opposite in small-town and rural Canada. The situation in Atlantic Canada certainly isn't restricted to our east coast. Most of non-urban Canada is populated by aging and increasingly retired populations who are less focused on acquiring stuff and more focused on preserving their shrinking assets. Nonetheless, there are opportunities in these places too: health-care services for aging populations, specialized financial planning for retirees, home retrofitting and service delivery customized for seniors—maybe even telecommuting options that will allow older residents to continue working. But for the time being, these are high-cost niche markets for a few specialized suppliers. And nothing will turn the slow decline into steady, sustainable, consumer-driven economic growth. Without economic growth, residents—especially younger residents—will continue to leave.

## What This Means for You

The decline of rural and small-town Canada is a major issue that few people are talking about and fewer still have a solution for. This is sad. We are turning a blind eye to perhaps one of the biggest issues confronting Canada this century. It has many implications for public policy and politics, especially when it comes to topics like economic development, immigration, and transfer payments that support important programs like health care. You will be part of this debate because of what is happening to our country's unity.

Most of our previous unity disputes were driven by sorting through the future of Quebec in the Canadian federation. **Today's unity dispute is different. This time it's about the economic and political grievances of relatively young and rapidly growing Alberta.** Aggrieved Albertans want to know why they should continue to support parts of the country that are both economically needy and politically hostile to their major industry: oil and gas. There's growing support for turning off the taps that allow what Albertans see as their money to flow mostly east to support national public services.

Opposition to oil and gas is being driven by the progressive elites who dominate our major cities. But Ontario, Quebec, and British Columbia have more financial capacity than our Atlantic provinces to survive a change in the way we pay for public programs. While it won't be one of the major combatants in this dispute, Atlantic Canada could experience significant collateral damage as a result. Hardest hit will be the small towns and rural areas that are most dependent on government transfers to survive.

# CHAPTER 8

# *The Rural Crisis*: What the Death of Small-Town Canada Means for All of Us

## Our Cultural Fabric

Annapolis Royal is emblematic of what's been happening to rural and small-town Canada overall. Just as there has been a big shift in the regional distribution of Canada's population, there has also been a major shift in the type of community Canadians live in. **The biggest migration in human history is taking place right now, and it's people moving from rural and small-town communities to urban areas.** Canada, like most other countries, is going through this transformation.

But aren't rural and small-town Canada the *real* Canada? That's what the rest of the world thinks of us. Sure, every few weeks we are thrilled to see another global index that ranks our big cities as among the most livable (if not *the* most livable) in the world. But when you speak with most people outside of Canada about this place, it's not walking down the bustling streets of Toronto or Montreal that captures their imagination (although there always seems to be a special reverence for the streets of Vancouver). It's our wilderness they crave.

Why wouldn't the world think that rural and small-town Canada is who we are? Look at the ads Destination Canada, the Government of Canada's tourism promoter, runs to attract tourists and their money to Canada. One recent effort was called "Exploring Canada," featuring video montages composed of selected clips of "Canada shared by Canadians" (it was supposed to show the world how we see ourselves). While there were a couple of recognizable cityscapes and urban activities presented, the clips were heavily dominated by scenes of our majestic wilderness and what you can see and do there: whales, bears, moose, skiing, hiking, skating on frozen lakes, snowmobiling, long drives (in a car or on a golf course), big views, mountains, oceans, copious snow, and the Northern Lights. Yup, this is exactly the stuff we all see and do every day in our local communities.

The appeal of the videos is easily explained. Canada's wilderness and rural and small-town communities add immeasurably to our cultural fabric with their unique identities, art, music, and cuisine. Listen to Canadians talk about "Canadian culture" or "what's great about Canada." It doesn't take long for their thoughts to drift to some bucolic country town they once visited, or to a wonderful vista or sunset they experienced in our great outdoors. Why wouldn't we tell the world this is who we are?

There was a time when "Canada shared by Canadians" was a more accurate portrayal of our country. In Canada's early days, the stereotypes about Canadians being rugged frontier people were mostly true. Statistics Canada catalogues the percentage of Canadians living in rural and urban communities as far back as 1851. At that time, close to 90% of us lived in places that Statistics Canada classifies as rural. Our economy was pretty much driven by what we grew, pulled out of the ocean or ground, or cut down in the woods. People follow economic opportunities, and Canada's opportunities then were mostly carved out of the wilderness. We were largely, as political economist Harold Adams Innis once described us, "hewers of wood and drawers of water."

## The Urbanization of Canada

Economies change over time, and human settlement patterns respond. People everywhere are migrating from the country to the city. In 2018, over half of the world's population lived in an urban area. That's up from 34% in 1960. By 2050, it's estimated that more than two-thirds of humanity will call a city their home. Put another way, the world's urban population is increasing by roughly 50,000 people a day. At that pace, over a month, that's a city the size of Prague (1.5 million people) springing up. Over a year, it's the equivalent of a country as big as Chile (18 million people) being created.

The trend in the rest of the world has been happening in Canada for about a century. **Fewer than one in five Canadians (18.9%) now live in rural communities.** That's still a lot of us, at 6.3 million (roughly three times our total national population in 1851). And it's true that our rural population is still growing, by 1.1% from 2006 to 2011. But the rest of Canada grew by 5.9% during that same time. In Ontario alone, the urban population grew by 15% between 2001 and 2011, while the rural and small-town population declined by 7%. That's a huge change in population density for our most populous province in just one decade, and this trend continues uninterrupted today.

So, yes, while rural and small-town Canada may still be growing overall, their relative weight in the Canadian population is getting lighter every year. Over a century, Canadians have morphed from country mice into city mice. This will just keep happening unless something dramatic—*really* dramatic—changes. Perhaps a large group of us will ditch urban life to telecommute from rural Newfoundland. Or maybe a big wave of retirees will move to a mining ghost town in the hinterland. Maybe the next couple of decades' worth of immigrants will all decide to farm the backcountry, like their predecessors did at the turn of the last century. That's the magnitude of population change that will be required to reverse the ongoing decline rural and small-town Canada are experiencing today.

## Why Our Rural Communities Are Endangered

Despite the image we have in our heads of the wide-open prairie spaces of the West, it's **Canada's eastern provinces that have the highest proportion of rural residents in our country.** The far west, British Columbia, is now tied with Ontario as Canada's most urbanized province. Only 14% of British Columbians and Ontarians lived in a rural environment in 2011, followed by Alberta (17%), Quebec (19%), Manitoba (28%), Saskatchewan (33%), Newfoundland and Labrador (41%), Nova Scotia (43%), New Brunswick (48%), and Prince Edward Island (53%).

What is a rural community in Canada today? That's a tough question to answer. From a statistical perspective, the definition is clear. Statistics Canada tells us that "rural" means "persons living outside centres with a population of 1,000 [or more] and outside areas with 400 persons [or more] per square kilometre." But this covers a pretty diverse range of communities. A Newfoundland outport isn't the same as a mining or cottage town in Ontario or Quebec. And a remote Prairie farm community isn't the same as an Indigenous reserve in the far north. All, however, would qualify as "rural" on a statistical basis.

Moreover, rural communities that have a connection or proximity to a major urban centre are in a very different position from those that are hours away by car or even by airplane. These days, **proximity to a major urban area is critical to the success of a rural area or small town.** Nearly 40% of Canada's rural population lives in areas with at least a moderate link to an urban centre. These are the lucky ones.

About a third live in remote rural areas with a weak link or no link to an urban centre.

What most of rural and small-town Canada has in common—unless they are fortunate enough to have a group of younger, affluent commuters who drive to the city from their hobby farms, cottages, or cabins—is that they are in big trouble in terms of population structure. Their best young people are leaving in droves, and they have been unable to attract and retain enough migrants or immigrants to offset these departures. It's not just that rural and small-town population growth has stagnated; these areas are also getting lighter on young, skilled, taxpaying workers at a time when their aging populations are becoming more dependent on public services.

Rural and small-town Canada aren't just aging because a lot of older people live there. They are also getting older because many of their young adults, age 15 to 29, who would under normal circumstances offset and support those older residents, have moved away. But while most of those leaving happen to be young, not all rural youth move to the city. The bigger problem is that those who do leave represent a significant share of rural and small-town Canada's best and brightest. These are the people who have the ambition to pursue higher education or better employment opportunities elsewhere. And when they achieve success, they rarely look back. The net result is a mass of hollowed-out hometown communities with a disproportionate number of seniors, diminished fertility, a shrinking skilled workforce, and a decreasing financial ability to support themselves due to a dwindling tax base.

Let's face it: Why would a young person with a whiff of ambition risk staying in rural or small-town Canada these days? Rural Canadian communities have relatively high unemployment rates, and even if a young person is lucky enough to find a job there, they can expect to earn about 30% less than their peers working in urban areas. It's even worse for a young person in our most remote rural and small-town communities. They can look forward to the lowest average earnings, the highest unemployment rates, and the highest incidence of government assistance of just about anyone in Canada.

So young people who sign up for a rural or small-town life are either very committed to the lifestyle regardless of the economic consequences, have been lucky enough to find a good job at home, or lack the educational achievement or ambition (or both) to pursue a job that offers them more earning potential elsewhere. It should come as no surprise, then, that educational achievement levels in rural Canada are, on average, significantly lower than they are in urban Canada. Just how low? According to the Canadian Council on Learning, rural communities have a higher high-school student dropout rate (16%) than urban communities (9%) and have lower average levels of post-secondary education.

Say what? A young person attending school in urban Canada is much more likely to graduate from high school than a kid living in the country? Really? How can this be? We've all heard about the challenges of getting a decent education in places like the rapidly growing and diversifying suburbs of Toronto or Vancouver. Teachers in these places say they are overwhelmed by the integration needs of students who have come to their classrooms from all over the world. Many have language and other cultural barriers to overcome that kids in the countryside never have to cope with. The poorer educational performance in rural Canada seems to be linked to rural poverty. While we can debate the cause, the results speak for themselves.

There's a lot going sideways in rural and small-town Canada. But I don't want to paint too grim a picture. It's not all doom and gloom. Not all rural and remote communities are in such rough shape. There are some with diverse economies that do well. Others have an economic focus that works for them, such as agriculture, forestry, mining, fishing, hunting and trapping, oil and gas, or tourism. But these are the exceptions, not the rules. Regardless of economic performance, **most rural and small-town communities have challenges related to aging and shrinking populations, keeping ambitious young people in the community, and convincing skilled migrants or immigrants to move there.**

## Canada's Farmers

One specific group of rural and small-town residents we should know more about are the people who feed us, Canada's farmers. Sure, we know they are out there. We see them when they come to the city to attend weekend farmers' markets and annual exhibitions like the Calgary Stampede, the PNE, the CNE, and the Royal Winter Fair. But what do we really know about them? To begin with, only about one in fifty-eight Canadians today lives on a farm, about 2% of our total population. Just under half of those are farm operators; the other half are members of their households. Given these numbers, think back to what Canada was like at the turn of the last century. You now have some perspective on how much we've changed in just a few generations.

Canada's biggest farm population is, believe it or not, in Ontario, at 174,905, or 1.4% of Ontario's total population. Ontario is followed by Alberta (129,810, or 3.6%), Saskatchewan (103,885, or 10.3%), Quebec (101,675, or 1.3%), British Columbia (64,650, or 1.5%), Manitoba (49,155, or 4.2%), and finally, Atlantic Canada (26,310, or 1.2%). While the proportion of farmers to the rest of the population is higher on the Prairies, the province with the most total farmers is Ontario. And even though the region with the greatest proportion of rural residents is Atlantic Canada, fewer of them make their living as farmers.

About 90% of our farmers live in rural areas, but only about 10% of rural Canadians claim to be farmers. And the farms that Canada's farmers work these days are rapidly evolving from a big number of small family farms to far fewer but much bigger commercial farms. In the old days, the emphasis in the phrase "family farm" was on "family." Sure, these were always more or less commercial operations, but farming used to be as much about family subsistence as it was about business. Today, the emphasis is moving from the "family" to the "farm." Twenty-five percent of farms are incorporated and, in many cases, **today's farmers would be better described as agricultural entrepreneurs or agrarian businesspeople.**

Apart from farmers being more likely to be male than female, they are also older—much older—than the average Canadian. The median age of a farmer in Canada today is 54, compared to 41 for the rest of our population. Farmers also tend to live in larger family units. The average farm household contains 2.9 people, compared to 2.5 for the general population. Maybe the truism from the past remains true to this day: more people on the farm equal additional free labour, while more people in the city are just extra mouths to feed.

Are all those early mornings grinding it out on the family farm worth it from a personal financial perspective? Here's the truth. The median total income for a Canadian farm family today is $82,456; that means half of all family farmers make more than this, and half make less. While at first glance this may seem like a pretty good living, the median family income for all families in Canada (not including single-person families) is $70,275. You can decide if making $12,000 a year more is worth ignoring the rooster and sleeping in.

One way to beat the odds and do better than the median Canadian farmer is to be careful about the type of farm you decide to operate. Farm families that do the best from a financial perspective are those involved in poultry and egg production. According to Statistics Canada, chicken farmers make a median annual income of $96,399. And there aren't that many of them to compete with. They represent only about 2% of all farm families in Canada. If you can get into this tightly controlled market, you will be the envy of all your new farmer friends.

Unlike much of rural and small-town Canada, which is a dead zone for new Canadians, farm life remains attractive for some immigrants. In the 2011 census, 44,790 immigrants reported their occupation as "farmer," which was nearly 7% of all farmers. Immigrant farmers seem especially drawn to British Columbia, where nearly 20% of farmers are foreign-born.

Certain countries are over-represented within the immigrant farmer population:

- Netherlands: 20%
- United Kingdom: 15%
- United States: 13%
- Germany: 9%
- India: 9%
- Switzerland: 5%
- Italy: 2%
- China: 2%
- Mexico: 2%
- Belgium: 2%
- Others: 23%

Bottom line—there are an awful lot of wooden shoes to be found in Canada's countryside.

While there are a surprising number of immigrants in the farming population, they are drawn mostly from the wave of immigration before the current one. Just over 33% came here prior to 1971, compared to 18.6% of our total immigrants. That's why the list above is dominated by immigrants from places other than Pacific nations (although China and India are both on the list). We should expect to see these proportions change over the next few decades, with more immigrant farmers coming from the Pacific and far fewer from Europe.

## What This Means for Your Business

The business future of Old Canada is not promising. Your remote customer base will shrink and age as the Canadian population increasingly concentrates in a few urban centres. But problems can also represent opportunities. **How does your business look through a rural and small-town lens? What solutions can you offer this part of Canada, which desperately needs a new direction?** Can you provide employment (remote jobs)? Can you provide essential services more cheaply and efficiently (distance medicine, distance training)? Can you deliver consumer products at prices comparable to those in the city (autonomous vehicles, drones)? If you have an idea, every level of government in Canada wants to hear from you. They are desperate for some new thinking. And they've likely got money for you too.

For governments, the only way to get rural and small-town communities to grow is to incentivize people, especially immigrants, to move there. The federal government has recently announced a new incentive program to encourage immigrants to move to more remote areas. It's too early to say if it will have any success, but it is a step in the right direction.

## What This Means for You

Rural and small-town Canada could represent a huge personal opportunity. **If your ideal life doesn't include commuting for hours a** day from the suburbs, and you can work remotely, there's a small town out there that would love to welcome you and your family. The money you would save on every aspect of life, but especially on real estate, will shock you. Don't believe me? Spend a couple of hours going over online real estate listings for your favourite small town and you'll see what I mean. You don't have to head thousands of kilometres away to have a completely different existence—a couple of hours should do it. Annapolis Royal is less than two hours from Halifax.

Also keep in mind that farther away isn't necessarily better. There's a point at which leaving behind access to large population centres means life gets more expensive and more difficult. To be truly remote, you'll need to head to the far north, but life there can be hard, especially for kids. If you do decide to go to the far north, stick to the bigger centres.

What about farming? Given the advanced age of Canada's farmers, there could be some opportunities there, although you will be in competition with industrial farm operators who also want the land you want. If you're lucky enough to find an older, sympathetic farmer who will sell to you, focus on poultry. In general, that's where the money is.

# CHAPTER 9

# *McFuture*: Why Suburbia Will Beat Out Downtown, Every Time

## The Real Canada

Leave it to the mythmakers at Disney to outperform our own national travel authority when it comes to presenting a balanced image of Canada to the world. You can see Disney's work in the Circle-Vision 360° video called "Oh Canada," featuring Canadian-born comedian and actor Martin Short. This fifteen-minute video plays at Epcot's Canada Pavilion at Disney World in Orlando, Florida, introducing visitors to the wonders of Canada beneath the shadow of a fake Château Frontenac hotel.

Sure, the video is as cheesy as its star and surroundings, and contains plenty of the same stereotypes (moose, whales, polar bears, winter sports, skating on the Rideau Canal, the *Bluenose*, the Musical Ride) that we've already discounted as the relevant cultural markers of today's Canada. But to its credit, it also takes a friendly swipe at the idea that Canadians spend their lives living like extras in the Disney movie *Frozen*. Partway through the video, Short accuses the offscreen Voice of God narrator of presenting a version of Canada that is "completely wrong." He then takes over the narration to lead us on a cross-country tour through some of our biggest cities—Victoria, Vancouver, Calgary,

Toronto, Quebec City, and Montreal (sorry, Atlantic Canada, your cities missed the cut). He then finishes up with praise for Canada's multiculturalism (which really exists only in our urban areas) and the strength we have found in our diversity.

Martin Short and Disney are right. Canadians today are increasingly creatures of concrete, condos, and commuting, and we're becoming more so every day. We are now an urban and suburban nation, with most of us living in large population centres that Statistics Canada calls census metropolitan areas, or CMAs.

## Population Concentration

In plain English, a CMA is a city plus its adjacent suburbs. There are thirty-five CMAs across Canada (Belleville, Ontario, and Lethbridge, Alberta, were promoted to CMA status with the 2016 census). **Any organization that wants to be successful in modern Canada must be hyper-focused on these thirty-five CMAs, because more than 70% of us (around 25 million people) live in them.** But our population is even more concentrated than that. Over a third of us now live in just three cities: Toronto (just over 6 million), Montreal (just over 4 million), and Vancouver (close to 2.5 million). Throw in Calgary (1.2 million) and that's almost 40% of the entire Canadian population living in just four large population centres.

This influence also translates into the job market. As Livio Di Matteo from Lakehead University has shown, there are six CMAs in Canada that stand out when it comes to employment levels and job growth: Montreal, Toronto, Vancouver, Ottawa-Gatineau, Calgary, and Edmonton. These are the only CMAs where total employment is greater than half a million jobs. Together, these six CMAs contain almost half of all of Canada's jobs. That's why more people move to them every day.

Not all CMAs are created equal when it comes to population concentration, growth, and economic influence. As we've already discussed, there has been a major shift in our population from east to
west, and from more remote communities to fewer, larger centres
close to the US border. This latter trend is especially true west of Quebec. Check out the population numbers below, and you will see the
effects of these big shifts on Canada's thirty-five CMAs. These are their
population growth rates in percentages from 2011 to 2016, according
to Statistics Canada:

- Calgary, Alberta: +14.6%
- Edmonton, Alberta: +13.9%
- Saskatoon, Saskatchewan: +12.5%
- Regina, Saskatchewan: +11.8%
- Lethbridge, Alberta: +10.8%
- Kelowna, British Columbia: +8.4%
- Guelph, Ontario: +7.7%
- Victoria, British Columbia: +6.7%
- Oshawa, Ontario: +6.6%
- Winnipeg, Manitoba: +6.6%
- Vancouver, British Columbia: +6.5%
- Toronto, Ontario: +6.2%
- Abbotsford-Mission, British Columbia: +6.1%
- Kitchener-Cambridge-Waterloo, Ontario: +5.5%
- Ottawa-Gatineau, Quebec/Ontario: +5.5%
- Barrie, Ontario: +5.4%
- Sherbrooke, Quebec: +4.9%
- St. John's, Newfoundland: +4.6%
- Montreal, Quebec: +4.2%
- London, Ontario: +4.1%

- Quebec City, Quebec: +4.0%
- Moncton, New Brunswick: +4.0%
- Brantford, Ontario: +3.8%
- Hamilton, Ontario: +3.7%
- St. Catharines-Niagara, Ontario: +3.5%
- Halifax, Nova Scotia: +3.3%
- Windsor, Ontario: +3.1%
- Trois-Rivières, Quebec: +2.8%
- Peterborough, Ontario: +2.3%
- Belleville, Ontario: +1.8%
- Saguenay, Quebec: +1.5%
- Kingston, Ontario: +1.0%
- Greater Sudbury, Ontario: +1.0%
- Thunder Bay, Ontario: 0.0%
- Saint John, New Brunswick: −2.2%

## Uneven Urban Growth

A few things stand out from these numbers. The first is the truly dire situation in rural and small-town Atlantic Canada. We already know their populations are stagnant from a growth perspective, but we now also see that the CMA populations in Atlantic Canada (except for Saint John, New Brunswick) are still growing. We know, too, that these provinces have lower fertility rates and higher death rates that aren't being offset by positive foreign or domestic migration, and that their working-age populations continue to leave for better economic prospects in other parts of the country (especially to the CMAs west of Quebec). So the CMA growth in the East is likely being driven by people vacating smaller town and rural communities to move to the bright lights of the closest city.

What's occurring in Atlantic Canada is also happening in Quebec and Ontario, but it isn't as pronounced just yet. In Quebec, the moderate-sized CMAs are still growing, but at a slower rate than the national average. And of Canada's big three cities, Montreal has had the least impressive growth, but it is still growing. Yes, Montreal attracts many immigrants, but not nearly the same proportion as the GTA, Vancouver, Calgary, or Edmonton.

In Ontario, we see a similar trend as in Quebec and the East, although Toronto is still growing at a faster rate than Montreal. It's Ontario's moderate-sized CMAs—especially those located outside of reasonable commuting distance to the GTA, which means they must rely more on their local economies for jobs—that are also sputtering. The CMAs that could be considered "commuter-accessible" to Toronto do a bit better. Headed in the wrong direction are old economy centres like Thunder Bay and Sudbury, which are now more aligned, from a demographic perspective, with centres farther east than they are with the rest of urban and suburban Ontario. Other Ontario CMAs that can be added to the stagnant growth list are places like Kingston, Belleville, Peterborough, and Brantford. These are the Canadian equivalents of the "rust belt" centres of the American Northeast. All used to be significant secondary hubs in the province, with hometown hero companies driving their local economies. Many of these heroes have now closed operations, have been acquired by bigger companies that have subsequently left town, or have left town of their own volition. It may be hard to hear, but **economic Ontario these days looks like New York City (the GTA and environs) surrounded by Michigan (all the rest).**

Across the Ontario-Manitoba border, and especially as we go farther west, population growth rates perk up. Winnipeg, which had been looking like an Atlantic Canadian city in population terms, has had a steady turnaround in growth since the turn of the century.

With growth of 6.6% from 2011 to 2016, it's ahead of comparable mid-sized CMAs in Ontario. This reflects the fact that Manitoba has found a way to attract immigrants (especially from the Philippines) at a much greater rate than, say, Thunder Bay.

CMA population growth really starts to take off once we cross from Manitoba to Saskatchewan. Saskatchewan's CMAs, which for decades have been stagnant in their population, have found new life in the twenty-first century. They are living proof that people follow economic growth. Former late-night TV show host David Letterman may have thought it was hilarious to say "Saskatoon, Saskatchewan," but with population growth of 12.5%, Saskatoon is nothing to laugh at. Regina is also near the top of the national league table, with growth of 11.8%.

Yes, Saskatchewan, like Alberta, has experienced an economic slow-down because of the decline in global oil and gas prices. But Saskatchewan has a more diversified economy than Alberta thanks to its significant agriculture, potash, and uranium production. These industries could buffer some of the impact of lower oil and gas prices on Saskatchewan's economic performance. The big question, though, is whether the decline in oil and gas prices is a short-term economic blip or a longer-term trend. Short-term blips don't have the same disruptive impact on population patterns as bigger, longer-term trends. The question that's up in the air is whether the migrants who moved west to ride along with Saskatchewan's prosperity will move on now that the boom is in jeopardy. And if they do, where will they go next?

Alberta is like Saskatchewan in terms of urban growth, but even more so. The growth of Alberta's CMAs has led all CMAs across the country. The volume of migrants moving to Alberta makes their CMAs—Calgary and Edmonton—look like Gold Rush towns from another century. Leaving aside foreign immigrants, over half a million Canadians have migrated to Alberta, mostly from Quebec and Atlantic Canada, since 1995. But we all know what happened to the Gold Rush towns: when the gold went, so did the people. Will that be Alberta's fate?

For much of the last two decades, Alberta has boomed along, with world oil prices trending at $100 or more per barrel. Now that the average price tends to be half this or less, Alberta is facing major economic challenges. Like Saskatchewan, the question for Alberta is whether changed economic circumstances will cause people to move. The initial speculation was that the slump in oil and gas prices would start a pattern of out-migration from Alberta, mostly to British Columbia and Ontario, where short-term economic prospects appear to be brighter. So far, this hasn't been the case. There has been some out-migration from Alberta, but not a mass exodus. Those leaving are most likely interprovincial migrants who could best be described as "last in, first out"—they have weak attachments to the province and have decided to simply move back home rather than ride things out in Alberta. However, even if interprovincial migration has trended slightly against Alberta, it has been more than offset by strong international immigration. On a net basis, many more people moved to Alberta than left in each quarter over the last few years. So Alberta's population continues to grow, especially in its CMAs. At least for now.

British Columbia is a mecca for many Canadians. With its temperate weather, breathtaking scenery, and laid-back lifestyle, it's a place many Canadians dream of living. The same can be said of international migrants, especially those from Pacific nations. So why isn't British Columbia leading the country in population growth? As we can see from the CMA data, Vancouver and Victoria are both growing, but not at the same rate as other western cities. Given what we know about what motivates people to move, British Columbia likely hasn't had as much economic pull as a place like Alberta. This may change now with the slump in oil and gas prices.

The CMA leading British Columbia in growth is Kelowna. Why? It's attractive to a very specific group of migrants: seniors. Kelowna has the oldest population in British Columbia. One-fifth of its residents (and growing) are 65 or older. According to Statistics Canada, it is the fourth-greyest metropolitan area in Canada (Trois-Rivières is the greyest). There are clearly some very specific places in Canada, like Kelowna, that will benefit from offering Canada's aging population a lifestyle they believe is worth moving for.

## The Draw of the Suburbs

Which communities are Canada's population growth leaders? These are communities with populations of 10,000 or more residents that have experienced extreme growth over the last few years:

- Milton, Ontario (Toronto): +54.3%, 84,362
- Whitchurch-Stouffville (Toronto): +54.3%, 37,628
- Chestermere, Alberta (Calgary): +49.4%, 14,824
- Beaumont, Alberta (Edmonton): +48.2%, 13,284
- Airdrie, Alberta (Calgary): +47.1%, 42,564
- Leduc, Alberta (Edmonton): +43.1%, 24,279
- Okotoks, Alberta (Calgary): +42.9%, 24,511
- Paradise, Newfoundland (St. John's): +40.6%, 17,695
- Sainte-Marthe-sur-le-Lac (Montreal): +38.7%, 15,689
- Marieville (Quebec City): +34.1%, 10,094

What these places have in common is that they are all suburbs. And almost all are located around the Greater Toronto Area, Calgary, or Edmonton. There's also one in Newfoundland (a suburb of St. John's) and two in Quebec (one a suburb of Montreal, the other a suburb of Quebec City). But all are suburbs.

The bottom line is that **while Canada's most robust markets are the growing CMAs, the real sweet spots are the suburbs, not the downtowns.** Downtowns will always have a strong attraction for younger, educated Canadians who are establishing themselves both in their careers and in their families. Some of them, when they start their families, may want to stick with the amenities that drew them to the city core in the first place. But the draw of bigger, more affordable homes and more open spaces in the suburbs appeals to immigrants with resources, older Canadians who want to stay in their suburban family homes, and younger Canadians who desire single-family dwellings but can't afford them in our increasingly expensive downtown cores.

## Urban Diversity

Our big cities are the core of Canada today, and they will become more so as we roll through the century. While we could spend endless hours debating over what are ultimately small differences among our big cities, the truth is that they have more in common with each other than they (or we) can sometimes comfortably admit. And they have more in common with each other than they do with towns even a hundred kilometres outside of their boundaries.

Don't believe me? Try an experiment. Next time you're in Toronto, Montreal, or Vancouver, spend some time strolling around. As you admire the landmarks, streets, and buildings, take some time to look at the people walking by. What you will see (and hear) is *diversity*. If it's Yonge-Dundas Square in Toronto, every second person who happens by will have been born in another country. If it's Robson Street in Vancouver, it will be two in five. If it's St. Denis in Montreal, it will be about one in five. You will see something similar in each city's suburbs.

While these cities vary in their amount of diversity, each will always be the most diverse community in their province.

Now drive a hundred kilometres outside the city limits. Stop in whatever town you like. Do the same thing you did in the city: look at the people walking around. With rare exceptions, they will be whiter, older, and much more likely to be conversing in one of Canada's official languages. You can look at the statistics as much as you like, but until you see it with your own eyes, it's difficult to appreciate what's really happening. **Canada is becoming two countries: big cities and the rest.**

I've inadvertently done this mental experiment many times while travelling around the country for work. After a while, it's hard to tell based on the people if you're in Brandon, Manitoba, or Sydney, Nova Scotia. And leaving language aside, the people in Trois-Rivières, Quebec, look the same as the people in Prince George, British Columbia. It's the same in the big-city suburbs. Surrey, British Columbia, looks like Markham, Ontario. But the people in Markham and Surrey look completely different from the people in Brandon, Trois-Rivières, and Sydney. Sure, there are exceptions, but these rules pretty much apply across the country. As I've said, we're becoming two countries.

## What This Means for Your Business

Canada is becoming two countries. One (cities) is the future; the other (rural and small-town communities) is the past. Medium-sized population centres beyond commuting distance from a big city exist in most regions, but like small-town and rural Canada, they too are beginning to feel the effects of lower fertility, aging, and lack of interest from immigrants.

**Our biggest cities and suburbs are now individual commercial zones spreading over the landscape. They are ground zero for business,** almost like the old city-states of ancient Greece or Italy. The challenge will be tuning into the needs of these metropolises—particularly their suburbs. Suburbanites now drive the Canadian economy *and* will decide who will win nearly every important election.

Who are our suburbanites? They are commuters with kids, mortgages, and private-sector jobs. They are increasingly new Canadians. They aren't having huge families, although they have more kids than other Canadians. They are older than you might think, but still younger than average. These are the consumers who will be essential to your business's growth and should occupy the central position in your future business planning. What are you making for them? How are you making their hectic lives easier? Politicians, what in your election platform will appeal specifically to them?

## What This Means for You

If you live in the suburbs, you are more important to our future than you appreciate. You may not feel important, because our cultural, business, and political leaders seem to have little understanding of how you live your life, and everything important seems to happen where you don't live—especially if you're part of the shrinking audience that watches television news or reads a daily newspaper. The Laurentian elite doesn't live where you live, appears uninterested in the issues you care about, and probably travels through your community only on the way to their cottage or cabin. But **the suburbs have the power, and it grows every day.** This is becoming more and more obvious with every election.

# CHAPTER 10

# *The Big Smokescreen*: Why the Urban-Suburban Divide Will Continue to Grow

## Toronto: Love It or Hate It

Toronto is Canada's Megacity. If an important population trend has taken place, it probably happened in Toronto first. Sure, every Canadian city is a bit different, but Toronto is usually a solid leading indicator for future change. **What's happening in Toronto spreads. It's just a matter of time.**

There are few neutral opinions about Toronto. You either love it or you hate it. On the love side, count in most of the people who live there. Survey after survey shows that if you can get past the traffic jams and high cost of living (by Canadian standards), you think Toronto's worth the pain. Why? Because you love Toronto's diversity, its sense of community, and all that it offers in terms of cultural attractions and experiences. As Peter Ustinov was suggesting in his backhanded way when he said Toronto is "New York run by the Swiss," Toronto is to Canadians what New York City is to Americans.

Nonetheless, even if you love living in Toronto, nearly all (90%) of your neighbours now agree that it's becoming too difficult for the average person to live there. As a result, even though they enjoy the lifestyle, nearly 40% of Toronto residents are at least considering giving up their big-city dream and moving away. This is especially true for young parents with lower incomes.

Aside from its residents, the other group that loves Toronto are the experts who create indices that rank the livability of the world's major cities. These days, most of the indices generated by the world's top think tanks, non-governmental organizations, consultancies, and media rank Toronto near the top of the world's livability list, along with Montreal, Vancouver, and Calgary. Also scoring well are the major cities in Australia and New Zealand, as well as European cities such as Paris, Vienna, and Berlin. Toronto was the seventh most livable city in the world in 2018 according to *The Economist* magazine's livability index, behind Calgary (fourth) and Vancouver (sixth). The world's least livable city is Harare, Zimbabwe.

With all this hometown and international love for Toronto, who hates the place? Sometimes it seems like it's just about everybody in Canada who doesn't call Toronto home. Go to any city or town outside of Toronto, drop by the local watering hole, and ask any of those bending an elbow at the bar what they think of Toronto. Check the second hand on your watch. The hate will start rolling in before it makes it back to twelve.

I've developed my assessment of what Canadians think of Toronto more systematically than by just hanging out in bars (although I've done that too). Over the last thirty years I've had the privilege of moderating hundreds of focus groups across Canada. I've moderated groups in every single province more than once, and in communities big and small across the country. When the groups are in a city, they're usually held in a specially designed room with recording equipment and one-way glass through which observers can watch the conversation without being seen. When they are in smaller towns, the groups are held in hotels or community centres. I've even conducted focus groups in temporary shelters in remote logging camps on Vancouver Island.

One of the hardest parts of conducting a good focus group is getting nervous civilians in the mood to talk, especially those who have never been to a focus group before (in the business, we call these people focus group virgins). It's an intimidating environment. They are sitting in an unfamiliar room with a bunch of strangers, waiting for who knows what to begin. That's why every good moderator has an introduction memorized to set the mood for the room and to ease everyone into the conversation. Part of my patter has always been to share something about myself. My thinking is that you need to give something to get something. So I'd talk a bit about my family and hobbies, nothing too threatening. Then I'd finish with "I live in Toronto."

The reaction from participants to this statement was instantaneous and almost physical, as if a noxious smell had just entered the room. Some in the group would ask how anyone could live in a place like that. "It's nothing but traffic, pollution, concrete, and crime." "Look at how beautiful it is here in (insert name of town). Any sane person would rather live here than in Toronto." Others in the room were defensive, thinking I'd come to their town to judge them. "You people from Toronto are all so smug and look down your noses at the rest of us." The only worse thing I could have said was "I'm from Ottawa and I'm here to help you." Over the years, I learned my lesson. My intro has forever switched to "I'm from Cambridge, Ontario." That always goes over much better.

## Canada's Power Centre

Focus group reaction notwithstanding, it is undeniable that Toronto has become Canada's great power centre. And it's becoming more powerful every day. That's because the Greater Toronto Area, or GTA, holds the largest concentration of people in the country. Even if the GTA is growing more slowly than some other Canadian population centres, it's starting from a much bigger, more diverse base. It's growing regardless of economic cycles. It will be very hard for any other Canadian city, including the fast-growing cities in our West, to catch up to Toronto any time soon.

According to Ontario's Ministry of Finance, the GTA is projected to be the fastest-growing region in Ontario over the next twenty-five years and will account for over 68% of the province's population growth during that period. This means the population of the GTA will increase by over 40%, from 6.6 million in 2015 to almost 9.5 million in 2041. That's the equivalent of adding nearly four new Calgarys to the GTA over the next quarter century. As early as 2025, the GTA will represent over half of Ontario's total population, and its share will just keep growing.

Leaving the population numbers aside, it's understandable why so many Canadians have a hate on for Toronto, especially the downtown. This bastion of the Laurentian elite can come off to the rest of the country like it sees itself as the centre of the Canadian universe, if not the entire universe. While it might grate on some sensibilities, there's some justification for Torontonians feeling this way. **Over the last forty years, there has been an enormous concentration of power in Toronto.** Almost all of Canada's major corporate and cultural headquarters are now clustered around Toronto (except for those anchored elsewhere for political reasons or by the resources they harvest). This includes all of Canada's top five banks, Canada's biggest stock exchange (the TSX), and most of Canada's media institutions. For example, all of Canada's major news organizations are now headquartered in Toronto, and two of our three nightly national television news broadcasts come from Toronto. Global TV's broadcast still comes out of Vancouver, but it relies heavily on content generated by resources based in Toronto.

Political parties find it very difficult to win a national election without carrying the GTA. Business leaders find it near impossible to run a successful large business in Canada without the country's biggest consumer market and source of capital in their corner. Cultural leaders eventually have to deal with someone in Toronto. Most of the gatekeepers and decision-makers for just about everything in Canada reside in Toronto. Sure, there are important exceptions. Montreal is the hub if you're working in French. For government, it's Ottawa. If it's oil and gas, you're dealing with Calgary. But the smart money plays to the rules, not to the exceptions.

## The Greater Area

While the contemporary image of Toronto is driven by pictures of the CN Tower, shining bank towers on Bay Street, tattooed hipsters on Queen West, or the new neon Toronto sign in Nathan Phillips Square, this isn't the real Toronto for most GTA residents. Downtown Toronto is tourist Toronto, or the Toronto that plays New York City or Chicago in Hollywood movies. Downtown Toronto is where the decisions get made, and where many locals work and play. But most of them don't live there unless they are members of the affluent 1%, struggling hipsters, or condo singletons. The reality of the GTA for most residents is in the first and third letters of the acronym, not the second. It's more about the Greater Area than it is about Toronto. The same is true for Canada's other two big cities, Montreal and Vancouver. **Canada's current population growth is really a story of the suburbs. That's where our new people power is located.**

This point was made by David Gordon, Lyra Hindrichs, and Chris Willms from the School of Urban and Regional Planning at Queen's

University in an important study on community growth in Canada. People who live in suburban homes and go everywhere in a car have been responsible for almost all of the growth in Canada's cities over the past decade. As their report notes, Canada is a suburban nation. More than 80% of the population of large cities, including Vancouver, Calgary, Toronto, and Montreal, live in suburbs. "Their downtowns may be full of new condo towers, but there is five times as much population growth on the suburban edges of the regions." And these suburbanites get to work almost exclusively by car.

The extent of Canada's suburbanization is born out by the population numbers for the GTA. While the growth of Toronto's population (which also includes what some consider to be inner Toronto suburbs of North York, Etobicoke, and Scarborough) is projected by the Ontario government to rise from 2.83 million to 3.74 million by 2041 (which is above the average provincial growth rate), the growth in the other census divisions of the GTA (Durham, Halton, Peel, and York) is projected to be significantly faster, with the addition of 1.9 million people to those areas. Provincial government analysts also project that Peel Region alone will see its population increase by 685,000 over the next twenty-five years—a rise of nearly 50%—while Halton Region is projected to be the fastest-growing census division in all of Ontario, with a growth of 63.6% during the same time.

Given these population trends, it's difficult to figure out (if one cares about evidence-based public policy-making) why Canada's biggest cities are obsessed with choking off car transportation with new bicycle lanes and other traffic obstructions in their downtown corridors. Picasso would be envious of their often abstract and whimsical handiwork with road paint and concrete. These anti-car initiatives serve an increasingly exclusive constituency of downtowners without considering the expanding population of suburbanites who have few options for getting to the city other than by car. Many of those who live in Canada's suburbs see commuting by bicycle or using today's transit options as realistic as riding a unicorn to work.

I don't mean to say that the environmental and other benefits of increased cycling and mass transit aren't worth pursuing, or that Canada's big cities don't need to find better ways of moving large numbers of people and enticing more of them to live closer to downtown. They absolutely must. But until they do, all that's happening, apart from self-satisfied virtue signalling by downtown activists and politicians, is that they're creating grounds for an ongoing political war with the suburbs, based on transportation. This was one of the big motivators behind Rob Ford getting elected as mayor of Toronto. He called it "the war on the car." And half of Toronto's voters, overwhelmingly in the suburbs, voted for him. It was also a big part of what elected Rob's brother Doug to the office of Premier of Ontario. The 2018 Ontario election was essentially the revolt of the suburban commuters against the values of the anti-car downtown elites.

## Suburban Population Growth

Why are Canada's car-commuting suburbs growing so quickly? In the GTA (but also in Montreal, Vancouver, and Calgary), it's because the suburbs now attract the lion's share of migrants (both international and domestic). Remember the stereotypical pattern of poor migrants starting downtown and moving out to the suburbs when they can afford to? That's much less likely now. **Today's migrants tend to start their Canadian adventure in the suburbs and then stay put.** Many of them arrive with means and skills, and can already afford to buy a bigger home in a suburban community that has a concentration of people from their home country. But this trend applies even to less-affluent immigrants, who can find more affordable housing options in the 'burbs, along with the necessary community connections to smooth their way into their new country.

For example, if you're an immigrant from China today, you are less likely to start your Canadian life in Toronto's old downtown China-town, as previous Chinese immigrants did. Instead, you will prob-ably settle in a suburban community like Scarborough, Ontario, or Richmond, British Columbia, where there's a large concentration of both recent and established Chinese immigrants. Similarly, if you are coming from India, you will likely settle in Surrey, British Columbia, or Brampton, Ontario.

The high cost of real estate in Toronto's desirable downtown neigh-bourhoods also directs newcomers and even current city residents to the suburbs. (This is also the case in Vancouver, but less so in Montreal.) Apart from helping to attract migrants to the 'burbs, real estate prices are also pushing Millennials out of downtown because most don't want to raise their kids in the downtown accommodation they can afford: shoebox houses or condos. **Canadians still believe the best place to raise a family is in a house with a yard where the kids can play.**

Seniors are also contributing to suburban population growth because they have decided to stay put in their suburban family homes. These seniors and soon-to-be seniors are content to age in place. So even if the share of seniors in the GTA is currently lower than the pro-vincial average (because the city attracts so many younger migrants), the senior population in the GTA suburbs is projected to grow by 160% by 2041.

Apart from wanting to stay in the family home for lifestyle reasons, seniors also want to be in high-density neighbourhoods near a city. As people age, they develop increasing physical mobility issues, and they also become more reluctant to drive. Being close to a city gives them easier access to specialized hospitals and other services they need, as well as a variety of transportation options to get them there. Access to these services is also a big motivator for seniors contemplating leaving rural and small-town communities. So not only are today's suburban seniors staying put, but seniors from other places are now moving to join them.

## Suburbs Are Made for Families

Family structures affect where we decide to live. The traditional family— a married opposite-sex couple and their biological offspring living in the same household—is becoming less common in Canada. **Canadian families now include as many flexible relationship combinations as we can imagine.** Some are a product of divorce, widowhood, or common-law living arrangements. Canada is also seeing more same-sex parents raising children, and more single men and women opting from the start to raise kids on their own. While the traditional family will remain an aspirational social preference for some, especially when it comes to raising children, it isn't a practical or workable arrangement in the real-world lives of a growing number of Canadians.

Raising children has a huge impact on where and how we decide to live. Because of what's happening in our most expensive and desirable urban and suburban real estate markets, we should expect to see more multigenerational families experimenting with living together in the same household, and city councils should get ready for this new reality. The logic is far too compelling. It's already happening. We all know of multigenerational immigrant families choosing to live together for cultural and/or financial reasons, especially when they are first transitioning into Canadian society. Immigrant families will continue to do this, especially if Pacific nations and developing countries remain our biggest source of immigrants.

Multigenerational families already established in Canada will increasingly consider experimenting with living under one roof, especially in

Canada's most desirable cities and suburbs. This trend is about employment location, a lack of desirable and affordable real estate, and the expanding need for unfunded senior care. In some instances, it will be because the younger generation (partnered or single) is not able to afford the right house in a neighbourhood close to work. In others, it will be that the older generation needs help from their children to stay in the family home. Remember, seniors prefer to age in place over selling and moving to an unfamiliar neighbourhood.

In both cases, some extended families may decide that it would be better for all of them to reconfigure the right family home into new living accommodations to fit multiple generations. They might see this as better than spending hours on the highway commuting to cities that are increasingly hostile to the transportation needs of commuters, or going into huge debt to buy a less desirable house in a worse location. Think of this as the shared family cottage arrangement, transferred to Canada's best urban and suburban neighbourhoods.

## Downtown Is for the Young

For those who are young and highly educated, Toronto's core (or the downtown core of any of Canada's big cities) is an urban playground. These are people who want to have easier, quicker access to all the cool jobs and fun stuff that a big city's downtown offers. They also want to live with people just like them. Researchers who study cities have long known that people with similar characteristics tend to gather in the same types of neighbourhoods. Go through any of Canada's big cities and you will immediately see these concentrations, whether it's Greektown in Toronto, Vancouver's Chinatown, or Montreal's Little Italy. The same applies to artists or finance folks. Like attracts like. The data underscore this point. The median age in Toronto's core is mid-30s, while in the rest of Ontario it's now above 40.

Downtown Toronto is also home to a lot of people with a post-secondary education—20% more in downtown Toronto than in the rest of Ontario. And despite what's celebrated about Toronto's diversity, downtown is relatively white in comparison to the increasingly ethnically diverse suburbs. Again, like attracts like.

Another noticeable aspect of life in downtown Toronto is fewer families with kids. The same goes for Montreal and Vancouver. In the downtowns of all three cities, the proportion of children age 14 and under is only about half of what it is in most peripheral areas. Canadians tend to follow the lifestyle and residential stereotypes. Once you decide to have kids, downtown's clubs, hipster bars, artisanal BBQ joints, and vintage clothing stores become a fading memory as you find yourself on the highway back to your split level in the 'burbs, with its ample parking for your minivan or SUV.

## Increasing Tensions Between Suburbs and Downtowns

Downtowns dominated by universities and the creative and service industries will be true outliers going forward because they are magnets for one of the rarest groups in Canadian society: upwardly mobile young people. Downtowns will be dominated by this affluent, well-educated, and less ethnoculturally diverse population, who won't have many kids. As you now know, having children typically triggers a move to the suburbs.

Tension between the suburbs and downtowns will continue to grow. The big fights will be over access to public services, transportation, and mobility. **Cities will continue to fight the war against the car, while suburbanites will fight for relief from their longer and longer commutes.** This will happen all over the country, but especially in the GTA and in the West.

There's no doubt that the mood will be increasingly tense among

Canada's generations and communities going forward. Older people will be living longer and demanding more and more in terms of public services. They will be staying in their desirable houses and jobs longer than the younger generations expected or want them to, and will flock from endangered rural and small-town communities to the affordable edges of the suburbs. They will need access to the services offered by a city, but not with the same regularity as commuters. Providing seniors with on-demand access to the city will be a big business opportunity.

## Rural Atrophy

If the future of urban and suburban Canada is about generations learning to live together in the same, increasingly crowded space, rural and small-town Canada will be focused on dealing with the opposite situation. The growing challenge for these communities—and for medium-sized and smaller cities outside of reasonable commuting distance from our biggest southern cities—will be how to keep from becoming ghost towns. Over the next decade (as over the last several decades), Canadians living off the beaten path will increasingly decide to relocate to large metropolitan communities. Making the move will be both older people who need reliable access to support services and ambitious young people looking to compete for the best jobs. This is not just a Canadian trend, it's a global one. Remember, by 2050, two-thirds of the world's population will be living in an urban area.

Also choosing to move to Canada's biggest centres will be the immigrants we absolutely need to keep our population numbers at least stable. Despite feel-good stories from well-meaning writers about little mosques springing up on prairies, these are and will continue to be very minor exceptions. Almost all immigrants choose to live in one of our large southern metropolises, even if they start off in a more remote community. Like anybody else with ambition, immigrants go to where the jobs are, but they also move to where people from their cultural community have established a beachhead for them, and that's almost always in a suburban centre. We should expect these patterns to persist, to the detriment of our rural and small-town communities, which desperately need an injection of younger people.

Commerce follows people, as well as the other way around. It is a virtuous, reinforcing circle. Unless Old Canadian communities can find ways to attract new businesses, more lucrative jobs, and younger people, things will just keep spiralling down for them. Of course, there will always be communities that buck this trend. For example, Kelowna, British Columbia, has found new life as a mecca for retirees. But Kelowna has the advantages of having a good climate and the critical mass of people to support the reliable and accessible public services that seniors need. Not all smaller, more remote communities have these advantages.

Nonetheless, there will be more Kelownas. It is inevitable. Inspired community leaders will see the writing on the wall and will come up with the necessary changes to infrastructure and services to seize the opportunity. Smart business operators will join in, remembering that seniors have money. The guaranteed huge increase in Canada's senior population will drive these changes. (Guaranteed as much as anything involving people can ever be guaranteed.)

Not all seniors will want to age in place. Many will decide to move to their own version of Kelowna. That's the opportunity. But for every new Kelowna, there will be many, many more communities like Cape Breton, Nova Scotia, which have little opportunity to follow suit. Cape Breton and communities like it will struggle to stay afloat with their aging, shrinking, and expensive populations, with few obvious prospects for turning things around. The statistics tell the tale: Cape Breton's population shrunk by 2.9% between 2011 and 2016; 24% of the population is 65 or older (compared to the Canadian average of 17%); and only 1.8% of the population is foreign-born (compared to 20% for all of Canada). This is what happens to a coal-mining community when the market demand for coal dries up and governments lack a plan or the will to confront the situation.

**In the next couple of decades, big swaths of rural and small-town Canada will be in serious atrophy and very much at risk of terminal decline.** Since businesses will struggle to find a commercial reason to invest there (they will be more likely to pull out than move in), it will come down to governments stepping up to fix things. The darkest days for established communities will coincide with the growing demands of suburbanites, who will want better commuting access to the cities where they work. The only realistic solution for commuters is major mobility and transit projects, which require big public bucks from all levels of government. Improving mobility and transportation will also offer huge opportunities for business.

At the same time as governments are struggling to respond to the needs of declining rural communities and suburban commuters, the growing senior population will be looking to maintain their health care, pensions, and other benefits. Governments won't be able to do it all. In a political system based on representation by population, Old Canada's voice—places like Cape Breton—will be getting weaker and weaker in the battle for scarce public dollars.

## The Hamilton Phenomenon

Sure, there could be some technological miracle that leads to the rebirth of rural and small-town Canada. That telecommuting thing might finally take off, like it was supposed to thirty years ago. Or maybe there will be another gold rush. But even that would have only a short-term impact on the communities that are lucky enough to have gold. Or perhaps young people will finally wake up to the possibility that there's more to life than an insecure entry-level job that requires them to be crammed into a city they can't afford. This does happen, and not just on TV. Just such a collective decision created a renaissance in the old steel town of Hamilton, Ontario, which some are now calling "Canada's Brooklyn." Young people, including artists and other creative types, have decamped in big numbers from expensive Toronto for a new life an hour west.

"The Hammer" may have been through a few tough decades with the decline of its steel plants, but it also has impressive, historic housing that many people desire but could never afford to buy in Toronto. In Hamilton, it's still possible, and that's a big part of the attraction. Unfortunately, as you read this, you may have missed your opportunity in Canada's Brooklyn. Cheaper than Toronto doesn't mean cheap. Hamilton is now one of the fastest-rising real estate markets in Ontario. And because it is only about an hour's commute (on a good day) from Toronto's jobs, it is a viable option for commuters who want a spacious single-family home but can't afford the more expensive, though closer, commuter towns of Mississauga and Oakville.

None of this, however, helps Timmins or Moncton. But there's a very real possibility that the Hamilton phenomenon will replicate itself across the country in more and more historic mid-sized cities and towns within commuting distance of big cities. There may also be an expansion of what is considered an acceptable distance for commuting. Hipster bar owners won't be the only ones moving in. Seniors from farther away will also come to town. We could see not just the revitalization of the downtowns in these places, but also an increase in residential subdivisions close to highways and other transportation links for commuters, as well as purpose-built seniors' communities. Again, the key accelerant for such a change is proximity to the opportunities, attractions, and facilities of a major metropolis, so building serious transportation infrastructure will be an even greater priority.

## What This Means for Your Business

**The two big opportunities for business emerging from Canada's urbanization, and especially suburbanization, relate to real estate and transportation.** These are also two of the biggest sources of anxiety for most metropolis-dwelling Canadians. Government has proven to be mostly incapable of dealing with these issues. Jurisdictional battles combined with a fear of raising taxes or clashing with community groups opposed to development have bogged down or destroyed almost every potential solution that has been brought forward. As the need for solutions increases, the tension grows.

While it might seem like a fool's errand to jump into this battle, it's a great business opportunity. Solutions will have to start small, neighbourhood by neighbourhood. Developers who can find a way to create affordable housing options that respect established neighbourhoods will be in demand. Think of mixed generations of the same family within purpose-built housing options. Make it work in one neighbourhood, and it becomes possible in other neighbourhoods.

Want to appeal to suburbanites? Find a way to make their commutes easier. You might, for example, develop real estate options that allow commuters to live closer to where they need to be for work. But the more immediate solution will likely involve a serious rethink of city transportation infrastructure. We need a truce in the war on the car. The only realistic way for that to happen is to provide car commuters with new alternatives, most likely some form of rail. No doubt, the costs will be enormous, and the jurisdictional and land use battles will be ridiculous. But it's really the only option. If that's the goal, then what's the solution? There must be a group of visionaries out there who can get this ball rolling.

## What This Means for You

**Despite the doomsayers, real estate remains a solid investment—especially real estate in the best neighbourhoods of our major metropolitan areas.** Our population continues to grow, and most people want to live where most people are already living. This includes the Perennials, who are staying put. There isn't enough supply, so demand will continue to grow, which means prices will keep going up. There will undoubtedly be fluctuations like those we've seen in Vancouver because of the new tax on foreign buyers; it's important, however, to not confuse fluctuations with trends. Yes, the market in Vancouver is down a bit, but it will rise again. It's inevitable. That's what happens to real estate prices when the sixth most livable city in the world has a growing population.

You might also look at investing in companies that are focused on creating transportation alternatives for commuters, whether these are new types of vehicles, new technology-based ride sharing options, or creative rail-based solutions. Financial companies and engineering companies who have new ways of financing and building transportation infrastructure will be a good bet too. The commuting situation in Canada will eventually become an emergency that will force governments into action. When that happens, companies that have recognized the problem and been proactive in preparing solutions will be at the front of the line for whatever projects emerge.

# PART 3

# WHO WE'LL BE

# CHAPTER 11

# *Everything Is Political*: Why Diversity Is Not Our Strength

## HISF and the Dark Cloud of Populism

It was a grey, cold, and rainy mid-November weekend in Halifax. It seems to be like this every year for the Halifax International Security Forum. This was an exclusive invite, and I was privileged to be there. HISF (pronounced "HISS-IF" by the initiated), is billed as the security and defence equivalent of the World Economic Forum, which is held annually in the Swiss Alpine town of Davos. But instead of attracting Hollywood celebrities and major corporate leaders to the Swiss ski slopes, HISF brings three hundred defence and foreign ministers, generals and admirals, diplomats, academics, and other experts from ninety countries to the Halifax waterfront. What HISF lacks in celebrity glitz, it makes up for in brain power. HISF truly is a who's who of the world's top international security experts.

Since the second year of the forum, Ipsos has conducted a twenty-four-country poll on what the citizens of the world think about security issues. I was in Halifax to report on the latest iteration of the survey. The brief from Peter Van Praagh, who heads the HISF team, was, as always, intended to inject a bit of the real world into the Forum's highbrow deliberations. Van Praagh believes, as do I, that it's just good manners to ask regular folks what they think before having the global security elite pronounce on what's best for them.

One of HISF's highlights is always the welcome dinner at Pier 21 on the Halifax waterfront. Pier 21 is where, between 1928 and 1971, more than a million new immigrants streamed into Canada after sailing across the Atlantic. It now hosts the Canadian Museum of Immigration, which tells the story of the people who came ashore here. If your immigrant ancestors came to Canada through Pier 21, you can look up their entry records at the museum.

The welcome dinner features the culinary wonders of Nova Scotia. To the delight of hungry delegates festooned with red and white plastic bibs, kilted bagpipers play in trays of steamed Atlantic lobsters born aloft by an army of wait staff. Perhaps this isn't the same as rubbing elbows with Clooney and DiCaprio over après-ski cocktails in Davos, but it's still pretty cool.

HISF was started by former Conservative Party defence minister and local boy Peter MacKay, along with important American congressional leaders such as the late Senator John McCain, global security organizations such as NATO, some inspired corporate sponsors, and, of course, the Canadian government. Ever the smart local politician, it wasn't lost on MacKay that local voters would welcome the filling of two thousand hotel rooms in Halifax's off-season. The Trudeau Liberals aren't dumb either: they've kept HISF rolling along in Halifax, where they won every seat in 2015. Truly, as legendary US Speaker of the House Tip O'Neill once observed, "All politics is local."

HISF says it "advances a unique and modern vision of security by promoting greater strategic cooperation among democracies." Heady stuff. But amidst all the talk about treaties, security regimes, and weapons systems, one topic of late hangs over both the formal and back-room discussions like a heavy, dark cloud blowing in from across the Atlantic Ocean: populism. Delegates spit out the word as if it were a toxic pill they had mistakenly swallowed. It's been like this ever since the election of Donald Trump in the United States and the Brexit vote in the United Kingdom. The global security elite, along with elites everywhere, struggle mightily to come up with a rational explanation for what has transpired in democratic politics over the last few years. How is it that populism, a historical phenomenon for most Western democracies, has taken root again in our time?

## The Drivers of Modern Populism

It's instructive to listen to experts talk about today's populism, as I have in Halifax. While there's always some acknowledgement of dark cultural motivations, with an aside to unscrupulous demagogues and interfering foreign governments, they eventually settle on economic disadvantage and inequality as the key drivers of modern populism. If it's Americans talking (Americans talk *a lot* at HISF, mostly about their own country), populism is driven by lower-middle-class white men in Rust Belt states who voted for Donald Trump because they wanted to get back at the political elites who had sacrificed their manufacturing jobs to foreign countries. For them, it's all about trade agreements and robots in factories. J.D. Vance's book *Hillbilly Elegy* provides the grist for their theory mill.

It isn't, however, just the Americans in Halifax who jump on economic causality. The Brits offer up similar explanations for the Brexit vote. Economics is also at the centre of the theories spun by continental European delegates attempting to explain outbreaks of populism in such diverse places as Hungary, France, Italy, Poland, Austria, Sweden, and Germany. Yes, the results of war and peace, cultural change, immigration, and racism factor into their theories too, but these are most often treated as shameful local nuances and embarrassing peculiarities, not as legitimate root causes worthy of serious consideration by intelligent people.

The Canadians at HISF regard these discussions about populism as if they were encountering a newly discovered exotic animal in a zoo. They have heard of this beast called populism, but they are pretty sure it will never survive in our special Canadian climate. Their proof? Canada has gone in the opposite direction of the United States and many other countries with its politics. Instead of electing populists, Canadians have opted to be governed by a proud, progressive Liberal Party that revels in its tolerance, inclusivity, sunny ways, and selfies. Canada's government is led by the ultimate anti-populist, Justin Trudeau. The Canadians at the forum remind anyone who will listen, both from the stage and in the back rooms, that Trudeau is a self-proclaimed feminist who wants to take a progressive approach to foreign and trade policy. "You've gone Trump, we've gone Trudeau," they say. And unlike Trump, the Trudeau government is committed to tamping down the economic drivers of populism by helping the middle class and those who want to join it.

All of these experts are wrong, including the Canadians. They don't understand what's driving modern populism. When you look closely at the global public opinion evidence, it becomes clear that **populism is rooted mostly in demographics and culture, not economics.** Sure, culture and economics are bundled together. But the jet fuel that's really feeding the populist firestorm is nativism, the strong belief among an electorally important segment of the population that governments and other institutions should honour and protect the interests of their native-born citizens against the cultural changes being brought about by immigration. This, according to the populists, is about protecting the "Real America" (or "Real Britain" or "Real Poland" or "Real France" or "Real Hungary") from imported influences that are destroying the values and cultures that have made their countries great.

Importantly, it's not just the nativists who are saying this is a battle over values and culture. Their strongest opponents believe this too, and they are not prepared to concede the high ground on what constitutes a "real citizen" to the populists. For them, this is a battle about the rule of law, inclusiveness, open borders, and global participation. The list goes on and on, but you get the picture. This is a fight for the soul of a country. It's not only or even mostly about the best way to reduce income equality.

Ultimately, Trump, Le Pen in France, and the Brexiteers didn't create this situation. They are symptoms, not causes. They and their fellow travellers just threw the match that ignited the explosion. And that's what a populism outbreak ultimately takes: a demagogic politician who is prepared to embrace populism as a political strategy, whatever the consequences for their nation's social cohesion. Sadly, these types of politicians aren't hard to find these days.

Even if populist voters are satisfactorily employed, they still support populist options. There's only a weak correlation between personal economic situations and populism. That's what the surveys Ipsos has conducted around the world demonstrate on this question. And the Western countries where populism has taken root continue to perform relatively well economically. Therefore, economics alone doesn't explain the rise of populism.

## Acknowledging the Primacy of Nativism

If the true roots of populism seem obvious after looking at the data, why is it such a difficult conversation for the delegates in Halifax to have? They are the intellectual offspring of great economists like Marx, Schumpeter, Freidman, and Keynes. But for the Halifax delegates (and, most other elites, including business elites), the only mature political debate worth having is about who has and who has not. They would never honour a nativist's views, which are not defined by economics, with serious consideration. To them, nativists are simply bigots who are to be scolded or ignored, like unhinged Millenarians predicting an imminent zombie apocalypse.

Since the end of the Second World War, Western intellectuals from both the mainstream left and right have expended most of their brain cells on questions involving economic class, including the size, shape, and responsibilities of the modern welfare state. Arguments over how far to go in ameliorating economic and social inequality can get heated, but the range of options at play are pretty much understood and agreed upon by most political leaders. Should we have higher or lower taxes? Should we increase the minimum wage? Should we have universal or targeted social welfare programs? Should we have freer trade or higher tariffs? None of this really strays into the cultural territory of what makes a "real citizen."

Furthermore, trade, income distribution, and tax conflicts are all relatively short-term issues that are easy to spot and control. They are the low-hanging fruit of public policy. Demographic change, and the cultural challenges it causes, is much higher up the policy tree. Cultural change happens at a slower pace, affects us much more deeply over the long term, and is much harder to effect through public policy tweaks once it gets rolling. Sure, you can see an emerging demographic trend that impacts culture (like declining fertility) coming from a long way off, but once it builds momentum, it is very difficult to stop. Similarly, the decisions being made today about Canada's immigration policy will forever shape our future population and will ultimately have a major impact on our culture. That's why they must be made carefully, and with a clear understanding of the cultural consequences for Canada.

**Elites won't acknowledge the primacy of nativism in driving populism because it opens a can of worms they would rather keep closed.** But ignoring the existence of nativism is dangerous for two reasons. First, it means that smart people are not engaging with this problem in ways that will solve it. We are purposefully misdiagnosing what's going on and substituting placebos for cures, which only encourages populism to flourish. And second, if one of the most effective claims populists can make is that they are the only ones who are prepared to listen to and respond to the interests of "real Canadians," the elites aren't helping their cause by seeming so out of touch with everyday reality.

## The Risk of Our Own Populist Firestorm

**Misunderstanding the relationship between nativism and populism is especially problematic for Canada because we have so much at stake.** Almost all of our population growth now comes from immigration. We have been able to pull off this big win with minimum social disruption because successive federal governments over the last three decades have both understood what was needed and managed immigration very carefully. They have made sure that our selection process skims candidates who are poised for successful integration, and they have embraced multiculturalism as a national project. Absent these conditions, Canada might right now be going through the same populist backlash to expanded immigration that we are seeing in so many other countries.

But we shouldn't be relaxed about this. A populist backlash to expanding immigration isn't inconceivable in Canada. It has happened before. What might drive it this time would be our leaders and other elites failing to understand serious tensions within Canadian public opinion about immigration. The tolerance that our political leaders like to tout at global summits and in speeches to the United Nations is noteworthy only because of the relative toxicity of the rest of the world. Canada might top global surveys on tolerance for immigration, but it's only because we are a shade above a very low global average.

Consider this: only 38% of Canadians are prepared to say immigration "has had a positive impact on Canada." Almost the same number (40%) believe it is causing Canada to change in ways they don't like. The United States scores 46% on the same question. So we are only marginally more tolerant than Trump's America.

Overall, the survey evidence shows that Canadians lean more negative on immigration and the cultural changes it brings about than our elites should be comfortable with. That's why it is not inconceivable that we could be laying the kindling for our own future populist firestorm. What will it take to light the fire? Apart from a political demagogue prepared to throw a nativist match, it merely requires our elites to go on believing that the best arguments for expanded immigration, especially from cultures distant from the Canadian majority, are about our national economy and celebrating our compassion. Those who are concerned about immigration will see this messaging as self-serving (either from a commercial or a political perspective) and tone-deaf. Why? Because we live today in a low-trust environment in which facts and direction from elites are regarded as ideological positions to be challenged, rather than objective truths to be believed. Therefore, **telling Canadians who are concerned about the cultural impact of immigration that they don't understand how this helps our country, that they lack heart, or that they are simply bigots is just asking for trouble.**

## Our Tolerance Is Our Strength

"Diversity is our strength" has become a common applause line in speeches by politicians, corporate leaders, and other elites these days. And why not? It would be an admirable achievement for Canada in this turbulent, divided world. But we need to think about what it communicates to a typical Canadian audience. What it says is that if you are at all uncomfortable with the cultural changes that diversity brings to your community (which surveys show many Canadians are), then you must be part of what makes us weak. You may even be a Canadian version of what Hillary Clinton called in a campaign speech the "basket of deplorables." Hardly an uplifting and unifying message.

"Diversity is our strength" is also an oxymoron. Just like the Party slogans from Orwell's novel *1984*, "War is peace. Freedom is slavery. Ignorance is strength." And as in *1984*, the public is expected to remain blind to its internal contradictions. In truth, diversity makes societies weaker, not stronger. It's obvious. If we're all the same, there's less to fight about. It's true for language, it's true for religion, it's true for wealth, and it's true for culture. Massive immigration increases cultural diversity, and increased cultural diversity creates more opportunities for social division and friction. It's folly to pretend otherwise. This friction has occurred throughout Canada's history, and will increase as immigration from more distant cultures keeps growing to compensate for our low birth rate. **Cultural friction created by demographic change is real. Therefore, it needs to be acknowledged, understood, and ameliorated—not dismissed or ignored by our leaders.**

So if diversity isn't Canada's strength, what is? It's our collective tolerance. This, more than any other value, defines our culture. Ultimately, tolerance is what makes Canada possible. What do I mean by tolerance? It's about live and let live, about fairness and equity of treatment. Equity of treatment means the same set of rules must apply to everyone, native-born and immigrant. These are not just political slogans or corporate talking points. **Tolerance is the core of what makes Canada work.**

Connecting with our core tolerance requires a very delicate balance. Canadians born or settled here need to believe that change in their communities due to expanding immigration is in their own personal self-interest. In other words, we need a good answer to the question "How is my life better because of this?" In addition, our political leaders need to acknowledge and deal with concerns about immigration's impact on cultural integration, job competition, security, and social services. These concerns shouldn't be swept aside by those in power as racist projections. Public opinion evidence shows that these are all strong mainstream worries in Canada today.

Specific stories of recent immigrant successes in Canada would be much more helpful than our elites endlessly repeating "Diversity is our strength." The more personal the stories, the better. The best stories are not about big numbers and the national impact. They are about real people next door, and the specific successes being achieved in communities across the country. This strategy, by the way, is not exclusive advice for our political leaders. Businesses can be helpful in delivering the message too. After all, these new immigrants are the next wave of employees, employers, and customers.

## Everything Is Political

If you're looking at populism from a business perspective, you might be thinking, *What does this culture stuff have to do with me?* It has everything to do with you. The private sector is no longer private. As the border between our private and public lives blurs, **what used**

to be regarded as a simple buying decision is increasingly an act
of political expression. Everything is political now. You can't watch
a late-night comedy show, an entertainment awards show, or even a
sporting event without something political popping up.

An Ipsos study showed that the number of people who have stopped
using products or services from a company due to its political leanings
or because of protests or boycotts is double the number who say they
marched in a protest or took part in the boycott of a company. It's not
just the left that does this, it's the right too. Political values are a minefield for brands now, and no brand is safe. Ask Canadian icon Tim
Hortons, which took a reputational beating because of a clash over
increasing the minimum wage for employees in Ontario. While this
was an Ontario issue, it has hurt Timmies' reputation across Canada.

In this age of populism, are we moving towards ideologically
defined brands? Possibly, which means you need to understand the
values of your customers more than ever. It's all about building trust.
**Trust is the most important asset any organization can have in this
turbulent world.**

Here's a practical example from a consumer's point of view. Is your
next dream car an all-electric Tesla or a Ford F-150 pickup? Sure, there
are practical, rational factors behind both choices, but the decision
is increasingly made based more on values than on automotive and
economic practicalities. It's now as much about the political person
punching the accelerator as it is about the car enthusiast appreciating
how long it takes to get from zero to sixty.

The car example is an obvious one. Car buying has always been
deeply informed by personal values and expressions of identity. Ask
anyone who owns a Prius or a Hummer. But this type of values signalling now extends to more mundane purchasing decisions—which
hardware store you shop at, which sports team you support, the beer

you drink, the art you enjoy. Every commercial act is becoming a potential political signal, even buying a double-double at Timmies or a latte at Starbucks.

## Pepsi's Fatal Blind Spot

Communicating amid this cultural battle zone is complicated and is getting more so every day. Ask the good people at Pepsi about the backlash they received because of their Kendall Jenner "Live for Now" street protest ad. This ad was an attempt by Pepsi to take the "diversity is our strength" message and connect it to the cultural and political divisions in the world today. Using a product ad to allude to larger social forces isn't a new idea. One of the most famous examples was produced by Pepsi's big rival, Coca-Cola, back in 1971. Coke's "Hilltop" ad, which featured youthful multicultural singers who shared the common goal of teaching the world to sing "in perfect harmony" (as they buy them a Coke), is widely regarded as a textbook example of effective socially aware, values-based advertising.

While "diversity is our strength" worked for Coke in 1971, it was a reputational disaster for Pepsi in 2017. Pepsi's ad was wrong for so many reasons: privileged supermodel as ersatz street protester, a pep rally masquerading as a serious protest, cultural appropriation for commercial exploitation—the list goes on and on. But the biggest problem was that it showed that Pepsi didn't understand the intersection between their brand, their message, and the contemporary cultural zeitgeist. Their ad might as well have said "Drink Pepsi and miss the point."

Why did the "peace and harmony" message work for Coke in 1971 and fail for Pepsi in 2017? Weren't the sixties and seventies also politically and culturally turbulent? Yes, but that turbulence was created by the rebellious offspring of the majority society. Nineteen seventy-one was about Boomers rebelling against the cultural conformity of their own parents. It was about long hair, peace, free love, and pop music. It was about generational tension, as opposed to ethnocultural transition. There was no imported foreign threat to challenge the dominant culture in 1971. Pepsi seemed to think its ad was plugging into the same generational tension as the Coke ad. Instead, they stumbled like a sleepwalker into today's most explosive cultural minefield: identity politics.

The irony is that Pepsi didn't get much pushback from right-wing populists for their ad, although they might actually have been going for that. Instead, it was the progressives, especially younger progressives, who flooded social media with posts attacking Pepsi. This was the very group Pepsi wanted most to connect with. So while the ad's targeting worked in terms of demographics, it delivered the wrong message to the right target group. Instead of saying "We want to bring everybody together in harmony" (as Coke did), Pepsi's ad said (or was taken to say) "We are about exploiting your deeply held personal beliefs for our commercial gain." The lesson? Using identity politics to market a consumer product is tricky and dangerous territory these days, especially if the advertiser happens to be a multinational corporation selling what activists might regard as an unhealthy product.

It's easy to roll your eyes at what happened to Pepsi. How could they have been so dense? I caution you not to be too quick to judge. The folks at Pepsi aren't stupid. Far from it. They have some of the smartest marketing and advertising people in the world working for them. Their advertising over the years has been incredibly successful. They wouldn't be where they are in the marketplace if it hadn't been. The point here is that if Pepsi can get it wrong, you can too. It's important to get past the tongue-clucking and move quickly to the lessons that should be learned from Pepsi's misstep.

Pepsi had a fatal blind spot. They were ignorant about how commerce and culture play against each other, and how much culture is changing along with identity. It was an easy mistake, because culture is a complicated and evolving topic. To better connect with Canadian customers you need to start with an understanding of who we are in ethnocultural terms and who we are becoming. For Canada, this means recognizing that we are increasingly a country of migrants. Our ancestors and more and more of our neighbours came from somewhere else. **Migration shapes us and will continue to shape us. It will increasingly define the Canadian marketplace.**

## Connecting with New Canadian Voters

One area where commentators get cultural connection wrong is in politics. These days, **you cannot win a national election, or an election in a large province, without winning the vote of new Canadians in the suburbs.** This is especially true in the 905, which describes both the telephone area code and the belt of suburban ridings that surround the City of Toronto. Stephen Harper won his majority there in 2011, as did Justin Trudeau in 2015, and Doug Ford swept it in the Ontario election of 2018.

There is a consistent belief among Canadian pundits that the way to connect with new Canadian voters in the suburbs is to connect with their cultures. This is wrong. New Canadians move to the suburbs for the same reasons anyone else does. They want to buy a home with a yard and a two-car garage, raise a family, and have a successful middle-class life. One big trade-off they are prepared to make for this lifestyle is commuting to work. Economic prosperity leads the list of issues they care about most, regardless of their ethnocultural heritage.

So why were three candidates as diverse as Stephen Harper, Justin

Trudeau, and Doug Ford all successful with new Canadian voters? Because they understood the middle-class focus of suburban commuters. Going into election day, all of them were in the lead on economic management. While this is easy to accept for Harper and Ford, it's a bit harder to explain for Trudeau. Trudeau didn't as much win on the economy in 2015 as Harper lost on it.

Here's a rule of thumb for handicapping Canadian elections. For Conservative parties to win, they need a double-digit lead over their main opponent on economic management. Harper had it in 2011, Ford had it in 2018. In 2015, Trudeau had it over Harper and Mulcair. How did Trudeau achieve this? Part of it was some good luck—Statistics Canada declared early in the election that Canada had entered what they called a technical recession. After that, Harper lost his ability to claim he was a superior economic manager. In addition, after nearly a decade of Conservative government, middle-class suburban Canadians were ready to hear another economic message: the hope and hard work of Team Trudeau. Did voters buy into the idea of running bigger deficits to promote economic growth? No, that still hasn't happened. However, the hopeful mood Team Trudeau communicated about what the future economy could be was a welcome change from the gloominess of the Conservatives.

In the end, then, connection with new Canadian voters doesn't mean treating them like they are different from other middle-class voters. When you move to the suburbs, you become a suburbanite like the rest of your neighbours. Sure, new Canadians want to know that politicians welcome and respect their unique cultures. But that's no substitute for connecting with them as members of the striving middle class. Harper figured this out first, Trudeau followed his lead, and so did Ford.

## What This Means for Your Business

**If everything is political, do you ever look at your business through a political lens?** Do you understand how people see you as a political actor? Not just how you want to be seen, but how you are *really* seen by potential supporters and opponents, including formal and informal groups from regulators, NGOs, political parties and leaders to Facebook groups and digital influencers. What do they think about your products or services—not in terms of quality or price, but from the perspective of whether they are good or bad for humanity and the planet? What about your employee practices? What about your board and management structure? What about who your customers are? What about your supply chain? All of this tells Canadians who you are.

If you don't know the answers to these questions, it's time to figure them out. In this world of instant communication, there's no time to find answers when a crisis hits. Single-use plastics are a good reference point for what can happen when your product becomes a political target: from habitual daily use by most consumers to political and social pariah in an instant.

Governments and policy-makers must come to grips with how Canadian culture is changing. Canada's major source of population growth is now immigration. Increased immigration is accelerating cultural change. Cultural change leads to political change. Political change isn't just about who wins and loses elections (although there are partisan and electoral implications to changing demography); it's more about changes to our power structure.

Big change is messy. We are seeing the political effects of migration-driven change all over the world, and much of it is ugly. So far Canada has dodged a major nativist political backlash—more by luck than by design. We are not immune to it. Both progressives and conservatives continue to play at the edges of this ugliness, which does not bode well for our future. Such a backlash starts with virtue signalling and low nativist dog whistles, but can move rapidly to a more dangerous confrontation. Canadians are a tolerant people, but that tolerance should never be taken for granted. It's time to move beyond the slogans and have a serious conversation about what we want for our immigration policy. **How much change can we tolerate, and how can we make change tolerable?** That's a great place to start.

## What This Means for You

If you're feeling more political these days, that's because both you and the world *are* more political. Increased educational achievement, expansion of the internet, instantaneous access to information, and global communication have seen to that. You would be well advised to start taking the political implications of your investments into account. **Think about what companies might be vulnerable to changing political values and how that could affect their viability in the future.**

I'm not necessarily talking about investing in ethical funds, which usually represent a progressive view of ethics. There are lots of companies that would never make it into these funds that have terrific financial performance. It's about how politics in general will play into the future of the companies you are trusting your money to. Are they on the right side of the biggest political and social trends, ensuring a bright future? Are they a *Titanic* about to hit a political iceberg? Or are they sufficiently below the radar that they should avoid political intrusion? If you don't know, it's time to find out.

# CHAPTER 12

# One Solitude: Why English Canada Will Continue to Dominate

## Our Two Founding Cultures

Other than language, the French and English dominant cultures have more in common with each other than they don't. They were spawned by almost identical political and economic systems with similar imperial aspirations. Indeed, the English and French would have been virtually indistinguishable to the Indigenous peoples they first encountered in the New World. Yet despite their similarities, their major difference—language—gets most of our attention. **You simply can't understand Canada without understanding language.**

For most of Canada's history, discussions about Canadian identity have focused almost exclusively on reconciling the frequently fractious relationship between Canada's English-speaking majority and its French-speaking minority. That has always been the animating issue for our ruling Laurentian elite. A report penned by Lord Durham that followed the violent rebellions of 1837–38 in Upper and Lower Canada famously described Canada as "two nations warring in the bosom of a single state." Lord Durham's report led to the Act of Union in 1840 that united Upper and Lower Canada into the single Province of Canada, helping to pave the way to Confederation for Ontario, Quebec, New Brunswick, and Nova Scotia in 1867.

Even after Confederation, Lord Durham's two warring nations kept at it. We've since lived through the hanging of Louis Riel, two conscription crises, three referenda on Quebec's future in Canada (two provincial, one national), a litany of constitutional and court challenges on language issues, Quiet Revolutions and not-so-quiet apprehended insurrections, as well as the patriation of a constitution that enshrined official bilingualism for our nation.

What has all of this dissention meant for Canada's two founding cultures? Leaving the cacophony of political rhetoric aside, the population numbers tell the story. According to Statistics Canada, back at the time of Confederation in 1867, 3.5 million people called our new Dominion home. Of those, 34% lived in Quebec, 46% lived in Ontario, 11% lived in Nova Scotia, and 8% lived in New Brunswick. Rolling the clock ahead by 150 years, the Canadian population has multiplied more than tenfold to over 37 million today. And even though Quebec has grown to a healthy 8.3 million residents, it now constitutes only 23% of Canada's total population. That's a decline of 11% relative to the rest of Canada since Confederation. If these demographic trends continue, Statistics Canada estimates that the population share of the Western provinces will surpass Quebec's in less than fifty years.

## The Fallacy of "Revenge of the Cradle"

What's responsible for the decline of Quebec's population relative to the rest of Canada? While the population proportions have shifted with the addition of several predominately English-speaking provinces since Confederation, that's not the whole story. **Most immigrants to Canada since almost its beginning have been non-francophones.**

In addition, the birth rate of Quebec has declined to the same non-replacement levels as the rest of the country. This is despite the government of Quebec's considerable efforts, through heavily subsidized child care and other state programs, to get Quebeckers to consider having larger families.

"Revenge of the cradle" still permeates discussions about Quebec's history. You've probably heard it before. The story goes that Quebec's much higher birth rate offset the demographic impact of the conquest, assuring the future of the French Fact in Canada. Except it didn't really happen, at least not to the level its adherents claim it did. Less political and more scientific analyses show that Quebec never had a huge, sustained birth-rate advantage over the rest of the country. Yes, Quebec was slower to urbanize than Ontario, and Quebeckers typically had larger families as a result, but that didn't last long. The truth is that the position of Quebec and the French language in Canada has always been more assured by politics and the rule of law that it has ever been by demography.

What have these evolving population patterns meant for our two founding peoples and their mother tongues? Since Confederation, **Canada has become an overwhelmingly English-speaking nation.** According to the 2011 census, just over one in five of us now have French as our first official language. And the percentage of French speakers continues to decline every year along with Quebec's weight in our national population.

Statistics Canada has developed a forecast to look at the growth of mother tongue populations in Canada up to 2036. What their model forecasts is that both our English and French mother tongue populations will steadily decline from their current levels. In 2011, 59% of Canadians identified English as their mother tongue; by 2036, this population is expected to decline to between 52% and 56%. In 2011,

21% identified French as their mother tongue; Statistics Canada expects this to decline to between 17% and 18% of Canada's population by 2036.

## Mother Tongue: Other

If the English and French mother tongues will represent smaller shares of our population in 2036, which group will pick up the slack? It will be Canadians who identify their mother tongue as "Other." In 2011, this was 20% of Canadians. By 2036, Statistics Canada projects that the group will make up between 26% and 31% of our population. **At some point in the 2020s, "Other" will overtake and pass French as a Canadian mother tongue in terms of the number of people who speak it.**

Two hundred different languages are "spoken most often at home" in Canada, including English, French, Indigenous languages, and immigrant languages. Also, nearly 25,000 people say they use sign language at home. Twenty-two immigrant mother tongues are each spoken by more than a hundred thousand people in Canada today. Sixteen language groups are spoken regularly at home, but only 6% of those with an immigrant mother tongue use it as their exclusive language at home. Of those who don't, 64% pair it with English.

There are five major allophone language groups, spoken by the following percentages of the population:

- Romance languages (Spanish, Italian, Portuguese): 18%
- Indo-Iranian (Punjabi, Urdu, Persian, Gujarati, Hindi): 17%
- Chinese: 16%
- Slavic (Polish, Russian, Ukrainian): 11%
- Semitic (Arabic, Hebrew, Amharic): 7%

**The fastest-growing language in Canada is Tagalog**, a language spoken in the Philippines, up 64% since 2006. The other fastest growing languages (compared to 2006 levels) are

- Mandarin: +51%
- Arabic: +47%
- Hindi: +44%
- Creole: +42%
- Bengali: +40%
- Persian: +33%
- Spanish: +32%

The biggest declines among the top twenty-five languages spoken at home are for Greek, Italian, and Polish.

Ninety percent of those who speak an immigrant language most often at home reside in one of Canada's thirty-five largest population centres, with 80% of them living in just six communities: Toronto, Montreal, Vancouver, Calgary, Edmonton, and Ottawa-Gatineau. By far the largest number—1.8 million—live in Toronto. This is two and a half times more than the next-biggest group of immigrant language users, who reside in Vancouver. The most common immigrant languages spoken at home in Toronto are Chinese dialects (16%), Punjabi (8%), Urdu (6%), and Tamil (6%), all languages originating in the Pacific region.

As for the other big population centres, Montreal has two main immigrant languages, Arabic and Spanish. For Vancouver, the predominant immigrant languages are Punjabi and Chinese dialects. For Calgary and Edmonton, they're Punjabi, Tagalog, and Chinese dialects. And for Ottawa-Gatineau, they're Arabic, Chinese dialects, and Spanish. Ottawa-Gatineau is almost a mini-Montreal, except that 87% of those who primarily speak an immigrant language at home live on the Ontario side of the river.

## The Dwindling Promise of a Bilingual Nation

Turning back to the status of the French language in Canada, it's not just the population growth of the predominately English-speaking parts of Canada that is putting pressure on French in our national conversation. French is under pressure from within Quebec too. The French-speaking population in Quebec is shrinking. Given this situation, over the next generation we might see the desire to preserve the usage of French in Quebec spawn even more strident political and policy reactions. Otherwise, the only other outcome is that French will be heard less and less in Quebec, especially on the streets of Montreal.

What's happening to the French language in Quebec and Canada is explained by a combination of global and domestic language and population trends that add up to a strong current of change that's difficult to counter with domestic policies. The most important of these trends is the decline of French as a global language, especially for business. Nowhere can you find credible data that shows this isn't the case. In fact, in a recent Ipsos survey in twenty-six countries, a quarter of those interviewed said they had jobs that required them to speak with people in other countries; 67% had those conversations most often in English, while only 3% had them in French. Focusing just on Canadian workers who participated in the survey, only 4% said they speak to international customers and colleagues in French; 85% do so in English. The bottom line is that if you aspire to at least a middle-class career in Canada today, you need to be able to communicate in English. Quebec is part of a national, continental, and global economy, which is likely why 90% of the increase in Canada's bilingualism has been in Quebec, especially among those in the age range of 15 to 49. **French speakers are learning to speak English, not the other way around.**

Immigration is responsible for "Other" being the fastest-growing category of language spoken at home not only in Quebec, but also in the rest of Canada. Bilingual immigrants are ten times more likely to pair their home language with English than French. This is true even with Quebec controlling its own immigration policy and prioritizing language in its selection criteria. Quebec also has restrictive language laws and an education policy that requires that all but a small share of students must be educated exclusively in French. But nothing so far has stemmed the steady decline of French in either Quebec or Canada.

In the 1970s, through official bilingualism, Prime Minister Pierre Trudeau championed a new vision of how French was to thrive in Canada. At the time, this was not about the survival of the French language; it was more about living up to our obligations as a nation to fully recognize the equality of the French language in our national life. This vision of Canada was enshrined in our new constitution, which was rejected by Quebec but was inserted into the federal presence across the country.

The dream of a bilingual Canada is a cornerstone value of the Laurentian elite. A lot of good has come from this vision. **The need to have a workable compromise between French and English has created an environment of tolerance that makes our national project possible.** This tolerance is also behind our ability to peacefully accept and integrate as many immigrants as we have over the last century. Compare our success with how other countries have dealt with immigration, and you will understand how special our tolerance is in the world.

While tolerance is a wonderful thing, just how bilingual is Canada after about half a century of official bilingualism? The answer is hardly at all. You can test this yourself. Pull up to a drive-through window anywhere in the country and order a burger or poutine in either French or English. Only the most doctrinaire bilingualist would reasonably expect to be understood when ordering a Timmies in French in Timmins or doing the same in English in Trois-Rivières.

The numbers show that Canada hasn't lived up to the promise of being a bilingual nation. Between 2006 and 2011, the number of people who reported being able to conduct a conversation in both official languages increased by 350,000 to 5.8 million. That gives us a claimed bilingualism rate of 17.5%. Ever the optimists, Statistics Canada tells us this number is likely to increase by 1% by 2036. But a lot needs to go right on the language front for this to happen. And most of what needs to go right has been going wrong, especially outside of Quebec.

What does "claimed bilingualism" mean? A person claims on the census that they can conduct a conversation in both English and French. But that ability is not tested. It's like the census questions on heritage and ancestry, which indicate simply what you're prepared to claim, not what is objectively verifiable. That's why I believe Ipsos has asked a more accurate question about a person's perceived level of bilingualism: Can you do your job equally well in the other official language? Just 9% of those surveyed said they could.

Let's call this 9% Canada's functionally bilingual population. These are the people who say without hesitation that if they landed a new job that used the other official language exclusively and had the same duties and responsibilities as their current job, they would be successful. This number is three times higher in Quebec than it is in the rest of the country.

Along with the small pool of Canadians who say they can work successfully in a bilingual work environment, only 11% feel they can comfortably read a newspaper in the other official language, and only 7% say they can easily debate in the other language. These numbers reveal just how few Canadians could be the leader of a national political party if one of the key requirements is that they are able to participate equally in the French and English national leaders' debates at election time.

In the end, then, is Canada a bilingual nation? Sadly, no. Not if numbers mean anything. Despite our best intentions and efforts to live up to the promise in our constitution (including the expenditure of a considerable amount of public treasure), **we've made almost no progress towards the goal of becoming a bilingual nation.** If the past is any indication, this could remain an explosive issue in both Quebec and Canadian politics.

## Indigenous Issues

Any discussion about Canadian cultural identity must involve our country's original inhabitants, the Indigenous peoples. Especially since the turn of the century, there has been an increasing national focus on both acknowledging the importance of Indigenous peoples to Canadian society (past, present, and future) and reconciling the wrongs committed against Indigenous peoples in our past. Reconciliation has involved everything from tearful formal apologies from our political leaders to legal rulings recognizing the political and territorial rights of Indigenous peoples. It's also behind the territorial and land acknowledgements you now hear at the beginning of many public events across the country. Since there are six hundred unique First Nations and Indian bands in Canada, there's a lot to acknowledge.

What's a territorial acknowledgment? If you've been to a recent public event, you've likely heard one. At the start of the event or ceremony, a dignitary comes forward and says those who have gathered together on that spot recognize they are on the traditional territory of the Indigenous peoples who first called this place home. For example, at the start of every Vancouver City Council meeting, there's an acknowledgment that the session is taking place on "the unceded traditional territory of the Musqueam, Squamish, and Tsleil-Waututh First Nations."

Territorial acknowledgements have spread rapidly beyond political meetings and awards shows to everyday activities and events across Canada. They have become almost an unofficial pledge of allegiance in many Canadian schools and now accompany the playing of our national anthem at the start of school days. The NHL's Winnipeg Jets and Edmonton Oilers now include a territorial acknowledgement as part of their opening ceremonies before every home game. You can't get much more mainstream Canadian than that.

Regardless of your personal experience with territorial acknowledgements, **Indigenous issues are incredibly important for Canada's future**, especially for any organization working in resource extraction or any industry where land use is a consideration. Several of the most intense political disputes we have had in Canada over the last thirty years have involved land use and Indigenous communities. There's no sign that this type of debate will decline anytime soon. The greater likelihood is that it will increase.

Indigenous communities are under a lot of pressure, particularly in the more remote parts of Canada. They are smaller than most of us know. Under the current Indian Act, there are 744,855 Status Indians in Canada. That's about 2% of the Canadian population. Just 44% (327,736) live on a reserve; 417,119 live off-reserve. So about half of Canada's Status Indians live on a recognized Indian reserve or on Crown land, located mostly in rural and northern parts of the country. The reason most Canadians rarely meet and don't have much understanding of Status Indians, especially those who live on reserves, is there aren't many of them and they tend to live where most Canadians don't.

While the Status Indian population has grown strongly in the past, it is about to hit a wall because the Indigenous birth rate has now fallen to 2.2—almost replacement level. **This generation of Indigenous Canadians will be the last to have above-replacement-level fertility.** Their fertility is declining for the same reasons as for the rest of the Canadian population: urbanization, the empowerment of women, increasing educational achievement, and declining poverty. These forces are also driving ambitious young Indigenous women and men away from their remote communities to pursue opportunities in the suburbs and downtowns of our biggest cities. Indigenous communities that want to maintain themselves into the future will need to create a reason for their young people to stay home. Opportunities created by greater political autonomy and economic empowerment could be just the ticket.

Along with declining fertility, Indigenous people are becoming a smaller part of our population for the same reason that French Canadians are: immigration. Every year since 1990, Canada has welcomed an average of 230,000 immigrants to our shores. There's no sign this level of immigration will let up. In fact, the federal government intends to admit 370,000 immigrants, and possibly more, every year going forward. This means every month, roughly 30,000 legal immigrants can move to Canada. We are now bringing in more legal immigrants every year than the total population of Status Indians on reserves. Yes, the Indigenous population has been a fast-growing and youthful group, but this level of immigration makes them a smaller part of our population every day.

## What This Means for Your Business

The issue of language in Canada is not yet settled. **While the language issue has been turbulent in Quebec in the past, it could become even more so going forward.** A culture under threat will take steps to preserve what is most important to its identity. For the Quebecoise, that's language. The potential for nativist political candidates or factions to become empowered by the need for language preservation is real. That doesn't mean the desire for sovereignty will necessarily increase, but an increasing need for language protection could have a big impact on how business is done in Quebec. Even bigger than it has today. *Plus ça change, plus c'est la même chose.*

The rise of other languages in Canada presents a combination of opportunities and threats. The threats come from not adapting quickly enough to properly service new language groups. Companies that act more quickly to reduce the friction caused by language barriers will have an advantage in the marketplace. We know **businesses that do a better job of making early connections with immigrants tend to establish lasting relationships.** So they will need to find ways of incorporating new languages into their business communications, aggressively hiring native language speakers to serve as ambassadors to the fastest-growing immigrant communities. That means hiring front-line staff who can communicate with new Canadians from India, the Philippines, and China. That's necessary diversity.

Most Canadian businesses will not be directly affected by issues involving the Indigenous community. There are too few Indigenous people living in the places where most business activities take place for them to represent a consumer marketing target. However, if you work in resource development or land use, Indigenous issues will be important to your business. Understanding and working with the Indigenous community is about building partnerships. Look for companies that have done this. They are the ones to follow.

**The next two decades will be critical for the future of the Indigenous peoples because they are on a path to becoming a smaller share of our population every year.** Declining birth rates and massive immigration will see to that. Now is the best time to achieve reconciliation. Down the road, a growing immigrant population that doesn't see itself as responsible for the mistakes of the past could be less interested in dealing with this critical issue.

## What This Means for You

If you care about realizing the goal of a bilingual Canada, the facts I have presented will be distressing to you. I have been told by critics that I have it all wrong. They say the number of bilingual people in Canada is increasing. They are right. But that's against a population base that's growing rapidly. In this case, percentages matter more than absolute numbers.

While I agree with Statistics Canada on most population issues, on bilingualism I don't. They subscribe to a watered-down definition of bilingualism that really isn't bilingual at all. They also underestimate the impact that increased immigration will have on bilingualism. Most of the projected increase in bilingualism will happen in Quebec, not in the rest of the provinces, which are slated to become even less bilingual than they are today. Is that really the goal of bilingualism? I expect the government of Quebec is looking at these numbers with growing concern.

If you are a unilingual anglophone, should you learn to speak French? As a patriotic act, I would say yes. Our constitution says we are a bilingual nation, so we should all do our best to be conversant in both official languages. However, **if you don't aspire to work for our national government, or live in Quebec, the practical need to be bilingual diminishes every year.** What a shame.

# CHAPTER 13

# *The Battle for Immigrants*: Why Our Biggest Challenge Is Our Biggest Strength

## The Low-Fertility Trap

Immigration will be increasingly important for Canada's population growth as we move through the twenty-first century. The contribution of fertility to our national population growth will lessen simply because the proportion of Canada's female population of child-bearing age will continue to decline. As noted already, fertility no longer contributes to population growth in Atlantic Canada because deaths there now exceed births. This trend will inevitably expand to the rest of our country, as it is has expanded in many other countries in the developed world.

Thinking through the national consequences, imagine Canada's population as it trundles into the future. At first glance, we should be happy with what we see. Our population is still projected by Statistics Canada to grow over the next few decades—an important achievement compared to the rest of the developed world. For example, the overall population of Western Europe peaked around the year 2000 and has declined ever since. But as we know, Canada is also being impacted by persistent low fertility and a shrinking pool of women of child-bearing age. This trend will especially hurt sections of our country that have weak immigration and don't benefit from interprovincial migration. Think rural and Atlantic Canada, which are already experiencing the repercussions. Quebec can expect to follow the same path within twenty years or so unless something significant changes there.

Since 2011, and for the first time since 1972, the increase in immigration is higher in the Prairie provinces than in other regions of the country, while fewer immigrants today are moving to Ontario (which explains the recent slowdown in its population growth). Regardless, even the Prairie provinces will have to attract more and more migrants every year if they want to make up for their steadily eroding fertility.

It should by now be clear that first glances at population statistics can be deceiving. Even though the total size of our population is still expanding, its structure is changing, especially in terms of age and fertility. You already know that Canadians—both men and women—are on average getting older. While men can produce children until quite late in life, women cannot without considerable medical intervention.

Sure, immigration is offsetting our lack of fertility, and it will continue to keep our population growing for several years to come. But the rest of the world, and that's the entire world, is now trending to lower fertility as well. Most countries now have older populations that are having fewer babies than even two decades ago. The world's population is aging at a faster clip than demographers, including those at the United Nations, have been predicting.

The surplus young people we need to come to Canada from other parts of the world are becoming scarcer every day, especially in the Pacific countries from which we currently draw most of our immigrants. As well, we will be in increasing competition with other countries who also need immigrants to offset their own population declines. Moreover, the world's middle class is expanding every day, especially in Asia, reducing the necessity for young people to emigrate to achieve financial success. They can now just stay home and help lead their own country's economic development.

Putting it all together, **there's a risk that over the medium term—say by mid-century—immigration will no longer be able to compensate for Canada's declining national fertility.** That's when we will really be in the low-fertility trap, and an overall population decline could be the result. Japan is already experiencing just such a decline today: there are more deaths than births (the pattern in Japan for about a decade), they have almost no immigration, and roughly a quarter of their population is 65 or older. Doesn't that sound like what's starting to happen in Atlantic Canada?

## Offsetting Factors

One factor that will somewhat offset the impact of low fertility on our total population numbers, at least for a period, is that the average longevity of Canadians will continue to expand. Since we've increased our lifespan by 30 years over the last century, who's to say we can't do the same over the next century? It may seem too good to be true, but there really is no natural limit, or best-before date, to a human life. If lifespans continue to increase as we've seen (and Statistics Canada predicts), it will delay when our population decline begins. But decline our population must. It's only a matter of time.

Another factor that could have a short-term impact on our population patterns is that a lot of young women who deferred starting their families to pursue an education and career are now expected to start having kids. At least, that's the thinking among demographers. What no one knows yet is how many children these pending mothers will have. There's the potential for a mini baby boomlet. However, if these women defy the forecasters and decide against having kids, or have fewer than expected, Canada's population could start to stall and age at a faster rate than Statistics Canada is forecasting. Based on what's happening in countries like the United States, where the birth rate for Millennial mothers is now around 1.0, this is not out of the realm of possibility.

## Population and Climate Change

Governments and other public organizations don't necessarily like to talk about scenarios that suggest declining and aging populations. It's a bit of a downer, and is considered unpatriotic in some countries. Suggesting that there will be fewer total people in the world also raises some uncomfortable economic and public policy questions. Think for a moment about a huge issue for today's activist governments: climate change. It's based on the premise (supported by a consensus of scientific evidence) that the activities of human beings have caused and are causing the warming of the earth's atmosphere, and that this is changing our climate in detrimental, potentially fatal ways. As the world's population grows, humanity's impact will naturally become greater, which is why fighting climate change today is, as many argue, the world's most pressing priority.

While I'm not one to quibble with climate scientists about the impact of humanity on the atmosphere, it's perfectly reasonable to challenge some of their assumptions about the size of the world's future population. For example, what if there are fewer humans on the earth to engage in climate-harming activities? There's compelling evidence that over the medium to longer term, the world's overall population will begin to shrink. What happens to the various climate-change scenarios if we change the denominator (world population) in the equation? Would the projections of global calamity be as dire as experts are predicting today? An interesting question.

## From Prejudice to Tolerance

Historically, Canada's population patterns were driven by discovery, conquest, economic exploitation, sanctuary, and settlement. Our population patterns today are driven by the pursuit of opportunity, whether it's refugees fleeing war and oppression or members of the new mobile global middle class seeking to maximize the economic return on their marketable skills. The modern wave of immigrants to Canada are here to live in what they see as the land of opportunity.

Immigrants to Canada have chosen well. This land and its people have offered better economic mobility and personal safety than most places they could have ended up. It is without dispute that most immigrants and their descendants have thrived here, and they have also contributed to building a more diverse, tolerant, and prosperous Canada. It is also without dispute that the majority Christian, Caucasian Canada hasn't always been the most welcoming place for newcomers. For example, anti-Orientalism was virulent on our west coast around the turn of the last century. Head and landing taxes, along with travel restrictions, were instituted to limit Asian immigration. At one point, to stop what was called the "yellow peril," authorities even refused entry to female Asian immigrants to prevent the settlement of Asian men who had come here as temporary labourers to build our railways. There were race riots in Vancouver in 1887 and 1907. This prejudice extended beyond Japanese and Chinese migrants to other immigrants of colour. In 1914, four hundred Indian migrants aboard the ship *Komagata Maru* were turned around by the Canadian Navy and refused entry to Vancouver.

These anti-Orientalist policies, combined with the internment of immigrants and their descendants from combatant countries (Japan, Germany, Italy, and Eastern Europe) during the World Wars and the deplorable treatment of Jewish refugees fleeing Nazi Germany, show that Canada hasn't always been as tolerant and welcoming as it is today. The embarrassing truth is that the last racial criteria in our immigration system, which favoured Europeans and Americans, weren't eliminated until 1967, when the points system was brought in. This new system favoured immigrants based on their qualifications, language, and job skills, as opposed to their country of origin. There's much in our treatment of various immigrant groups and their descendants that Canada's governments have been right to apologize for.

Despite these rough spots, Canadians today revere tolerance. Tolerance defines us. It has certainly made it possible for Canada to manage a level of demographic and cultural change that few societies have been able to accommodate without serious social friction and even violence. Look at the way many European countries, and even our American cousins, have reacted to the Syrian refugee crisis and compare that to our reaction. That's Canadian tolerance in action.

Where did this tolerance come from? I believe it grew out of the need for our two founding cultures, the English and the French, to find a way to live together. From there, the significant immigration that was required to build our nation, combined with official multiculturalism, entrenched the idea that Canada, for its own survival, must be a tolerant and welcoming place. **Our defining creed is less about life, liberty, and the pursuit of happiness, and more about live and let live.** Therefore, harmonious demographic and cultural change has been and continues to be possible in our country.

## Historical Immigrant Waves

Although Canadians now embrace tolerance as a defining national value, immigration has tested its boundaries. The first big test came with Irish immigration to Canada in the mid-nineteenth century. The Irish came here out of desperation, not as part of some grand plan to build an economic or political empire, to convert the locals, or to flee the new American Republic. They crossed the Atlantic Ocean to make a better life for themselves and for their families.

What the Irish experienced when they first arrived here was not our prime minister greeting them at Pearson International Airport with smiles, selfies, and taxpayer-funded winter coats. Their arrival was marked by tragedy. After a harrowing trip across the Atlantic on a "coffin ship," they were greeted by overwhelmed government and church officials who immediately quarantined them. The government of Lower Canada established a quarantine station at Grosse Isle in the Gulf of St. Lawrence to contain a cholera outbreak among immigrants in 1832, and it remained active up to the 1930s.

After the Irish, the next big wave of immigrants focused on settling what our government of the day advertised as the "Last Best West." Western settlement was more like current immigration to Canada in that many of those who came here in the late nineteenth and early twentieth centuries were, for want of a better term, recruited. Clifford Sifton, Canada's Minister of the Interior from 1896 to 1905, was responsible for a government marketing program to attract settlers from places other than the United Kingdom. Sifton famously said, "I think that a stalwart peasant in a sheepskin coat, born on the soil, whose forefathers have been farmers for ten generations, with a stout wife and a half-dozen children, is good quality."

To find his peasant farmers, Sifton's recruiting program focused on bringing in large numbers of Western, Central, and Eastern Europeans who understood how to farm the lands available in Canada's West but spoke neither English nor French. He got lucky because his preferred homesteaders were surplus population in their home countries, with few opportunities, and they were anxious for a new lease on life. They included Russians, Finns, Swedes, Danes, Norwegians,

Macedonians, Dutch, Romanians, Icelanders, Swiss, Ukrainians, Germans, and Poles, among others. Also among the homesteaders were migrants fleeing persecution in their home countries due to their religious beliefs (Jews, Mormons, Mennonites, and Doukhobors).

This new wave of immigration up to 1914 and the start of the First World War was one of the most important periods of population growth for Canada. The year 1913 was the peak for Canadian immigration, with 400,000 newcomers arriving on our shores, a record to this day.

There's no doubt that Sifton's immigration program worked. Maybe not always in the way he intended it to, but it certainly brought a considerable volume of new residents to Canada. By 1913, the year before the First World War began, the Canadian population was roughly 7.6 million—double what it was at Confederation, less than half a century before. In the first decade of the twentieth century, the Canadian population grew by more in percentage terms than at any time in our history before or since, largely thanks to Sifton's efforts.

The next big phase of Canadian immigration came at the end of the Second World War. Canada's expanding peacetime economy created a need for more industrial workers. Initially, they came from among the million-plus displaced persons and refugees in Europe. Many of these people didn't want to return home to countries that had been overrun by the communists or had been ravaged by war. Canada offered them an opportunity for a new life. However, unlike the mass migration that was prompted by the opening of the Canadian West for settlement, postwar immigration was not about pushing people into agriculture or rural industries like forestry or mining. Canada came out of the war a more urban, industrial power than it had been, and it needed workers to fill the many manufacturing jobs its growing industrial economy created. It also needed construction workers to build the infrastructure needed by the new economy and increasingly urban population.

With the growing requirement for more workers, the Canadian government started to take a more open-minded approach to source countries for immigrants. While immigrants from the United Kingdom and United States were still preferred, there was a diminishing pool of Eastern Europeans available because of the Cold War, so there were new opportunities for immigration from countries in Southern Europe, like Italy, Greece, and Portugal, which had previously been discouraged. These migrants went almost exclusively to the cities, especially the big cities. Many of Canada's population centres already had a Little Italy, Little Portugal, or Greektown started by early adventurers who made it here despite the official obstacles, but they really began to fill up in the 1950s, 1960s, and 1970s.

Along with immigrants looking for better economic opportunities, Canada also became a haven for refugees. Plotting out when specific ethnic groups made their way to Canada is like tracing the history of geopolitical tensions in the mid- to late twentieth century: Hungarians in 1967, Czechoslovakians in 1973, those fleeing oppression and war in Uganda, Chile, Africa, and the Middle East, as well as Vietnamese boat people in the early eighties. More recently, Sikhs, Tamils, Somalians, Afghans, and Syrians have sought refuge here. Roughly 10% of all immigrants these days come to Canada as refugees.

As European economies recovered from the Second World War and their birth rates began to decline, fewer Europeans were moving to Canada. In the 1970s and 1980s, the slack was taken up mostly by Pacific nations, which coincided in the 1990s with a big increase in the number of immigrants Canada was prepared to accept. In addition, in the 1980s, the concept of business-class immigrants was created—that is, immigrant investors and entrepreneurs who came to Canada with the capital and skills to have an immediate impact on our economy. Business-class programs tended to benefit entrepreneurs from Hong Kong (fleeing from the reversion to Communist China in 1999), the Chinese mainland, Taiwan, and Korea.

## Immigration Today

**Economic necessity continues to drive our immigration policy today.** Yes, there's still compassion in who we decide comes to Canada, but it takes second place to filling out our labour force. Just over 60% of Canada's recent immigrants were admitted under various economic categories, while 27% were admitted under the family-class category (joining relatives already in Canada) and about 12% came in as refugees. Almost half (48%) of Canada's recent economic immigrants came in as skilled workers, with 27% coming in under a provincial or territorial nominee program. There's been an uptick in refugees and asylum seekers, and they get the lion's share of the media attention, but the truth is that most of our immigration is used to fill in gaps in our labour force, as it always has been.

Canada's population has continued to grow into the twenty-first century. We have led the G7 in population growth for the last decade. An increase in immigration numbers has been the main source of growth because our birth rate has been steadily shrinking over the same time. For the last two decades, Canada has been bringing in roughly a quarter-million immigrants each year—the equivalent of adding two new Torontos to our population over that time frame.

Most years Canada battles it out with Australia as the country bringing in the most immigrants per capita in the world. However, due to recent refugee crises in the Middle East and Africa, some Middle Eastern and European countries have entered the running as they struggle to accommodate a massive movement of refugees and other migrants. Unlike Canada, though, these countries are responding to an immediate humanitarian crisis, as opposed to implementing a long-term, purposeful policy to grow their population through immigration. The approach to population management that Canada has adopted would be difficult to sell almost anywhere else in the world, as recent populist reactions show.

The impact of our approach to immigration is significant. Today, close to 22% of Canadians are immigrants. That's the same as the record for foreign-born residents noted in the 1921 census, which is the highest percentage recorded since Confederation. And it's not slowing down. Between 2011 and 2016, 1.2 million immigrants came to Canada, 3.5% of our total population. Statistics Canada estimates that, if this pattern holds, by 2036, Canada's foreign-born population could grow to as much as 30%.

**In 2006, Asia passed Europe as the region where most foreign-born Canadians came from.** By 2016, 62% of recent immigrants were from Asia, with 13% coming from Africa and only about 33% coming from Europe. Estimates are that by 2031, 55% of our total foreign-born population will be from Asia, compared to 20% from Europe. This changing demographic trend is also reflected in the median ages of European and Asian immigrants today. Europeans who came to Canada in the 1950s, 1960s, and 1970s are now older, while the more recent Pacific immigrants are younger. The median age of Canadians born in Europe is now 57; for Canadians born in Asia, it's only 40, close to the median age for Canada overall.

The switch from European to Pacific sources of immigration is apparent when you compare the top ten source countries for immigrants to Canada in 1970 to what they are today.

## Top Ten Countries of Birth of Recent Immigrants to Canada

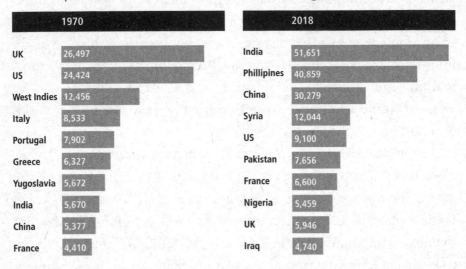

| 1970 | | 2018 | |
|---|---|---|---|
| UK | 26,497 | India | 51,651 |
| US | 24,424 | Phillipines | 40,859 |
| West Indies | 12,456 | China | 30,279 |
| Italy | 8,533 | Syria | 12,044 |
| Portugal | 7,902 | US | 9,100 |
| Greece | 6,327 | Pakistan | 7,656 |
| Yugoslavia | 5,672 | France | 6,600 |
| India | 5,670 | Nigeria | 5,459 |
| China | 5,377 | UK | 5,946 |
| France | 4,410 | Iraq | 4,740 |

What's notable in the data, apart from the shift from European to Pacific source countries, is how long the United Kingdom topped the immigration table. Back in 1871, our first census showed that 84% of immigrants were from the British Isles. The United Kingdom was still our top source of immigrants right up to the mid-1980s. Through the late 1960s and early 1970s, a lot of Americans were moving to Canada to escape the Vietnam draft. And while China made it into the top ten source countries for immigrants in 1970, those immigrants were almost exclusively from Hong Kong. Today's Chinese immigrants are drawn almost exclusively from the mainland, and many more of them (six times more) are coming to Canada now than in 1970.

## Immigrant Distribution

Following the pattern that started after the Second World War, **most of today's immigrants settle in the major metropolitan areas of four of our provinces—Ontario, Quebec, British Columbia, and Alberta—and the majority choose cities west of Quebec.** Over 90%

now live in one of our thirty-five largest population centres, compared to 63% of people born in Canada. A third of Canada's census metropolitan area (CMA) population is foreign-born, compared to only 7% in other areas. Most immigrants settle in the largest cities, especially Toronto, Vancouver, and Montreal. They usually cite having family and friends living there or job opportunities as the motivation for their choice. By 2031, about 55% of people living in CMAs will be either immigrants or children of immigrants, compared to 19% in the rest of the country.

Toronto and its suburbs have the largest number of immigrants. It is truly astounding the number of foreign-born people who reside in Canada's most populous metropolitan area. The Greater Toronto Area now has the highest per capita foreign-born population of any major city in the world—higher than London, New York, or Tokyo (the world's largest city).

Montreal, Canada's second-biggest city, hasn't kept pace with Toronto when it comes to attracting immigrants. While 50% of Toronto's population was born in another country, it's only about 20% in Montreal. This isn't due to a lack of trying by the government of Quebec, which is the only provincial government in Canada that exercises direct control over immigration. The problem is that even when immigrants can be persuaded to move to Montreal, they don't stay there in the same numbers as in Toronto. This is especially true of immigrant businesspeople and entrepreneurs: about 60% leave Quebec once they can move around Canada. The situation is even worse in Atlantic Canada: about half of *all* immigrants—not just business immigrants—who start there eventually leave for another province.

When it comes to attracting and retaining immigrants, Vancouver and other cities in the West are more like Toronto. Even with the downturn in resource prices, Canada's western cities continue to be magnets for immigrants (as well as for interprovincial migrants). Sure, immigrants who move to a western city may start in one city and move to another (these days it's from communities in Alberta to those in British Columbia). But there's enough action across the region that a combination of immigration, interprovincial migration, and a younger population having more kids keeps the provinces growing, so much so that even Manitoba and Saskatchewan have reversed the population declines that plagued them for decades. These successes aren't happening in Atlantic Canada. Which begs the question, what have Manitoba and Saskatchewan done that Atlantic Canada can learn from?

This is one of the most serious challenges for rural communities in general: How will they compete with Canada's top urban areas as preferred homes for new immigrants? Small towns and rural areas have too few kids and too many seniors to maintain sustainable populations without significant immigration.

## The Impact of Visible Minorities

The newest wave of Canada's immigrants share many traits. In addition to being younger and much more urban than the Canadian population overall, they are also more likely to be visible minorities and much less likely to be Christian.

Visible minority status is determined in Canada by the definition in our national Employment Equity Act. **By 2031, around 30% of Canadians will qualify as visible minorities** under the act. This is up from 5% in 1981, a six-fold increase. Canada is moving from being a predominately white population focused in Ontario and Quebec to being a browner population focused more in Ontario and the West.

By 2031, 96% of Canada's visible minorities will be living in one of the thirty-five biggest population centres, with 70% choosing Toronto, Montreal, or Vancouver. Looking at two additional markers for recent immigrants, 91% of allophones and 95% of non-Christians will live in a CMA. About 60% of the residents of Toronto and Vancouver will be visible minorities, compared to only about 30% in Montreal and less than 5% in St. John's, Sudbury, Trois-Rivières, Quebec City, and Saguenay. Small cities, as well as small towns and rural communities, are simply becoming aging versions of what they have always been: almost exclusively Christian and white.

Where visible minorities tend to settle depends in large part on their source country. South Asians and Chinese are the two largest visible minority groups in Toronto and Vancouver. In Montreal, it's blacks and Arabs. Montreal Arabs have come primarily from French-speaking countries in North Africa, predominately Muslim countries such as Morocco, Algeria, Tunisia, Libya, and Mauritania. They choose to settle in Montreal because of the importance Quebec's immigration policy places on language in their selection criteria.

The visible minority population isn't increasing due to immigration alone. These groups also have, for the time being, higher birth rates than Canadians in general because they are younger on average, and many also come from source countries with cultures that favour higher birth rates. One visible minority group that bucks this trend is Chinese immigrants. Time will tell, but today's Chinese immigrants may turn out to have a lesser long-term impact on Canada's population than other immigrant groups have had or will have. They could have a one-generation population effect but drop off precipitously over the longer term. More on this in chapter 14.

Arab immigrants have the highest fertility rate among Canadian immigrants. Conversely, Europeans, Americans, and East Asians have lower birth rates. This trend is reinforced when we look at birth rates by religion. Muslims have a birth rate of 2.4, Hindus 2.0, Sikhs 1.8, and Christians and atheists 1.5 (which is the Canadian average).

If world trends are a guide to what to expect for Canada, the greatest likelihood is that we will see a short-term positive population effect from higher-birth-rate immigrant cultures, but these rates will decline over subsequent generations. Affluence, freedom, and modernity create an environment in which women have greater control over their reproductive choices. In these circumstances, women tend to pursue an education and a career, marry later (if at all), start their families later, and have smaller families as a result. There's only one country in the world—Israel—where, under similar conditions, birth rates have increased rather than declined.

## Diversification of Religious Practices

By 2031, about 14% of our population will be non-Christian, up from 8% in 2006. About 50% of the non-Christians will be Muslim. Islam is the fastest-growing religion in Canada thanks to increasing rates of immigration from Muslim nations, and because women who follow Islam tend to have more children than the average non-Muslim woman, at least for the first generation moving to Canada. By 2031, 64% of us will be Christian, 7% will be Muslim, and 1% will be Jewish.

There's also significant growth in the number who say they have "no religion." The category of non-believers will go from 17% in 2006 to around 20% by 2031. While we may think this growth is because a significant number of people are turning away from the practice of formal religion, it's also because Chinese newcomers are unlikely to bring a formal religion with them to Canada.

## The Immigrants of the Future

Going forward, the largest visible minority groups in Canada will be South Asians and Chinese, at least for the next while. But over the longer term, the fastest-growing groups will likely be Arabs, West Asians, and Africans. From there, it will all depend on who comes to Canada next (which is determined by domestic conditions in home countries), and what they do once they settle here. For example, will the daughters of Arab women have as many children as their mothers did, or will they take their cue from the majority society and opt for smaller families? The evidence is that new immigrants tend to take on the fertility norms of the majority society within about a generation.

If Canada's population is to continue to grow, we will have to find immigrants in new places with surplus populations. Where will that be? Look at the world's fertility statistics by country, and you will see that, today, it's Africa and some parts of the Middle East. When they get here, these immigrants will continue to go to the cities and suburbs. Unless there is an economic boom in the East that can't now be foreseen, immigration will not help arrest the accelerating decline of Atlantic and rural Canada. Perhaps these communities need to find another Clifford Sifton, whose job this time will be to populate the "Last Best East."

There will continue to be crises around the world, produced by both nature and human tragedy, that will create displaced populations. However, accommodating refugees is not an immigration policy; it is a response to random occurrences. Besides, people who come from the calamities that create refugees constitute a short-term burden on taxpayers because they arrive with little beyond their own lives. Yes, over time they will contribute to the Canadian economy, but not right away. However, given our fertility rate, simply adding people to our population is still a necessary step in the right direction.

## What This Means for Your Business

It's clear that you should be preparing yourself to deal with a base of customers, employees, and neighbours who are very different from what you are used to. They will look different, they will speak different languages, and they will have different cultural practices. **Get used to dealing with Canadians who are increasingly visible minority, non-Christian allophones from Asia and the Arab world**, especially if you're living in one of Canada's larger urban areas, as more and more of us are every day. If you live in smaller-town Canada, you will continue to deal with Canadians who are mostly French, English, Christian, and white. They will also be old, and getting older every day.

Your new Canadian customers will vary by geography. If your business operates predominately in Ontario and the West, your new customers will be from India, the Philippines, and mainland China. If you are strong in Quebec, they will increasingly be from French-speaking countries of Africa. What do you know about your new customers' buying habits and tastes? How do they shop? What do they eat? What real estate options do they prefer? How do they like to invest? How can you help them quickly adapt to life in Canada? Being the first to know and address their needs will give you a big advantage in creating a customer base for life.

## What This Means for You

If you live in Old Canada, you will be seeing the effects of immigration on the news, but you won't experience it much in your day-to-day life. If you live in a major city or suburb, though, you will have even more of the world at your door. Embrace it. The range of options you will be exposed to is thrilling. **Soon, the mix of immigrants moving into your neighbourhood will likely be changing again, increasingly coming from African nations.** This new wave of immigrants will bring lots of change with them, just as immigrants always have. How will your neighbourhood adapt? There's an opportunity here for you to help, because adaptation and integration at the community level are our biggest challenge when it comes to immigration. Without community-level acceptance, we will be in big trouble.

# CHAPTER 14

# *Gender Wars*: Why Women Will Power the Market

## Global Birth Rates

For every 100 women alive in Canada today, there are just 98.6 men. It doesn't start out that way. If nature is left to her own devices, more boys are always born than girls. This is true everywhere, not just in Canada. The global birth ratio of boys to girls is 107:100. In Canada, it's a bit tighter at 105:100, but it still favours boys. The difference between Canada's 105 and the world's 107 is material and not a matter of chance. The global numbers are thrown off by some large-population countries, such as China and India, tipping the scales even more to the advantage of males. In China, for example, the gender birth ratio is 115:100. In some Chinese provinces, it can run as high as 130:100. This is the influence of China's now defunct one-child policy meeting up with a cultural preference for male offspring. In China, if you can have only one child, for most parents it must be a boy. But you don't need an official one-child policy to create an artificially large gender imbalance. A ruthless cultural preference for male heirs can be enough to accomplish the same goal. That's why India, a rigidly patriarchal society, has a male-to-female birth ratio of 111:100.

Behind these unnatural gender imbalances is the cruel epidemic of gender-selective abortions. Estimates are that both China and India are missing around 60 million women from their populations due to this practice. One unintended consequence is the social havoc it creates when it comes time for couples to marry and start families. There are huge swaths of men in both countries who will never marry because there are no brides available for them. They simply don't exist. Many of these men will never be fathers or husbands. Political leaders in these countries rarely talk about the issue of the missing women, but it is a hugely disruptive cultural problem for which there is no easy solution.

Lest you think source country fertility practices are left behind when people immigrate to Canada, there's evidence that they persist here. While most immigrant cultures take on the fertility practices of Canadians within a short time of arriving, some hang on to their old ways for longer. For example, while the disincentive for Chinese immigrants to have larger families doesn't exist here, **Chinese women still have the lowest birth rate of any of our major immigrant groups.** Even though they have moved away from the one-child policy of their former home, the cultural norm for smaller families has moved here with them. There's also emerging evidence that some South Asian immigrant families continue to try to improve the odds for male births beyond what nature provides for, especially if the parents have already had a girl or two.

## Population Dominance

So if there are always more boys born in Canada than girls, why are there more women than men in the Canadian population? Men dominate our population at the start but quickly lose out to women over the longer term, and unless something big changes for Canada's men, this gap will continue to widen as our population ages through the century.

**The average Canadian woman outlives the average Canadian man by about 4.5 years.** While it is true that life expectancy for men is improving faster than it is for women, for the foreseeable future, women will continue to dominate the older age categories. By the age of 30, whatever advantage in numbers men had at birth has been wiped out. After that, women start to outnumber men. By the time a woman reaches Canada's median age of 41, 50.2% of her age cohort will be female, while 49.8% will be male. And this disparity accelerates as women get older. At age 65-plus, the proportion of senior women in Canada is 56%. At age 85-plus, it's 67%. By age 100-plus, centenarian women outnumber centenarian men by a ratio of 5:1!

The gender and age patterns we see in Canada are basically the same in most of the developed world. The global numbers are thrown off by the artificially created excess of male births in China and India, but even in these two countries, by age 50 women make up for the huge early gender imbalance and start to outpace the number of men in the population as they age.

## Why Women Live Longer

Why do women outlive men in Canada? A couple of significant factors are improvements in maternal health care and declining teenage pregnancies. Childbirth used to be a big killer of Canadian women, helping to explain why men outnumbered women in the Canadian population until 1971. Childbirth was especially hard on teenage mothers. Dramatic improvements in maternal medicine and a substantial decline in birth rates (thereby reducing the opportunities for maternal deaths) have made what was a common tragedy for our great-grandmothers much rarer today.

Biology also contributes to shorter lives for men. Some studies have suggested that estrogen (the female hormone) and testosterone (the male hormone) have differential health effects that favour women. **Men, especially younger men, are also more likely to engage in risky lifestyle behaviours**, including smoking, drinking alcohol, and taking drugs, but also choices that expose them more often to homicide and fatal accidents. Riskier driving by young men explains why young women pay so much less for car insurance than young men do.

Moreover, men are stubbornly unaware of how to manage their personal health compared to women. They are more likely to be overweight, and are less likely to make changes to improve their health. Women are more likely to have consulted a medical doctor in the last year and to follow through on their doctor's advice. This is especially true for younger women compared to younger men.

And tragically, suicide is the seventh-leading cause of death for Canadian men, who are three times more likely to end their own lives than Canadian women. Men between 40 and 59, and particularly men who are single, divorced, or widowed, are at highest risk of suicide.

## Women's Growing Educational Advantage

In the end, then, **a big reason for the emergence of female power in Canada is that women have the growing advantage of numbers, especially as our population ages.** As we know, the weight of numbers matters a lot. But it's not just the number of women that is increasing their importance in Canada; it's also how their lives are changing at all ages.

Several years ago, I was asked by the federal government to conduct a series of focus groups across the country to help them better understand how young women and men looked at the link between education and careers. This was the era in which everyone in government was talking about lifelong learning. They were interested in revising student assistance programs to encourage more young Canadians to get a university or college education, to help them prepare for our future economy. Those watching the focus groups, including me, were surprised by the difference between how young men and young women talked about their education and careers. While opinions varied, young women had a distinct tendency to link better education to better jobs. Young men, not so much. The women seemed almost fixated on acquiring credentials. They believed that having an accreditation or degree meant they wouldn't be judged as much based on their gender by future employers, as if getting a degree inoculated them against the sexism they expected to experience once they joined the workforce.

I tucked that observation away and didn't return to it until recently, when I started looking again at how Canadian men and women have been performing at school and in the workplace. It turns out that what those women were saying didn't apply only to them. A generation of women see a link between education and work. What is the net effect of these changing views? Simply put, **women are not only Canada's longevity champions, they are increasingly our smarter sex.** Women earn better grades and are more likely to graduate from high school than their male counterparts. They are more apt to pursue a post-secondary education, and to graduate with a degree when they do. Women now account for 60% of Canada's college and university graduates, and this advantage is steadily growing. Men still dominate in trade schools and some professional schools, such as architecture, business, and anything science- or math-related (the STEM disciplines). But the number of women in those programs is increasing every day too.

Women's growing educational advantage hasn't closed the income gap, though. Women earn 87 cents for every dollar a man earns. We should be careful about jumping to any conclusions here. This fact does reflect sexism in the workplace, no doubt. But it is a complicated topic with many moving parts. Anyone looking at the relationship among gender, income, and education must consider, for example, type of education and level of degree, among many other factors. Women in "physical and life sciences and technologies" and "health, parks, recreation and fitness" earn more than men in the same fields at the same age, and earnings for Ph.D. and master's graduates are nearly identical for men and women of the same age with the same degree.

What's undeniable is that **improvements in educational performance and qualifications are contributing to improved incomes for Canadian women.** Although increasing education will continue to boost women's incomes, simple generational replacement is also having a big impact. Men and women at entry level today are more similarly qualified than their parents and grandparents were. As older workers leave the labour market and are replaced by younger workers, men and women will bring similar qualifications and expectations to the workplace. This will help to further narrow the income gap.

## Women in the Workforce

One of the biggest changes in Canadian society over the last century has been the growth of two-income families in which both partners work outside the home. Such families are now Canada's social norm. This change has contributed to huge productivity gains in the Canadian economy and a massive increase in Canada's workforce, and has contributed to declining birth rates. How big a change has it been? Back in the early 1950s, about 25% of all Canadian women had a job outside the home. Today, that number has more than tripled, to 82%. Nearly half of Canada's workforce is now female. While it's true that men, at 90%, are still more likely to be in the workforce than women, the gap continues to shrink. And for university-educated men and women, it's already effectively zero.

Women particularly dominate in part-time work. While there's a persistent belief that women work part-time because they have a hard time finding full-time employment, in reality it's men who are more inclined to say they face this challenge. Women typically say they work part-time because they believe it's a better fit with their other life choices, such as school and home responsibilities (child and senior care). Senior women are also more likely than senior men to have part-time jobs outside the home, and are more engaged with volunteer work in their communities. There may be a social aspect to being active outside the home, either for pay or not, that's more motivating for women, especially older women, than it is for men.

Here's a surprising fact that gets little notice when it comes to gender and workplace participation: the income gap hasn't been closing just because more women are now working; it's also because fewer men are working. Workforce participation among men has dropped by around 5% since the 1950s. Some of this reduction is due to fathers choosing to stay home to care for their children while their partners work, but there are also a significant number of men who have, for all sorts of reasons, simply drifted out of the workforce. According to Statistics Canada, economic downturns hit men harder than women, especially in the construction and natural resources sectors, where men are overrepresented and which tend to get hammered hardest when the economy sours.

If women are underrepresented in the construction and resources sectors, in which industries are they overrepresented? The data show that some biases die hard. Women are still concentrated in traditional female occupations such as teaching, nursing, health, clerical, administration, sales, and service jobs. But these numbers are all gradually coming down. And in the occupations that have traditionally been dominated by men, women are becoming more of a presence (even in construction and natural resources). In some previously male bastions, women now dominate. For example, women now make up 55% of Canada's doctors, dentists, and other health-care workers. These numbers will keep growing, because 60% of Canada's medical students are women. And that percentage is growing too.

## Equality in the Workplace

While the hard numbers are encouraging, the real question is whether women believe all this change has created equality in the workplace. After all, their beliefs are based on each woman's personal reality. In a major 2018 survey that Ipsos conducted with the advertising agency McCann, three-quarters of the women interviewed said Canada has not yet achieved equity in the workplace. They believe there's still more to do, and that the gender gap remains strong and persistent, particularly in the top jobs. We can have a debate about why this is so, but the facts, in the minds of most women, are undeniable. The evidence of inequality gets stronger the higher you go up the ladder, especially into the executive suites.

The lack of true employment equity has motivated Canadian women to introduce new expectations and rules of behaviour to the workplace. They want to be treated the same as men when it comes to opportunities and pay. Almost as important, the men who answered the survey said they wanted the same thing, both for their female co-workers and for themselves. Neither wants gender to be a factor in how the Canadian workplace operates.

Despite the strong desire for workplace equity held by both genders, the roles that women play in their families still affect their work lives in ways their male colleagues don't experience. A woman's decision to become a mother has an especially negative impact: **there's a clear "child penalty" in terms of income that isn't an issue for fathers.** That penalty grows with the number of children a working mother decides to have. These facts are clear in the income data. While the difference in earnings for married and single women isn't large, and earnings are also about the same for both single men and single women, those who earn the most are married fathers. Being married and becoming a father tends to greatly improve the job status and income of men, but the same can't be said for women—even the 30% of working women who earn higher incomes than their working male spouses.

Finally, while we tend to talk about gender as the single defining element of every woman's identity, we know this is an incomplete picture. A woman's heritage, beliefs, and other factors also need to be considered when assessing career status and income. For example, immigrant women are more likely to have completed a university education than Canadian-born women. Statistics Canada tells us that's because our immigration policy focuses on educational and occupational qualifications. In addition, immigrants who arrive at a young age are more inclined to get a university education because their immigrant parents tend to be highly educated, and parents' educational aspirations strongly influence their children. When it comes to marriage, a factor that affects both workplace participation and incomes, more immigrant women are married than Canadian-born women in all age categories. They also tend to get married at a younger age.

## Gender Equity at Home

If women are our stronger and smarter sex, what's behind the persistent perception of gender inequality in Canada? Their family life at home certainly plays a role. You might be too young to remember the American TV series *Leave It to Beaver*, which ran from 1957 to 1963. If you did see it, it was probably in syndication, long after it originally ran. That's when I saw it too. The images it portrayed of family life and gender roles were indelible and appropriate for the time it was made.

The Cleaver family lived in the suburbs. Dad (Ward) commuted to the city for work, while Mom (June) was a full-time homemaker. The show was driven by the comedic trials and tribulations of the two Cleaver sons, Wally and his younger brother, Beaver. Where the show was inaccurate from a demographic perspective was in the number of children it placed in the Cleaver household. Based on the American birth rate in the early 1960s, there should have been four Cleaver kids, not two.

*Leave It to Beaver* was a show about American family life, but it could easily have been about a Canadian family at that time. Instead of living in the American suburb of Mayfield, the Canadian Cleavers could have lived in Canada's first planned modern suburb, Don Mills. The gender roles and family responsibilities of the Canadian June and Ward Cleaver would have been the same. Ward would have been the breadwinner, and June the homemaker. Both were exclusive roles. June didn't work outside the home, and wasn't expected to. And Ward's household responsibilities were limited to some yardwork, dealing with the car, and serving as the male role model and source of discipline for Wally and Beaver. The title of a later American TV series—*Wait Till Your Father Gets Home*—accurately describes Ward's parenting function.

While Ward was off in the city, winning the family bread, everything to do with running the Cleaver household fell to June. She took care of the boys, cooked the meals, and managed the family's community interactions. When Ward got home, dinner was always on the table, and all four family members ate together. How did you know Ward was home? He switched his suit jacket for a cardigan. But the collared shirt stayed on, and so did the tie. Business casual was still a distant dream.

Compare your family today to the Cleavers. For most of us, there is no similarity, even in households with two opposite-sex, married parents raising two kids. Instead, today's Canadian families look more like those depicted in the contemporary American TV show *Modern Family*. *Modern Family* features a range of family types that would be familiar to most Canadians these days, including blended families, same-sex families, and more traditional families (like the Cleavers). What's also noteworthy is that the range of household roles portrayed on *Modern Family* are as varied as the families themselves. In *Modern Family*, men are not exclusively responsible for financial security and women for household management. Even the curmudgeonly patriarch of the show, Jay Pritchard, who is on his second family, is expected to play a different role as a husband and father in his current blended family than he played in his first family. Some of the best comedic tension in the show is driven by Jay's struggles to be a father to his older children as he adjusts to new parenting responsibilities with his younger child and stepchild.

As in *Modern Family*, gender roles in Canadian families are in transition. We see gender expectations about how to split up household duties being altered by both men and women. And the transition is a source of tension in our homes just as it is on TV. In the best cases, the new arrangements create households that achieve the equality many of us say we want. But most men and women in Canada don't live in best-case scenarios. Only 59% of women and 50% of men say they believe gender equality really means equal responsibilities at home. That's hardly unanimous.

For many women, when they enter the workforce, their responsibilities at home don't change. As a result, they now believe they are expected to serve double duty. **"You can do it all" has become**

**"You *must* do it all."** Once an aspirational badge of feminist honour, today's double-duty life has become a major source of tension in our households, especially for mothers who work outside the home. Working mothers say they spend twice as much time on child care as fathers do, and 50% more on other household responsibilities. What makes it worse is that men think they are making more progress on equalizing chores than women believe they have. Three-quarters of men say they have an equal share in household chores, but only 57% of women agree. At least, that's what they told Ipsos and McCann, and those findings confirm Statistics Canada reports.

The Ipsos-McCann research shows the serious level of mental strain double duty creates for working mothers. Time management and work-home balance are their big issues. The reality of double duty is an ongoing internal narrative featuring a never-ending to-do list. What haunts women is the constant thinking ahead, knowing where everyone is, knowing what everyone has going on, and making sure nothing falls through the cracks. This mental juggling is something men seem to be either less aware of or less involved in. Again, the statistics tell the tale: two-thirds of women believe they do more mental juggling than men do.

**What we really need in Canadian households, then, in response to transforming gender roles, is a new model of how women and men can work together as partners in a family and in the working world.** If we look at households as successful partnerships made up of individuals with unique strengths, weaknesses, and personal preferences, a whole new picture emerges. A successful partnership is one based on an equitable distribution of household responsibilities, regardless of gender. There's no need to put a value judgment on it. The equalization of household and family responsibilities is a necessary evolution based on the realities of the modern Canadian family.

## Transforming Our Workplace Culture

Home and family life also have huge implications for the Canadian workplace. Although we say our goal is to treat women and men the same at work, they still come to the job from different life situations. Home life plays a big role in workplace success. As the income data show, **if you're a married dad, today's working world is set up for your success. If you're a married mom, not so much.** It can't be good for Canada if the excessive burden of managing work and family keeps women from achieving their full potential in both roles.

What have Canada's policy-makers and employers been doing to help working mothers struggling with double duty? So far, not much. Most of their focus has been on symbolic hiring initiatives. While gender-balanced cabinets and board appointments signal positive steps towards a commitment to equity, they don't make it easier for the average working mother to balance her stressful work and home life. What would be much more helpful is a serious transformation of workplace expectations, policies, and incentive structures. Access to affordable child care is part of this equation, but won't alter the deeply ingrained workplace cultures that somehow end up working better for married dads.

The good news is that even if this issue isn't getting serious attention yet, it is, as they say, in the mail. **Throughout this century, we must continue to change our workplaces to better fit the needs of working moms.** If we don't, our already below-replacement-level birth rate will just keep getting lower. In addition, employers who want to attract the best talent, which is increasingly female, will miss out. Ultimately, change is inevitable.

## Delayed Motherhood

Change also means that those dark corners of Canadian society where patriarchy, oppression, and poverty still lurk for women will continue to be illuminated and eliminated. As this happens, some empowered Canadian women will not only opt to become mothers at an older age than their mothers and grandmothers did, they will also be more likely to decide to have only one or two children, if they have any at all. Exceptions will always exist, but they will be rare, and they certainly won't represent the aspirational social norm for most Canadian women. As in urban China today, large numbers of children in single households will increasingly be regarded as cultural curiosities in Canada. Not quite as much of an oddity as the Dionne quintuplets, but not far off either.

As we move through the century, we will increasingly feel the power of the growing number of single women in the marketplace. **Many women are now taking their own path and accumulating wealth on their own terms.** Every year, more Canadian women in their 20s will be choosing further education and starting a career over getting married and having kids. These shifting priorities are becoming more the norm around the world every day.

Women will spend their 20s and 30s building their careers and will eventually, but belatedly, confront the big questions about their future family lives. Should they get married or form another type of life partnership? Should they try to have kids while they still can? Should they freeze some of their eggs? How many kids should they have if they want them? Should they embrace living alone on their own terms? Should they buy a home on their own? Should they buy a Harley-Davidson motorcycle?

## The Power of Senior Women

There's an important group of Canadian women who get almost no attention from our country's consumer marketers: older women. When was the last time you saw an ad featuring an older woman that wasn't about a drug, especially one designed to cure erectile dysfunction? Even then, she's relegated to the role of supporting player. A survey of older Canadian women by Ipsos and McCann found that 68% of older women think people like them are not represented in advertising. Marketers see older women as, at best, a narrow specialty segment outside the mainstream consumer market. When you look at the population statistics, though, it becomes clear that this view must change. **There's a growing number of older women in our country, and they are sitting on a lot of Canada's wealth.** Big numbers plus money equals power. You already know that women outlive men, and the proportion of older women is also growing compared to younger women, a function of declining fertility rates and increasing longevity. That's what happens when a country stops having kids and gets better at keeping people alive. Both population trends combine to increase the power of older women in the marketplace.

Despite the growing presence of older women in our population, we are still holding on to a persistent but inaccurate image of their dependency. How many times have you heard politicians talk about senior women living a lonely life, on the edge of poverty? For all but a small segment of older women, this simply isn't true. One of the biggest declines we've seen in low-income situations in Canada is for seniors. Only 3% of Canadian senior families are now classified as low income, down from 18% in 1976. Seniors, especially senior women, have more money than they have ever had.

In addition to having the money to support a comfortable lifestyle, senior women have a higher home ownership rate than senior men. Once an older woman decides to remain on her own, she tends to stay in her family home (especially if she has been widowed) or move into single accommodation by herself. By the age of 65, 25% of women live alone, compared to only 14% of men. By the age of 80, it's 54%

of women and 24% of men. As the number of senior women grows in Canada, so does the number of single-person households, contributing to the urban and suburban condo boom.

While senior women are more likely to live on their own than senior men, they don't describe themselves as lonely. They regard living alone as a choice to be personally independent. Senior women are also more connected to their families and communities than senior men are. Indeed, almost 60% of senior women say they are leading a fuller life today than when they were younger, compared to about 40% of senior men.

Since, for the foreseeable future, Canadian women will still outlive Canadian men, and many don't remarry after becoming widowed or divorced, there will be a growing number who elect to remain single. As a contact at Royal Bank of Canada told me, one associated trend is that widowed or divorced women often change financial advisors because they tend to have different financial needs than they had as part of a couple.

**Businesses will increasingly be forced to respond to the growing buying power that older women have.** They represent a growing market segment of optimistic, active, life-affirming potential customers equipped with the assets to make a difference to our economy. Who has twigged to this power and changed their product and marketing strategy to give senior women what they want? Almost no one.

## Let's Not Forget Canada's Men

There's lots going wrong for Canada's men today, and hardly anyone is talking about it. Why are we oblivious to so many young men dying before they reach the age of 30? Why does our health-care system fail men so badly? What are we doing about the epidemic of suicides among men? Why is our education system less able to connect with men? What will we do for the men who will be hurt by the coming changes to our natural resource and manufacturing sectors, where they are disproportionately employed?

**We should all be worried about Canadian men.** Our social cohesion is dependent on all of us, including men, believing that our society works for everyone. While women certainly have valid grievances about how Canada works, conditions for them are improving in almost every way that can be measured. The same can't be said for Canada's men.

Newton's third law of motion states that for every action there is an equal and opposite reaction. While Newton was talking about the interaction of physical objects in the world, in my experience, something similar happens with human relations. Will a serious activist men's movement emerge in reaction to this situation? Maybe. But it's more likely we will see aggrieved men clustering behind conservative, even populist, political options. There has always been a weak gender cleavage in our politics, but since we have traditionally operated within the confines of the Laurentian Consensus, which was more about moderating language and regional tensions, gender cleavage wasn't a focus. As the Laurentian Consensus falls farther into our history and our politics becomes more ideological and identity-based, we could see gender emerge as a more decisive factor in our elections. It certainly seems headed that way these days.

## What This Means for Your Business

The issue of gender is messy and complicated. The public discussion is dominated by strong voices on both ends of the scale. While some of you might snort with an "of course" and dismiss an advocate as hopelessly idealistic or antediluvian in their views on gender, real Canadians live with these issues and frictions every day. Whether you're dealing with gender in terms of employees, customers, or voters, it's more complicated than we think and is sure to become even more complicated as our population ages and younger women with strong career aspirations and demands for change become a greater part of the workforce.

If I can offer any advice, it would be to go back to that most quint-essential of Canadian values: tolerance. Expect that while there's a general view that equality of opportunity is a relatively hard value, there is some tolerance for difference in outcomes. It's as much about the intentions of those running the system as it is about what they achieve in the moment. However, the best proof of your intentions is the outcome. So it is an incredibly difficult equation to balance.

A lot of effort is being made these days by many organizations on what could be called symbolic equity, and there's justification for this. For women to strive to achieve more, they need to see that more is possible. But what the Ipsos-McCann survey tells us is **most women are not struggling so much with access to promotions or greater pay as with the omnipresent double duty that overpowers their lives.** For them, the most relevant change is anything that alleviates the stress of double duty in their households and work lives. The smartest organizations will figure out how to help with this.

What are you offering that makes the lives of working mothers easier? What are you doing for senior women? These are two big and growing opportunities that will define the future Canadian market-place and issues agenda.

## What This Means for You

For women, especially older women, your commercial, workplace, and political power is growing. The question now is what you will do with it. There are big battles left to fight. The biggest one is changing the rules of the workplace to better accommodate the needs of working mothers. **It's not just about doing what's fair; it's also about making it possible for women who want to have it all (education, a career, and motherhood) to realize their dream without penalty.** The benefits will accrue not only to mothers and their families, but also to a country that has a below-replacement-level birth rate.

For men, the challenge is to become the fathers their families need (and they already believe they are). It's time to have a serious conversation about the role of men in tackling the endless family to-do list. Unless we change what happens at home, changing what happens in the workplace won't have as much of an impact on women's lives as it needs to.

**We also need to face the fact that something is going horribly wrong in the lives of Canadian men.** When I mention this to audiences, the first reaction I get is usually a knowing laugh that suggests *Yup, men sure are dumb.* But later an audience member will often offer up a tragic story about a man in their life who has been added to the sad statistics. The issue starts with our education system. What can we do to get more men through school? If our need for skilled workers in Canada is growing, we need more well-educated and well-trained men to meet the demand. There has been some discussion around the margins of this issue, but we have no comprehensive national strategy that even recognizes it as a problem or an opportunity.

How can we modify our health-care system to better meet the needs of men? We have women's health specialists and pediatricians, but no resources specifically focused on men's health. Yes, there are specialists in diseases that particularly affect men, but few clinics specialize in men's overall health. Men need to learn to address their health issues expeditiously and to better follow the advice and treatments recommended by health professionals. There must be an app for that.

Finally, the tragedy of male suicide must be addressed. Why are men these days so prone to killing themselves? (Women kill themselves at alarming rates too, but men are especially drawn to suicide.) Part of the problem could be demographic transition. Men by themselves don't do as well as women by themselves. Whatever the cause, this issue needs to come out of the shadows for some serious attention.

PART 4

# WHAT'S NEXT

# CHAPTER 15

# *The Silver Tsunami*: Why a New Wave of Older Canadians Matters Most

## The Battle of Young Versus Old

Let's apply what we now know about Canada's generations to the emerging marketplace. I seem to be doing this a lot these days. Here's an example. Over the last few years, I've had the privilege of speaking on several occasions to major gatherings of people from Canada's restaurant and hospitality industry. These meetings, hosted by Restaurants Canada, the industry's trade association, bring together our country's significant food and hospitality players to learn about emerging food and hospitality trends. Attendees include representatives from the big hotels and restaurant chains, the major food and beverage suppliers who sell to the hospitality industry, franchisees, restauranteurs, and even celebrity chefs.

This is an audience I especially enjoy presenting to. It's the who's who of Canadian restaurants. Not only are these people important leaders in their industry, but they are also at the cutting edge of social and cultural change in Canada. Along with language, cuisine is a major cultural marker for people. Our comfort foods come to us from the cultures we were raised in. Therefore, food isn't just about physical sustenance. It also reflects who we are as people, and what we value at a very primal level.

If the Canadian population is changing, one of the first places the change will have a meaningful impact is on our restaurant and hospitality industry. All of us, regardless of age, gender identity, income level, religious practices, or ethnocultural background, need to eat. That's why, at one time or another, we all eventually find our way through the door of one or more of the restaurants represented at this meeting. Or the restaurants will eventually find their way to us: we are very big in Canada on takeout, delivery, and drive-through eating. And this share is growing. Going out for a meal is only 38% of our restaurant spending today, and a declining share. Off-premises eating is gaining ground because of technology, convenience, and portability. It allows us to eat what we want, where and when we want to.

Restaurants are important to us culturally, but they are also important to our collective prosperity. According to Restaurants Canada, **going out to a restaurant is the number one preferred way for Canadians to spend time with family and friends.** We do this at ninety-five thousand restaurants across the country, generating $80 billion in sales annually, which equals 4% of Canada's overall economic activity. Restaurants are also Canada's fourth-biggest employer, with a workforce of 1.2 million people, or 6.9% of Canada's total workforce. Getting trends about future consumers right, then, is a big deal for both the industry and Canadians.

In 2016, I spoke at the Restaurants Canada show at Toronto's Liberty Grand, a beautiful banquet facility located on the CNE grounds on Toronto's waterfront. Everything anyone would want to know about trends and new products in the food and hospitality industry was on display. I was speaking at a breakfast event, and the spread Restaurant Canada's members put on for attendees was second to none. Who knew there were so many amazing foods and beverages available for Canadians to start their day with?

Restaurants Canada asked me to focus my talk on how various demographic changes will affect the restaurant industry in the future. Before my presentation, they showed the audience a video clip to set the scene. It featured a TV comedy troupe doing a takeoff on Millennial hipster chefs obsessing over how to use caribou testicles in recipes.

Funny as it was (and based on the laughs from the restaurateurs, it was very funny), the clip hit on a relevant and contentious point within the restaurant industry. Just how much should restaurants focus on satisfying Millennial foodies and their obsession with the new and different? One side believes younger foodies offer growth potential for the industry and restaurant operators need to adjust their offers to meet this emerging trend. Others see them as a distraction from the mainstream market, where the big money is. To these restaurateurs, foodies may make for interesting shows on the Food Network, but they represent only a niche, non-leading, unrepresentative market that's not worth chasing. Later in the day, this issue was debated to a standstill by a panel of prominent industry players. Both sides have their committed advocates, and there appears to be no clear consensus in sight.

I was up first to speak at the event and had taken my place at the podium as breakfast started. By now, you are familiar with my views on demographic change and the emergence of the new Canadian mainstream, so you already know what I talked about. I had only twenty minutes to speak, so I focused on the one big element of the story that I thought would be most interesting to this audience: what restaurants are doing for older Canadians, not as a specialty consumer segment but as the emerging mainstream market. After all, there are lots of seniors and soon-to-be seniors in Canada, and there will only be more of them over time. Just as important, they are sitting on most of Canada's wealth.

After establishing the statistical justification for my argument (which isn't as boring as it sounds), I offered some advice on how to appeal to older Canadians. "Why don't you turn down the music so older customers who have trouble with ambient noise can have a conversation? And turn up the lights so they can see the menu. You should also make it easier for people with mobility issues to get to and around your restaurant. And while you're at it, put some items on your menu that cater to older palates." I returned to my seat to polite applause.

I was followed on stage by a restaurant expert from one of the major consulting agencies. His presentation went in exactly the opposite direction. It was all about catering to Millennials and Gen Z. Why? Because his statistics told him that they were the most active audience: younger people go out more often than older people, and they spend more of their disposable income on dining and other types of entertainment. From his perspective, for future success, restaurants need to focus more attention on the integration of technology into the dining experience—everything from how customers access the restaurant to how they interact with the menu to how they pay their bills to how they talk about their dining experience with their friends. In the end, he said, a strong social media presence with a loyal customer base is the key to building a successful restaurant.

After the session, the restaurant consultant and I each found ourselves surrounded by people asking follow-up questions. Those who came to me said my presentation resonated with them because they had been thinking about the same issues. I'm sure the people talking to the restaurant consultant were saying the same thing to him. But in the end, both presentations had something important to say. It's not an either-or situation. No business will be as successful as it could be if it excludes any significant group of potential customers.

## The Obsession with the Youth Market

There are many aspects of generational marketing I could look at. But the question I hear most often these days is reflected in the seemingly contradictory presentations given at the Restaurants Canada meeting. What is the better growth strategy for most businesses? Is it meeting the needs of younger people, or meeting the needs of older people? Yes, it's all important. But if they were to lean one way or the other, how should they lean?

Most marketers I deal with deem this an easy question to answer because they have a very clear bias when it comes to generations. In their opinion, most organizations should lean towards satisfying the needs of the younger generation. They believe that if you get a customer when they are young, they will stay with you for life. These marketers also consider young people the market's tastemakers: what they decide to buy determines what everybody else will eventually be buying, regardless of age.

Since the start of the Baby Boom, marketers have been right to lean this way. The massive injection of young people into the Canadian marketplace after the Second World War meant that they were the dominant demographic cohort, and they represented the mainstream for half a century. As noted earlier, the dominant demographic group sets the direction for the entire marketplace. Remember, it's important to focus on the rules and not get distracted by the exceptions. Whoever has the numbers always wins. So over time, advertisers and marketers have developed a built-in bias when it comes to generational marketing. To them, mainstream almost always means what younger people want.

I talked to an advertising expert, Mary Chambers, about this bias. At the time of our conversation, Chambers was the chief strategy officer at McCann Canada, our country's longest-standing ad firm. She was the strategic mastermind who pulled it all together for McCann and their clients. She is unusual in the ad game in that she understands both data and the creative process of making ads. Chambers gets that, as entertaining as an ad might be, if it doesn't move the sales numbers, it's a waste of an advertiser's money. That's why data, including demographic data, matter to Chambers.

Today's ad agencies aren't like those you see in *Mad Men*. There are far fewer drinks cabinets and corner offices now than at Don Draper's fictional ad agency, Sterling Cooper. McCann's Toronto office, like those of most major ad agencies I've been to, is all about communal workspaces and inspirational zones for sparking spontaneous conversations and creativity. In truth, it looks more like an airport lounge or a lobby in a hip downtown hotel than an office. Everywhere you look, you see young creatives walking back and forth, cradling their laptops in their arms.

While there are lots of hipster beards and tattoos, there's savvy and experience too. That's what Mary Chambers brought to the table. Thoughtful, precise, calm, confident, direct, and articulate, she's exactly who you would want to direct the show in front of a nervous client. Chambers is the adult in the room. Not in a patronizing way. There's lots of respect for the youthful "creatives." But she understands that their youth bias makes it difficult for them to think about a consumer who is older than they are. Chambers takes pride in being the one in the room who understands the issue of age bias. She also gets that, despite appearances, advertising is a serious business. In the end, it's all about inspiring consumers to buy a client's product.

I asked Chambers if marketers are reflexively predisposed to focus on the youth market to the exclusion of older consumers.

"Yes," she said. "They are."

In her view, that's because the aging segment is not a sexy market for advertisers. They tend to ignore it. While they might accept the statistical facts about the growing consumer power of seniors, they don't find them interesting. There's a consensus among marketers that tomorrow will always be defined by a different cohort than the one that defines it today—and the different cohort will always be a younger one. Younger cohorts have always been the big spenders, so it's legitimate for marketers to be obsessed with them. It's a life stage thing. Youngsters are the people having kids and buying houses. If not today, then soon. Retirees are past all of this and therefore simply don't represent the same commercial opportunity that young people do.

I couldn't agree more. Mary Chambers nailed it. It's what the restaurant consultant said in his presentation, and it's what I hear most often from marketing experts. But what if they are all missing something? Chambers made this point too. That is, **what if the senior life experience is in transition? What if the size of the older cohort is growing? What if seniors are living longer and livelier, and what if they continue to sit on the lion's share of Canada's wealth? Because all three points happen to be true.** And what happens to the consumer marketplace if seniors become the dominant age cohort in the new mainstream? Because that's going to happen too. It's already happening right now.

And what about the next generation of young people—the one that is supposed to define our future marketplace? What happens if Generation Anxious lives up to its moniker? What if they don't buy new homes at the same rate as previous generations (because older people are aging in place and blocking them from the market)? What happens if the sale of new furnishings and other goods that go along with home ownership don't take off as expected? What if Generation Anxious eschews expensive new cars because they are paying off student loans, or because they become urban renters and don't need a car? What happens if they have fewer kids and don't buy kids' clothes, furniture, or toys? Sure, young people will still constitute a big number as we move forward, but not as big as the growing number of older people. And the financial circumstances for both groups, especially when it comes to access to disposable income and capital, will be different from what it was in the past.

## Older Consumers Are Loyal Consumers: Insight from the Music Industry

I still haven't answered the question I initially posed to the attendees of the Restaurants Canada show and to Mary Chambers: Which generation should Canadian businesses focus on in the future, the younger generation or the older generation? One has the right behaviour but less money, the other has the money but lacks the right behaviour. So should you focus on the one everybody focuses on or the one they most ignore?

The music industry offers some interesting insight on this question, as I learned during a conversation with a close friend who books tours for major musicians. What he said about the different generations' impact on the music business was very revealing. He walked me through the economic realities of today's music business. Given what the internet has done to record sales, he said, live performance and touring are now the major sources of income for most musicians. But the internet has also damaged the music touring business, thanks to the growth of digital music and streaming. Almost no one buys albums with multiple songs anymore; they buy or stream singles (the exception is older people, who still buy CDs). Our music choices today are much more individual and diverse, with minimal intervention from outside curators.

Back in the day, radio programmers and hard-core music fans who worked at local record stores had a big influence on what local kids listened to. They were the curators, and they created the audience for most new music. Not anymore. Online music is so voluminous, diverse, and easy to access that it requires a big investment of time to sort through what's on offer and to winnow it down to what you like. There are just too many choices in too many places. Gen Z loves this, but the music business certainly doesn't.

My friend observed that young people today no longer have a common music experience like the Boomers had. There are no more albums like *Hotel California* or *The Dark Side of the Moon* dominating the charts for months and building the audiences to support big concert tours. Today, a new artist may have a greatest hit, but it's much, much harder to have multiple greatest hits. And you need greatest hits to build a big enough audience for a profitable concert tour.

A quick review of 2016's concert tours underscores this point. I could have picked any year in that decade; the pattern is the same. According to *Pollstar*, the music industry magazine, the top hundred tours in North America in 2016 sold forty-four million tickets and grossed $3.34 billion, up 7% over 2015. Concerts are clearly a big and growing business. But which acts moved the numbers? That's where it gets interesting.

For the top twenty tours of 2016, only seven of the artists could be regarded as "non-heritage" artists. I consider a heritage artist (my friend's term) to be one that released their first significant work prior to 2000. Sure, they may still be producing great new music today, but they first started building their audiences last century. Also noteworthy, only four acts in the top twenty that year—Adele, Luke Brian, Justin Bieber, and Drake—had released their first album in the previous decade. Even current, younger hot artists are making only a minimal mark on the concert scene, where musicians now make their income.

As for ticket prices, older audiences are prepared to pay a premium to see their favourite artists from back in the day. In 2015–16, the collection of major heritage acts charged $20.61 more per concert ticket than the six non-heritage acts combined. That's a premium of 18%. Even for similar artists from different eras, there's still an added cost. An average ticket to see Céline Dion will set you back a third more than an average ticket to see her contemporary equivalent, Adele.

**Who says older consumers prefer to sit at home and won't part with their money? Only those who haven't taken the time to look at the facts.** This quick analysis shows that older audiences are loyal audiences. They support the concert tours of their favourite artists well past the time they produced their most vital work. And they are prepared to pay a premium for the privilege of seeing those musicians. As my friend told me, without heritage acts, the concert business would go broke.

What's a younger act to do, then? They need to tour to make money, but since the turn of the century, very few of them have broken through as stadium headliners. So to make a living, they must play smaller tours and festivals. And changing demographics are creating another big impediment to the success of smaller tours. Many live venues in cities like Toronto and Vancouver are shutting down because of increasing property values. Most of the population growth in Canada is in our larger urban areas. Because of the increased demand for residential space in our metropolises, it's becoming more lucrative to convert concert venues into hip condos than it is to keep hosting concerts. Many owners of long-standing Canadian music venues are now facing the financial music and selling out.

As developers put up condos and new residents move in, an additional problem is created for urban live music. Live music venues, bars, and restaurants, which used to make these downtown neighbourhoods cool, are now being forced to move out or to close. It's not just the money from condo developers and big-box retailers driving this trend. Neighbourhoods that were once known for the music wafting through the night air are being silenced by new neighbours who prefer a good night's sleep to the sound of electric guitars at two a.m. They are pushing municipal politicians to bring in noise bylaws that make it more difficult to operate downtown music venues. Navigating this new regulatory morass makes it a lot more trouble than it's worth for many club owners to stay in the music business.

As live music venues close, the best places for new acts to get audience exposure are increasingly music festivals, both destination/camping festivals and travelling festivals. The big destination festivals are the ones you have likely heard of: Glastonbury in the United Kingdom, Bonnaroo in Tennessee, Lollapalooza in Chicago, WayHome or Boots and Hearts in Oro-Medonte, and the biggie, Coachella, in California. These are festivals that feature multiple stages and bands. The headliners attract the big audiences, but smaller bands get a chance to build a fan base by keeping audiences occupied until the big acts hit the main stage.

Festivals are great for bands, especially the newer ones, because they provide an opportunity to build a larger audience faster than they could by playing a small tour across multiple Canadian cities—especially when appropriate venues are getting tougher to find. Festivals also tend to pay well and are cheaper for bands than going on tour. Festivals, therefore, are good for everybody involved: the bands, the promoters, and the audiences.

For younger generations, these destination festivals have become rights of passage, as Woodstock or Monterey Pop were for Boomers in the sixties. A bunch of friends drive a beat-up car across country to a remote location where the festival is being held over a long weekend. You pitch a tent, get drunk or stoned, and watch as many bands, familiar and unfamiliar, as you can cram in. Sure, it might be uncomfortable standing with fifty thousand of your closest friends in a field all day and night, but the bragging rights and memories will last forever.

Festivals are also one of the most successful and lucrative segments of today's concert business. Surely, this must prove the point, then, that attracting younger customers is the key to success. Coachella in 2015 is Exhibit A for this argument. It set an all-time music event record for sales at $84 million dollars! If you were lucky enough to get a three-day VIP premium pass, which sold out, it set you back $799. That's clearly not chump change.

Sure, Mom and Dad might have been tempted to go to Coachella and put up with standing in a field for hours to see AC/DC, but only if they could sit (as opposed to stand) for Tame Impala, Interpol, Alesso, Alabama Shakes, Ride, Nero, and the other numerous younger acts who came on before AC/DC. As for the headliners on the other nights of the festival, Jack White and Drake clearly weren't booked to attract older audiences.

Coachella has been a huge success since it started and continues to roll on. A three-day VIP premium pass in 2019 sold for $999. Being successful with youth audiences clearly remains a lucrative business.

But Coachella's record as the most successful single music event ever was smashed by another festival, put on by the same organizers, in the same place, in 2016: Desert Trip. Desert Trip set a new world single-event record, earning $160.1 million from a two-weekend bill featuring the Rolling Stones, Paul McCartney, Roger Waters, Bob Dylan, the Who, and Neil Young. That's twice what Coachella 2015 pulled in.

Desert Trip, which was mockingly called "Oldchella" at the time, was specifically targeted to an older, affluent crowd. The average age of the audience was 51, and the average age of the headlining acts was 72. The VIP pass was priced at $1,599—twice the level of the equivalent product for Coachella in 2015. As Gary Bongiovanni, editor-in-chief of *Pollstar*, put it in an article written by Peter Larsen, "It's designed for the baby boomer generation. Essentially the same people who were fans of these bands 40 years ago. They just have more money today and can afford to do this."

What else was different about Desert Trip? The emphasis the organizers placed on the physical comfort of the audience. Instead of standing in a field, concertgoers were assigned comfortable numbered seats. Gourmet foods and the best wines were available, as opposed to the usual junk food and overpriced beer that are sold at youth festivals. And a special effort was put into making sure the washrooms at the event were both plentiful and clean.

What's the lesson? The trick to appealing to the older market is to accommodate it. Remember, Desert Trip was still a festival concert, and didn't differ from Coachella in most respects. But how it *did* differ made all the difference. The organizers understood that just because people in the music festival business tend to think of what they do as being for young people, that doesn't mean older people don't want in on the experience. Desert Trip proved that the festival concept, with a few tweaks, can be sold to older music fans.

The same concept applies to restaurants and any another other consumer services or products. **If you accommodate an older audience, they will buy what you are selling. And they may be willing to pay a premium for it.** So I say again, restaurateurs, turn down the music, make it easier for people with mobility issues to get around your restaurant, and put some items on your menu that cater to older tastes. If you build it, they will come.

## What This Means for Your Business

Do you focus too much on youth? Most companies I deal with do, because we have a built-in bias for younger consumers. But **the future will increasingly be about meeting the needs of older consumers.** There are lots of them, and they have most of the money. However, they lack the right behaviour. They probably already want what you're offering, but you may have to modify it to better meet their needs. Your product or service may simply need a few tweaks, or you may need to develop something new to appeal to the older market. The trick here is to not treat seniors like seniors; instead, create options that let them in on what you're already doing for the rest of the market. I bet your marketing team or ad agency hasn't discussed this with you, but it's time you had a chat. Your future success depends on it.

In politics, a lot of attention is given to attracting the youth vote. This is a mistake. The most reliable voters (and the fastest-growing segment) are older voters. Younger voters tend to have a weaker attachment to the political system, which makes them unreliable voters. If I was asked to run a political campaign, the voter group I would focus on the most is women over 45. There are a lot of them, and they are civically engaged. What they need is a candidate or party that takes them seriously. Is that you?

## What This Means for You

Which companies are figuring out that older consumers are more than a niche market? Get them into your investment portfolio. Consider technology companies making products modified for seniors, companies developing transportation options for seniors, restaurant chains focused on older diners, and entertainment options that don't exclude older consumers.

# CHAPTER 16

# *The Authenticity Dilemma*: Why Trust Is Your Most Important Asset

## Building Trust

Every worthwhile relationship is based on trust. You either have it or you want it. Those who have it hold an incredible advantage over those who are struggling to build it. In business, having your customers' trust means you will spend less money marketing to them, they will be more willing to listen to and believe your pitches, they will be more likely to try out your new offers, and you may even be able to charge them a premium for what you're selling. **Without trust, you will struggle to be heard in an incredibly crowded and noisy marketing environment that gets louder and more confused every day.** You will also be forced to compete more on price (welcome to commodity hell), and your customers will leave you as soon as they can get your product or service cheaper from someone else. In today's global marketplace, that someone else could be located anywhere in the world.

Sure, there are businesses that succeed as discount suppliers. They make their profits from huge volumes and cheap processes, including labour. But this is a precarious position to be in, and most Canadian businesses lack the scale to win a price war with a global competitor that's truly committed to and built for this strategy. Ask any Canadian retailer who has lost market share to Walmart or Amazon.

In addition to building trust with customers, businesses also need to build trust with a wider group of social actors who can influence their outcomes. Regulators, the media, interest groups, and specific communities can all affect your business. When you hear the term "social licence," that's what it refers to: permission from society to operate your business or organization. **The private sector in Canada is no longer private.** If you want to run a successful business these days, you need to be working hard at building both the best products and your social licence to operate. Failure on the latter can kill your business just as quickly as failing on the former. Ask anybody trying to build a pipeline, open a mine, build a housing subdivision, or site a waste treatment facility in Canada these days.

## Adding a "T" to the 4Ps

Over the last few decades, conversations I have had with marketers have tended to be peppered with references to some version of what they call the 4Ps: product, price, promotion, and place. It's axiomatic in the marketing world that if you have a desirable product that's priced and promoted appropriately, and if it's placed where it needs to be at the right time, it will sell at its optimal volume. Manipulating or getting the right mix of the 4Ps is what sophisticated, modern, and ultimately successful marketing strategies are all about. That's what they teach you in MBA marketing courses, and it's certainly what you learn if you work with any of the world's leading consumer packaged goods companies, such as Procter & Gamble, Unilever, or Coca-Cola.

The 4Ps are central to defining the modern science of marketing. Marketing today is absolutely a science—especially when you consider market mix modelling (the 4Ps in action). Market mix modelling brings together different streams of consumer data, including survey-based data, behavioural data, and real-world sales data, to name just three. It then combines these streams with massive computing power and advanced mathematics to create a 360-degree view of a dynamic marketplace. This is "big data" for marketers.

Big data gives numbers geeks the huge volumes of information they need to power advanced mathematical analyses that reveal subtle but meaningful correlations in the world of buying and selling. Think digital geniuses on a treasure hunt for patterns of meaning among what seem to the rest of us to be random masses of unrelated numbers. It's like the opening scene in the movie *The Matrix*, when the stream of green digits rolls down the screen. To data modellers, there's undiscovered meaning in every line of code, as Neo, the prototypical data modeller, soon finds out.

While *The Matrix* is fantasy, the same stream of potentially correlated numbers exists in the real world. For example, if a country is hiring more nurses, does this mean investors should avoid investing in funeral homes (health-care spending is going up, so fewer people will be dying)? If a retailer offers a coupon at X level and their competitor offers one at Y level, what happens to their respective shares of the market? If long-term weather forecasts suggest a cold summer, should beer companies adopt an early discount strategy to offset the potential decline in consumer demand? For modellers, there are answers to these questions and more in big data.

I've had the privilege of working with some first-rate data modellers in both politics (yes, there's lots of big data in politics) and business over the years. What always interests me most is not what their models explain, but what they leave out. Every model has what's called an error term. The error term fills the space between what's happening in the real world and what most models don't or can't explain—that little bit extra that remains a mystery after the computer has done its work.

Modellers treat error terms as tolerable wastage, like a tailor who throws away trimmed material they can't use. It's not central to the 4Ps, so the amount of time and effort it takes to figure out the error term isn't worth it. The error term is still reported as a mathematical value, but its content is left a mystery. To me, this seems like a wasted opportunity. Since everybody else in the marketing world is fighting a war of attrition over the 4Ps, there's little to be gained from knowing more about them. But what would happen if someone could figure out a way to differentiate themselves in the marketplace based on understanding error terms? That smells like opportunity. As baseball Hall of Famer "Wee Willie" Keeler was famous for saying, "Hit 'em where they ain't."

The more I've looked at error terms over the years, the more I've realized they aren't always unexplainable data noise. Sometimes there is a pattern or signal hiding among the errors. That signal is often what can best be described as trust. I approach marketing issues conditioned by my background in politics and public affairs, where trust is essential to success. And, just as trust is central to establishing a transactional relationship with a voter, so too is it the key to establishing a transactional relationship with a customer. Trust is the "T" that needs to be added to the 4Ps.

## Behavioural Economics and Nudge Theory

I certainly get why modellers and marketers might be uncomfortable with trust. It's not an easy concept to measure or control, since it can be emotional, illogical, and irrational. **Trust is based more on a sensory reaction than on a rational calculus. Something feels, sounds, smells, or looks to us like it can be trusted—or not.** That's a different part of the brain working than the one that rationally reviews packages on a shop shelf and compares their value according to their relative prices and sizes.

Emotional reactions are at the heart of behavioural economics, the hottest trend in marketing today. Behavioural economics comes from the work of Daniel Kahneman, a Nobel Prize–winner for economics. Kahneman observed that human beings either react or think when confronted with a decision. "Fast" thinking ("System 1") is our immediate instinctive or emotional reaction, while "slow" thinking ("System 2") is deliberation based on logic. Thanks to the ubiquity and influence of Kahneman's work in today's marketing world, you will hear a lot of marketers talking about fast and slow thinking or System 1 and System 2 decision-making.

You will also hear about Kahneman's work in government, except there it is called nudge theory. A "nudge" is creating the right decision-making context so that citizens will naturally do what the government wants them to do without being forced to do it. A well-known example of nudging is when the authorities at Amsterdam Airport Schiphol decided to put the image of a housefly into their airport urinals to improve the aim of their male patrons. What guy doesn't like to aim at a target? Better aim equals cleaner washrooms. That's a "fast thinking" nudge in action.

## Personality Heuristics

Successful politicians have always known in their bones what Kahneman is talking about. Citizens don't go into a voting booth carrying a copy of each party's platform and a calculator to make a rational (slow, or System 2) decision. Instead, we bring a lot of System 1, or fast thinking, in with us. Do you trust Brian Mulroney? Does Jean Chrétien look like someone who will embarrass Canada on the world stage? Does it feel like Stephen Harper has a hidden agenda? Who would you rather have a beer with, Jack Layton or Michael Ignatieff? Does Justin Trudeau seem like he's ready?

She looks shifty, he seems happy and positive, she seems out of her depth, I hate his eyes, she's hiding something, I don't like his hair. These observations represent us struggling to find a way to evaluate the trustworthiness of candidates whom most of us will rarely meet other than through the media. Our first instinct is to construct a fast-thinking personality heuristic (like a checklist or cheat sheet) to help us make an efficient decision. It's like the reflexive list we all go through when we meet someone new in our day-to-day lives. In plain English, it's a first impression or gut reaction to the question "Can this person be trusted?"

Here's an example of how powerful personality heuristics can be. Over the years, I've tested many draft TV ads for clients, using what the advertising industry calls animatics. Animatics comprise cartoon drawings, or storyboards, that show the main shots planned for an ad. A video is made of the storyboards in sequence, a voiceover is added, and then the draft ads are taken out to focus groups for early evaluation. The advertising agencies use animatics to avoid the expense of producing and running a bad ad.

Each time I use animatics, the following happens: I'll show the clip a couple of times and ask the group what they think about it. Without fail, someone from the group will stick up their hand and say something like, "While I like what's being said here, I really don't like the person saying it. They just seem a bit shifty to me." Remember, these are *drawings*. They are the paper-and-ink equivalent of mannequins.

The first time this happened I was slightly shocked. I remember gently reminding the group that it was a cartoon and not a real person. This got some nervous laughter and an admission that what had just happened was a bit silly and illogical. Of course, everyone would acknowledge, a drawing doesn't have a personality. But not fifteen minutes later, we were back at it again—can I trust what this cartoon "person" is saying about the issue or product in the ad.

While it's not possible to trust a cartoon drawing, we still try to evaluate its trustworthiness because nature has programmed us to default to our emotion-driven personality heuristics as a first reaction, essentially our fight-or-flight instinct. Each of us has built a personality heuristic through trial and error based on our entire life experience, and we continue to use it successfully every day. It's just easier and safer to go with our gut.

Consumers bring their heuristics to their purchasing decisions all the time. Like politicians, smart marketers understand this. It shouldn't be a surprise; if we use heuristics to evaluate cartoons, why wouldn't we use them when we are deciding what to buy? For example, marketers in the over-the-counter drug industry know there's little 4P rationality going in to how their customers make buying decisions. Instead, it's about whether a customer trusts that the product will relieve their symptoms. How do they make the decision on which cold medication to trust? Maybe they saw an ad that claimed four out of five doctors said it would work. Maybe they saw an ad in which a person wearing a lab coat who seemed kind of sciency said it would work. Either way, they trusted the advice enough to buy the product.

## Building a Trustmark

As amorphous as trust is, it's becoming more and more important in the commercial world, forcing us to re-evaluate the 4Ps and the marketing mix. We no longer buy things only from merchants located next door or down the street. Instead, we now buy anything from anyone, anywhere, at any time. Online commerce and the global marketplace are not restricted by time or space. **Sales of any product or**

**service can be choked out of existence by a lack of trust.** Can I trust that online vendor located in another country to deliver what they say they will? And most importantly, can I trust them with my most private financial information? The transaction only works if trust is at the centre of it.

The term "trustmark" hammers home the importance of trust in the marketing mix. In the overcrowded online world, the most reliable signals come from brand names we can trust. A trustmark goes well beyond a good brand name, or trademark. A brand is simply how we begin relating to a product. Potential customers want to know if the information coming their way from a company is trustworthy. They aren't just seeking a signal about the quality of the product, they also want to know about the character of the producer. Are these good people I can trust, or are they bad people I need to avoid? It's as much a question of character as it is a question of price and packaging.

What is the value of a high-quality trustmark? Research from Ipsos shows that **there is a strong correlation between a company or organization's level of trustworthiness and its ability to successfully market to its consumers or stakeholders.** For corporations, a strong trustmark translates into more cost-effective marketing communications, an increased likelihood for consumers to try products marketed under their company's corporate brand, and a greater ability to charge a premium for their products and services.

Having a trustmark working for you also means facing fewer communications headwinds. Among non-consumer stakeholders, such as government regulators, the media, and potential activists, a trusted business will get more favourable community buzz and potentially more sympathetic policy decisions. Financial stakeholders will be more likely to recommend investing in your organization and business partners will be more likely to collaborate with you if they value your trustmark. After all, to them you are one of the good guys. Everybody wants to be associated with and support the good guys.

## Get Known and Build Familiarity

How does a company build a trustmark? This is where politics and commerce cross lines. It all starts with awareness, also known as "mindshare" in the marketing business. In politics, if they don't know you, they can't vote for you. In business, it's the same: if they don't know you, they can't trust you, and they will be much less likely to buy from you than from someone they know.

Justin Trudeau, for example, didn't have an awareness problem when he entered politics. Given his family's legacy, his personal story, and his visually attractive presence, he was the best-known rookie in Canadian politics, ever. Because he had a high mindshare, he quickly and easily moved on to the next stage of building trust—creating familiarity.

Most businesses don't have Justin Trudeau's mindshare, or even the level of awareness that has been earned by a modestly advertised domestic consumer brand. If you think your target market knows who you are, just plug your name into Google and see if that's true. You might be pleasantly, but more likely unpleasantly, surprised. It's a crowded and confusing marketplace out there. **If you haven't claimed your piece of online mindshare, that's your first and most important mission:** *get known.*

After your company is known by potential customers, the next hurdle is building familiarity—making sure you are known for what you want to be known for. Justin Trudeau wanted to be known for change in the run-up to the 2015 election. He and his team used his campaign communications to make the Liberal Party brand, and his brand, synonymous with change.

To seize change, the Liberals came out of the gate in 2015 with a progressive campaign platform—so progressive, in fact, that many observers described it as being to the left of the NDP's platform. The centrepiece of the Liberal platform was a commitment to increasing the deficit to stimulate the economy. Did the public buy into bigger deficits to stimulate growth? Not really. But what the promise did was create a buzz around Trudeau and the Liberals as being serious about shaking things up. He was making himself most familiar as an agent of change.

Thomas Mulcair's NDP decided to go in the opposite direction: "safe change." If Trudeau isn't ready, we are, said the NDP. How would they prove it? On fiscal policy, they promised to stick to the low-deficit strategy of previous, responsible, mature governments. Scary socialists? Not the NDP of 2015. This NDP was mature and ready to govern, like those fiscally responsible Prairie NDP governments. The party that isn't ready to govern is the one with the scary big-deficit ideas. That's not us.

These days, "safe change" as a winning political strategy is a myth. Yet there's no shortage of candidates who try it. If every election campaign is about change or stability, and you're the change candidate, then you need to own it. When the public hits the change button, they mean it. Trying to portray yourself as "safe change" means you're for the status quo. If you don't believe me, ask George Smitherman (who lost to Rob Ford in the Toronto mayoral election), Thomas Mulcair, or Hillary Clinton. They were all safe change candidates who lost against opponents seen by voters as being more authentically committed to change.

Of course, purporting to stand for change and acting in opposition to your public stance can and will hurt your brand. Justin Trudeau learned this the hard way in his first term as prime minister, no more acutely than in 2019. First, in February, he became publicly enmeshed in the SNC-Lavalin scandal. Attorney General Jody Wilson-Raybould alleged that Trudeau and his team had actively tried to compel her, against her own judgment, to intervene in a corruption case brought against the company. Wilson-Raybould pushed back and was ultimately removed as the AG. After this news exploded in the media, Trudeau ousted Wilson-Raybould and Jane Philpott, another high-profile female MP, from the party for publicly contradicting the Liberal party's stance that they had done nothing wrong. (The federal ethics commissioner would later disagree, saying that Trudeau "directly and through his senior officials, used various means to exert influence" over Wilson-Raybould in particular, a violation of the Conflict of Interest Act.) And then in September 2019, mere weeks before voting day, videos and photos surfaced of Trudeau in blackface and brownface as part of costumes dating back two decades. Canadians, rightfully so, were shocked and horrified that the leader who had promised change had instead become representative of the kind of insensitive and hurtful behaviour many felt had all but disappeared in Canada. These two scandals, given the Liberal's platform of inclusion and transparency, would have doomed the prospects of most candidates, but Trudeau's brand, as tarnished as it was, won out over the uncharismatic and less savvy leader of the Conservatives, Andrew Scheer, who lacks a brand, and the Liberals managed to hold on to power, although in a minority government.

## Familiarity in Marketing

If owning change represents the right kind of familiarity in politics, here's a good example of how familiarity works in marketing. Many well-known industries have struggled to create the familiarity that builds public trust. Several years ago, the nuclear industry, which uses nuclear technology to generate electricity for our homes and businesses, asked me to help them develop an ad campaign to educate Canadians on why nuclear power needs to be an important part of Canada's future energy mix.

It was a tough sell, but it wasn't easy to see exactly why. The draft ads were visually solid and featured sound copy that communicated what, on the face of it, seemed to be a compelling message about nuclear power's reliability, safety record, and benefits for the environment. The ads featured credible spokespeople who had lots of scientific bona fides to back up their claims.

Why didn't the ads work? While they moved the focus groups through the logic of why nuclear would be good for Canada's future energy mix, they could only get so far. At some point, the conversation would always break down. What we kept hearing back from the groups was, "You might be right about all of this, but nuclear just makes me uncomfortable. Despite everything you say, I think nuclear is dangerous. I don't trust it."

This feedback was frustrating for the ad agency and industry representatives (mostly engineers) who were watching the groups. They couldn't figure it out. "Why won't these people listen to our logic? This is science, after all." Since I was in the room with the focus group participants, I could feel the hesitation and chilliness in the air, but I couldn't get those watching the groups to appreciate what was happening. I had to find a way to break through, to show them what they were up against.

For the next group, I decided to go off-script. During the break, I put a pencil and a blank piece of paper at each participant's place. Once the new group was ushered in and seated, I ran through my usual introductions, but I didn't tell them what we would be talking about. Instead, I asked them each to write down the first thing that came to mind when I said the words "nuclear technology." When they were done, I had them turn over their paper so no one else could see what they had written down. Then, one at a time, I had them flip their paper back over and read aloud what they had written. All the words were negative—"death," "bomb," "Hiroshima," "waste," "Chernobyl," "explosion," "dangerous," "missile," "weapon"—not just bad, but deadly. Sure, nuclear technology is well known by the public, but for the wrong things. We were talking about nuclear power, not nuclear weapons, but it didn't matter. When we said "nuclear," they could only think *bomb* or *disaster*. No wonder the ads, good as they were on the facts, couldn't break through.

Nearly seventy-five years of bad press—Hiroshima, the Cold War, Three Mile Island, Chernobyl—will do this to any industry. (This campaign was prior to the Fukushima Daiichi disaster.) What I told the ad agency and industry people was that they needed to create some positive associations with the word "nuclear." Granted, this would be an almost impossible task, but unless they could accomplish it, it would be very difficult to make any progress on getting Canadians to trust nuclear power. They needed a different kind of familiarity.

In the end, the industry ran some ads featuring doctors and scientists speaking about how important nuclear medicine was in the battle against cancer. This was the best, most positive association we could find with nuclear technology at the time. Did it work? Maybe a bit around the edges. But the industry simply couldn't buy enough advertising to counter the huge weight of negative familiarity they were up against.

More recently, the nuclear industry has had better luck with its communications efforts, given the growing concerns about climate change. Now that they can present themselves as a "green energy" alternative, they finally have a chance to build some positive familiarity with their product and industry.

## The Favourability Stage

After familiarity, the next stage of building trust is favourability. If they know you, and are familiar with what you do, do they have a favourable or unfavourable impression of what you're doing? Along with building familiarity, the 2015 Trudeau campaign focused on building their favourability. If elected, Trudeau and his progressive Liberal Party promised to bring about "real change for you." So not only was it change you could agree with, but it would make better what you cared about most. This promise allowed them to specifically direct their policy proposals to the key segments of voters (especially suburban, middle-class new Canadians, working women, and Millennials) that they most needed to win over. Sure, they targeted other groups of voters too, but winning those particular groups from the Conservatives won them the election.

The favourability stage is where the other well-known and familiar actors in the campaign—Stephen Harper and the Conservatives—tried to fight back against Trudeau and the Liberals. They knew they were fighting against change in an election about change. They had to make real change look like risky change (like associating nuclear with disaster). But they lost their ability to do so when Statistics Canada announced that Canada's economy had been in a technical recession. The risk to our economy associated with big change looked a lot less risky given that what the Tories were doing wasn't working. After that, the Conservatives were no longer an effective competitor in the election and the battle shifted to picking their replacement.

The favourability stage of building trust involves an important difference from awareness and familiarity. **Favourability is more about belief than it is about knowledge.** When considering favourability, we add a value judgment to our knowledge. Our personality heuristics kick in. We start assessing the supplier as if they were an actual person: Are these good or bad people we are dealing with? If you are lucky enough to have a trustmark associated with your personality, building favourability is much, much easier to do.

## Corporate Philanthropy

Moving beyond the 4Ps and focusing on the "T"—building a trustmark—is what smart marketers are doing these days. Learning from politics, they recognize that their customers and other important stakeholders are evaluating them the same way they evaluate people. Therefore, companies are now working hard to present themselves as "good people" with "good values." Put simply, we make good products, but we also want to do the right thing in the world. As per Spider-Man, with great power comes great responsibility.

Companies using their resources to benefit the community is nothing new. Around the turn of the last century, many libraries and other public buildings in the United States were built by steel magnate Andrew Carnegie. At the same time, Swedish chemist Alfred Nobel used the wealth he had accumulated from inventing dynamite and various military weapons to fund the Nobel Prizes. It is now society's expectation that those with wealth will try to make the world a better place.

There's a lot of corporate philanthropy going on in Canada. Big companies do it in a big way, but even little companies are sponsoring community events or local sports teams. There's a transformation under way in this area. Companies are shifting away from handing out money to whomever asks to aligning all corporate activities, including philanthropy, with the personality values they want to present to the world, and especially to their customers and key stakeholders. Companies recognize that their customers are evaluating them based on character, not just on the price and performance of what they produce.

That means they need to reinforce positive perceptions of their corporate personality.

The trend in corporate character-building is also moving away from what could be considered charity to problem-solving. Bill and Melinda Gates deserve a lot of credit for leading the way. They built an organization, the Bill & Melinda Gates Foundation, that focuses on solving inequality issues around the world. Their goals are very specific, and they measure the effectiveness of their activities in the same way a company would assess the rate of return on an investment. For them, and many other switched-on organizations, it's not about virtue signalling but about real, measurable problem-solving.

We will be seeing more and more problem-solving in philanthropy as companies look for new ways to build and reinforce their trustmarks. A case can be made for doing good that does not rely solely on the argument of responsibility. In fact, **companies can do good in the world while doing well for themselves through creative and strategic planning.** Corporations have a great ability to do good—even more so than governments in some cases, given their wealth of resources, their global reach, and the freedom to innovate outside of the bureaucratic and geographic limitations of governments.

Corporate sustainability or social responsibility programs are a big part of a company's efforts to do good, and they have benefits beyond being a responsible member of the global community. In addition to delivering a reputational boost, carefully designed programs can deliver meaningful change that builds authenticity for the company's social responsibility efforts. The key word here is *authenticity*. Sure, it's an overused concept these days. Everybody wants to be seen as authentic. What they sometimes forget, though, is that to be seen as authentic, you need to actually *be* authentic. There's no such thing as authentic spin. You need to live it and deliver.

A company also needs to pick the right problems to solve. Social responsibility efforts that clearly and demonstrably align with the company's values and actions throughout the business are more likely to strike their customers and stakeholders as authentic. In other words, problem-solving needs to be a natural part of what you do. A moving company might help families relocate to safe places during emergencies. A publisher can support literacy programs. A bank can sponsor financial literacy courses for new Canadians. These are all examples of philanthropy efforts that fit authentically with their sponsor's expertise.

## What This Means for Your Business

A commitment to building a trustmark takes a conscious effort from an enlightened organization that understands that the world of marketing has changed. A company's success is no longer determined solely by its income statement or the size of its market cap. **The public's permission for conducting business in this increasingly complicated and challenging world will come from people who are looking to buy from or align themselves with someone they can trust.** Sure, the 4Ps will always be important, but more and more you will need to be thinking about building and supporting your customers' trust. The key is authenticity. What you do has to fit with the community's priorities. You must be the right organization to deliver it.

## What This Means for You

We want to feel good about the products we buy, the manufacturers we buy them from, and the investments we make. Which companies do you feel good about? You likely have a positive association with them because they have given you a good customer experience—not just because their product worked well or you paid a fair price for it, but also because dealing with them made you feel good at a deeper level. Companies that are accomplishing this are worthy of your attention. They understand modern marketing. You might want to buy their stock.

# CHAPTER 17

# *Plugging In*: How to Connect with Consumers in the New Canada

## Establishing a Relationship with New Canadians

Canada is a nation on the move—the movement of immigrants (mostly from Pacific countries) to Canada's big suburbs, and of Canada's rural and small-town residents to more urban environments. In addition, the weight of Canada's population has shifted from our east to our west. **Canada's new consumer mainstream is becoming more visible-minority, more suburban, and more focused on our Pacific coast than at any time in our history.** How do you build a connection of trust in this New Canada?

One person who understands these issues is Mary DePaoli, the chief brand and communications officer at our country's biggest bank, Royal Bank of Canada (RBC). Most businesspeople I meet could be described as either thinkers or doers. When you talk to DePaoli, it's clear that she's a rare combination of both. Not only is she thinking about how Canadian consumers are changing, but she's already experimenting with how to make that work for RBC.

Over a breakfast of coffee and muffins at a downtown hotel in Toronto, DePaoli and I had a lively conversation about Canada's future marketplace. While I'm used to marketers being either surprised by or somewhat dismissive of my views on population change and the Canadian marketplace, she was well ahead of me, so much so that she was practically completing my sentences. She told me that she and RBC are paying very close attention to Canada's demographic transition and are actively seeking ways to adjust their business to it.

For example, while I usually surprise businesspeople by telling them that the Philippines is now one of Canada's largest source of immigrants and Tagalog is our fastest-growing language, DePaoli was not only acquainted with these trends, but was already acting on them. She told me how RBC had recently adjusted its sponsorship activities to appeal specifically to the Filipino market, sponsoring a Canadian tour by Philippine pop star Piolo Pascual. DePaoli was thinking about Canadian consumers using what she called a "global frame of mind." This strategy means considering both Filipino customers who already live in Canada and those who are considering immigrating here. While she and her team didn't know much about the Philippine music scene, they knew that associating RBC with a Filipino pop icon would help them build brand awareness with an important and growing immigrant community.

Building familiarity for your brand among new immigrants isn't just about making sure that your brochures and ads are available in languages other than English or French, although that's an important first step. It's increasingly about establishing a relationship with immigrants as early in their Canadian experience as possible, which includes getting to them even before they arrive in Canada. Building brand awareness by sponsoring the tour of a Filipino pop star makes good business sense. Increasingly, establishing these early connections and relationships is part of the marketing strategy for Canada's big financial service providers, mobile service providers, and others.

Jim Little, the former executive vice president and chief marketing and culture officer at Shaw Communications in Calgary, confirmed the efficacy of RBC's strategy. It's something Shaw has been doing too. Incidentally, Little is one of Canada's most experienced marketing professionals and, like Mary DePaoli, also served as chief marketing officer at RBC, among many other high-level marketing jobs he's had. The little guy in the bowler hat featured in RBC's ads? That was his brainchild, as are the various mascots that are now associated with the Shaw brand.

For Jim Little, another close reader of demographic data, building market share for Canada's telecoms (and other businesses) is about understanding the dynamics of our changing demographics. As he told me one very cold morning at Shaw's offices in downtown Calgary, "Growth now comes from movement." People aren't having kids like they used to, and making money from movement means that facilitating easy transition is an important selling point for any service provider. The easier you are to work with, the easier it is for a consumer to become your customer." **New Canadians need to know that you will make the move to Canada easy for them, and that you have a specific offer that meets their needs.** New Canadians are big internet users, but also strong value buyers. Even if you have a good offer suited to their needs, they will trade it for something not quite as good that's cheaper. Knowing this, Shaw can create an offer for new Canadians that's internet-heavy, easy to access, and also price-competitive. That's smart.

Like Shaw, RBC reaches new Canadians when they start their transition into Canada by putting financial advisors who speak immigrant languages in bank branches close to community centres and other cultural facilities. RBC's in-community financial advisors are there not just to sell financial services to newly arrived immigrants, but also to smooth overall integration into Canadian society. They assist with everything from getting clients properly documented for all levels of government services to accessing cellphone and internet services (one of the first things most new Canadians want right away). By being of service at the start of their customers' Canadian journey, RBC hopes to build a loyal relationship for the long term.

## Event-Based Marketing

Shaw, like RBC, is a big believer in event-based marketing. It's the easiest way to target new Canadian communities. It's about being where they are, being friendly and familiar, and being easy to access and use. Succeeding at event-based marketing means sponsoring and being present at community-based festivals and other gatherings. Mary DePaoli provided another interesting insight on why community and cultural sponsorships are good marketing opportunities, as opposed to, for example, sponsoring sporting events. As she puts it, "Unlike at sports events, concertgoers always leave happy. Nobody loses."

Despite this mantra, RBC still sponsors sports. They look at their sponsorship through a changing demographic lens, at what DePaoli and others believe about the impact of population change on Canada's emerging mainstream marketplace. By this metric, **basketball may be becoming a better investment of sports sponsorship dollars than hockey is**. The reason, according to DePaoli, is that basketball is associated with both the individual players and their teams. Basketball players are much more a part of the zeitgeist than hockey players are. They are part of a much bigger ecosystem. Basketball players are associated with fashion, music, and celebrity culture in general. For immigrants just starting out in Canada, the cost of hockey equipment could be prohibitive. The cost of entry for basketball—like soccer—is cheap by comparison. You just need a ball and a hoop. Hockey has a high barrier to participation, especially for new Canadians. Hockey is not something you can participate in alone, and learning to skate is difficult for people from warm climates where skating is unfamiliar.

Whether it's a cultural festival, a concert, or a sporting event, RBC counts on more than physical presence to establish a connection. They also confirm that connection by distributing content from the event afterwards, through social media and through their customer loyalty programs, to those who were there or wish they were there. "Here's a picture or song download from that great concert you were at and RBC sponsored," DePaoli says. It's all about building trust, which starts with familiarity and connection.

## Connecting with Fluid Identities

Regardless of how they start, new Canadians change over time, becoming their own version of what it means to be a Canadian. "Identity in Canada is a fluid concept," says DePaoli. People develop hybrid identities that blend their old culture with their new one. Their commercial activity is another variable added to this equation. RBC tries to create content that connects with all points of Canadians' blended identities. Music, sports, and food are all good examples of identity markers that everybody has an intimate relationship with. They all go to your background and reflect what's important to you. Identity markers help RBC decide what content to get to their individual customers. "Content is cheap," says DePaoli. "It is easy to produce. If it is relevant, it creates a connection with customers. By giving people what they want, we build trust. It shows that you get them as an individual."

**The idea of fluid identities is becoming increasingly relevant for all consumers, not just new Canadians.** Your fluid identities include your perfect self (for the world to see), your more private self (for your good friends to see), and your family self (just for your close family). For marketers, the goal is to connect with each identity in the right way. "The challenge for companies is, which identity am I speaking with?" suggests DePaoli. "How do companies connect with each identity in a relevant and trustworthy way?"

Connecting with fluid identities is also a major challenge that clients are bringing to advertising agencies. Mary Chambers from McCann has some interesting insights. She believes making a connection means appreciating that effective marketing isn't about targeting ethnic groups. You first need to deal with a person's values, which aren't derived from their ethnicity alone. "The new definition of the Canadian mosaic is not understood by business," says Chambers. "It's all happening faster than they can keep up with. For those businesses that are already comfortable in Canada, they would prefer to ignore it. But they do so at their peril." Their resistance isn't philosophical. "It's just that the world is different than they think," Chambers continues. "They migrate to the familiar and resist the unfamiliar."

There is some hope on the horizon, though. The culinary world tends to be an entry point for change. "Food is relatively harmless. It allows you to experiment with what's different without having to fully embrace it," says Chambers. As a country that's only just over 150 years old, Canada hasn't had time to establish its own cuisine, unlike other cultures that have been developing their cuisines over generations. Younger Canadians in particular are more willing to experiment with food and other cultural choices because they are less likely to see colour, ethnicity, or gender than their parents do. According to Chambers, these are all becoming less meaningful constructs. "The markers of identity are breaking down." Which means that "ethnic marketing" misses the point.

## Appealing to a Blended Mosaic

Another iconic Canadian company that understands that a new, blended mosaic is being created by changes in the population is Loblaws, the country's biggest grocery retailer. I spoke with Grant Froese, their former chief operating officer, about how their marketing focus is being affected by population change. For Froese, adjusting to the changing demographics of consumers requires grocery retailers to move past the normal population segments marketers used to think about and start looking at the marketplace as collections of individuals. Sure, people in any given community might have several things in common, but to market to the whole person requires that you also appreciate their differences. (This is what Mary DePaoli, Mary Chambers, and Jim Little were all getting at.)

Grocery retailing in Canada has historically taken a one-size-fits-all approach to what gets stocked on the shelves. Now, community composition, especially due to immigration, dictates a need for difference. But it's important not to emphasize the differences. The truth is that 80% to 90% of the items on most shelves are still the same everywhere. It's the final 10% that reflects the difference and helps to establish the customer connection to a specific retailer.

In the past, grocers offered more processed and dry groceries. That's now changing, as new Canadians focus more on fresh foods than native Canadian consumers do. The fastest-growing, immediate competitors for Canada's grocery retailers are the multicultural independents (like Asian wet markets, which sell fresh meat, seafood, and produce), who tend to focus on fresh foods and cultural delicacies that bigger retailers have a hard time providing at scale.

To compete in the new grocery retail market, bigger Canadian players like Loblaws need to get right both the 90%—natural foods, organics, and health and wellness products for our aging population—and the 10%, which is driven by specific local ethnocultural communities. "We now look at clusters of stores and what works for specific communities," says Froese. "We need to figure out how to make the Singhs and the Lees, as well as the Smiths, happy." Grocery retailers build customer trust and, ultimately, loyalty when they cover most of the relevant bases correctly. Customer loyalty, especially over the long term, is a growing challenge in grocery retail, due to increasing competition from both Walmart and Amazon.

## What About Rural Canada?

If Canada's corporate marketers are making changes to adapt to our changing ethnocultural population, what are they doing to accommodate the decline of small-town and rural Canada (which also covers the shift from east to west)? The truth is, not much. They are just matching their market presence to what makes business sense for a declining market. RBC might be experimenting with mobile bank branches, but they certainly won't be building many new brick-and-mortar branches north of the suburbs.

What most players are hoping for is that small-town and rural Canada will be amenable to technological solutions that provide access to services, such as FaceTime interactions with financial advisors. As long as Canada Post still provides service to a community, shopping online for anything you need is a viable option. Are Canada's marketers sitting up at night worrying about how to sell to remote Canada? Not even a little. Their eyes are on our growing urban and especially suburban centres.

## What This Means for Your Business

With most of Canada's growth now coming from immigration,

**immigrants and their children will be an increasing share of your customer base and employees.** For politicians, they will be a greater share of your voters. What do you know about them? They are not the same everywhere. Groups of immigrants vary by region. Which groups are growing where you operate? What do you know about their customs, tastes, shopping habits, and political and religious beliefs? What can you do to make their transition to Canada easier? How can you build an early relationship with them? Those who get there first, with the best understanding of this increasingly important group of Canadians, have the best chance of building a lasting relationship with them.

Some major players in Canadian business are already getting there fast. I suggest you follow their lead. Tailor your offerings to the needs of immigrant Canadians, matching the stage of the Canadian journey they are at. Go where they are—don't expect them to find you. Cultural festivals are a good place to start, but some companies are trying to get to incoming immigrants even earlier by establishing relationships with them before they move to Canada. Focus on their important cultural markers, such as music, sports, and food. How can your product or service be modified to take these markers into account?

Most important, understand how you look through their eyes. Keep in mind that the identity behind those eyes is fluid. That's true for all of your customers and employees, not just new Canadians. How can you make an authentic connection with each identity?

## What This Means for You

What it means to be Canadian is changing. Get used to it. If you embrace the change, this will be an exciting time. You will have an unprecedented opportunity to learn about different cultures, try new cuisine, and be exposed to a bigger world on your doorstep. And as

Canada opens its doors even wider in the future, the cultural change will accelerate with continued diversification. Yes, these changes will be mostly in our urban areas, but some effects will be felt everywhere.

If you buy into this vision of Canada—as most of our political, business, and cultural elites do—all will be well. However, as we've seen in too many places in the world, including the United States, the journey can be fraught with peril. **The biggest driver of populism in the world today is pushback against the demographic and cultural changes brought about by immigration. We would be foolish to believe that Canada is immune to it.** Expect immigration to be a hot-button issue for some time to come.

# CHAPTER 18

# *Winning the Future*: Ten Key Strategies

Canada is experiencing a population shock. Over the next couple of decades, we will transform into an older, more female, more ethno-culturally diverse, more western, and more suburban country than the one we know today. But what does all this mean for our day-to-day lives? Who will our neighbours be? What will our households look like? What sports will we play and watch? What music will we listen to? What restaurants will we visit? Which cultural markers will grow or fade away? How will our grocery shopping change? How will our community infrastructure adapt? What should we invest in? Where should we build? Whom should we recruit? What should we sell? Which programs should we fund? Who will dominate the market-place and the public square? What will "Canadian" even mean?

While every person and organization will have their own take on how the population shock will affect them, the following key take-aways are a good place to start.

## Focus on the Perennials

Boomers and their parents (basically, everyone 55 and older today) will dominate both the marketplace and our electoral politics for the next two decades. Perennials have the numbers, and they have most of the money, but they aren't feeling the love from a world obsessed with youth. It's time to stop ignoring them. They will be Canada's enduring mainstream market. The challenge going forward, for both businesses and governments, will be to increase the engagement of Perennials in both the economy and society in general.

Learn from the concert promoters who put on Desert Trip and adapt what you're doing to get older customers in the door. The pay-off can be huge. This isn't about a seniors' specialty market, although that will grow too. It's more about understanding that the mainstream is changing, and the sweet spot in the market is older than too many businesses assume. Look at what you're offering through the eyes of an older consumer. Are you excluding them from your restaurant or store because you haven't considered their access issues? Is the font in that awesome app you're directing customers to use too small for older eyes? Are you playing music in your store for the Gen Z kid at the cash or the customer with the cash? Little things can make a big difference.

## Remember that Women Will Dominate Canadian Life

Women at both ends of the age spectrum are becoming independent and powerful actors. They will increasingly be making major commercial decisions based on what is good for them personally, as opposed to what's good for their kids and spouses. Fewer of them will have kids and spouses to think about. The emerging power segment in the marketplace will be female Perennials. They have the numbers and the financial resources to have a significant impact on the market-place. But they are invisible in most marketing campaigns. When was the last time you saw a political party focus its campaign strategy on appealing to older women? When was the last time you saw an ad featuring an older woman in a mainstream context? Organizations need to stop ignoring older women, or they will miss an important opportunity to grow.

A growing segment of the population is older women living on their own. The image of poverty and loneliness that just popped into your head applies to only a minority of them. Most are happy, healthy, engaged with the world, and relatively affluent. What do you have for them to buy? If you're a renovator, most seniors want to stay in their family home if they can. What can you build to help them do that? If you're a real estate developer, older (and younger) single women are big buyers of real estate. What design features can you incorporate into your project that work specifically for them? If you sell fresh produce and other perishable items, what options are there for health-conscious older women who want fresh food but live alone in a small condo? What about services such as home and outdoor maintenance, dry cleaning, and transportation, staffed by women to promote feelings of safety and connection? If you're a charity organization, you're undoubtedly short on volunteers. Don't recruit Millennials—go after their moms and grandmas.

## Acknowledge the Challenges Affecting Boys and Men

While Canada's women and girls are making impressive strides in personal empowerment—especially in education and employment—the statistics for Canada's boys and men are grim and getting worse. Canadian males are having a hard time adjusting to the transformation of our country, and particularly our economy, in the twenty-first century. To the extent we talk about gender issues in Canada these days, there's almost no focus by anyone in authority on the plight of boys and men. The biggest challenge here is for our education and health-care providers. How do we help men get the education they need to be successful in the transitioning economy? How do we keep them from dying before their time?

## Engage with the Millennial Malaise

Connecting with Millennials starts with ditching the easy stereotypes and accepting their truth. Life for them is a grind. All their adult life decisions have been delayed or disrupted. What's the opportunity, then? Discovering a way to help them meet their arrested life goals. What Millennials want is not dissimilar from what our older generations wanted: a good career, an affordable home in a great neighbourhood, the ability to raise a family, and the potential for an affordable retirement. How each of these goals is achieved might be different for Millennials than for previous generations, but the means don't change the ends. Finding creative ways to help Millennials meet their life goals is a big opportunity for businesses and will be an increasing challenge for governments.

Let's start with homes. We need a big rethink of residential options in our biggest cities. Millennials need affordable housing options in desirable neighbourhoods. Our cities need the economic dynamism and vitality Millennials bring. Our environment and kids need parents to spend less time in cars commuting to work. Businesses that have creative solutions to the housing problem have a hot future ahead of them.

The next issue is debt, including both student debt and mortgage debt. Millennials need businesses and governments to come up with more creative solutions to get younger people into advanced education (which our economy needs) and into adequate family housing (which Millennials need to start a family). We must find new ways to finance education and mortgages. Our borrowing markets were designed for a different demographic epoch. Baby Boomers already have the assets they need and aren't going to be taking on debt at the rate they did in the past. The new borrowers are Millennials, who have a different need profile than their parents and grandparents had. The price of education keeps going up, and the rules for residential mortgages keep getting tougher. Sure, our financial regulations may be taking the heat out of the housing market, but they are also taking the joy out of Millennial lives. The debt issue isn't going away. It will be an important and fractious political topic as we roll through the century.

One final issue for Millennials is employment. Employers need to realize that there are financial rewards in stability. Millennials are being trained to be disloyal, not because they are flighty or lack commitment, but because their employers have been disloyal to them. We are rapidly moving towards a seller's market for skilled workers. What Millennials are looking for is stable employment and advancement potential with a loyal employer. It's time to stop thinking of junior and intermediate workers as disposable expenses if the quarter is down a bit. Very soon you will need them more than they will need you. Robots can't do everything.

## Learn What It Means to Fly Solo

The fastest-growing and largest number of households in Canada are people living on their own. This fact has huge implications for what we build, what we sell, and how we service customers and citizens. It also affects our ability to create cohesive, functioning communities. What do you sell to people who live in one-bedroom condos or apartments in the suburbs or city? They have limited floor space. What are you making for them? It's time for an entirely new definition of "family size."

One big issue is storage. Singletons need to figure out where to store everything from power tools to sporting equipment, and from bulk groceries to family heirlooms. Flying solo and living in smaller spaces means many of us no longer have basements, garages, spare rooms, pantries and freezers in which to keep stuff out of sight and out of mind. The storage deficit is a big opportunity for urban rental storage companies, but a big problem for companies that sell the items we tend to tuck away and use only occasionally, if at all. It also represents an interesting challenge for developers, architects, and builders of the solo residences of the future. What economical storage solutions are possible?

We must also rethink the community facilities in our cities and suburbs. In the past, these facilities have mostly been designed around what families with kids need. The future will increasingly be about the needs of older singletons. For example, urban school boards will have a lot of unfilled schools they will have to either sell or repurpose. In their place, we must create new facilities that get older solo residents out of their homes and connected to the bigger world. Otherwise, social cohesion in our urban communities will be in big trouble.

## Plug into the Power of the Suburbs

If older women are the growing demographic power segment, then our growing geographic power segment is the suburbs. Canada is becoming a suburban nation. Our commerce will be dominated by the needs of suburbanites, and so will our politics. Mobility is the big issue, in every way you can look at it. Governments must create commuting options for suburban workers, but also help suburban seniors get around. Disputes over transportation issues between the downtowns of our major cities and their suburbs will dominate our politics.

What can business do for the suburbs? It starts with housing. Millennials need affordable places to live, especially after they start having kids. As crucial, though, will be addressing the needs of the Perennials who are staying put in their family homes. The suburbs are designed for people who are raising kids and driving everywhere. The infrastructure needs to adapt to support a population that, on average, will be older and less mobile. Businesses can come up with solutions that make it easier for people to take transit or walk to shopping, entertainment, and community facilities—or find a way to bring all these things to them. Delivery and transportation services in the suburbs are going to be huge.

New Canadians dominate Canada's suburbs and will be a greater share of the suburban population every year for the foreseeable future. Businesses that are interested in connecting with this new source of customers and employees must be a part of what's happening in the suburbs. That means on the ground and engaged. You want to build a new store? Ditch downtown and head for the 'burbs.

## Go West

Most of Canada's population growth is now in the West and in the suburbs of Toronto. If you want to plug into Canada's growing market, the western provinces—and especially their suburbs—will need to be an increasing part of what you do. That means if you're creating a new facility to service Canadian customers, the numbers will be pulling you west. It's the same for politics: winning in the West will be a bigger part of winning a national election.

Think about it. Do most important things in Canada really need to be located in Toronto, Montreal, or Ottawa? While it's convenient for the lifestyles of the Laurentian elite, it's terrible for Canada's national unity. As the population of the western provinces continues to grow throughout the century, the pressure for recognition will grow too. This won't be just a political issue; it will become a business issue. Businesses need to be where their customers are, both for convenience and to build affinity, trust, and loyalty. It's time to start thinking about whether you really need another store in Mississauga, or whether it's time to build something in Edmonton or Saskatoon.

## Support Diversity

Today, support for diversity is usually seen as a statement about the values of an organization. "We are good people because we believe in diversity." Diversity has become a necessity because we are running out of working-age people. It's a matter of numbers. The increasing skilled-labour shortage requires organizations to access all the potential talent pools—women, new Canadians, and older workers. We must embrace diversity, because we can't afford not to.

A significant rethink of the rules of the workplace is required. As just one example, what can we do to make it easier for working women who want to have children? In the past, women would start a family in their early 20s and spread out the time for any subsequent children, which meant thinking about maternity and work on a baby-by-baby basis. That's not what happens now. Working women today start their families in their early 30s, and, if they have multiple children, have them very close together. Yet all maternity plans are still structured on a baby-by-baby basis. There is a huge career and financial penalty for a woman who decides to have two kids close together. HR consultants, any ideas on creating a more holistic career family plan?

## Take Advantage of African Markets

Canada's biggest sources of immigrants are Pacific nations. But these countries are now experiencing the same population shock that started for Canada a couple of decades ago. Immigration is a young person's game. And China, India, and soon the Philippines are running out of young people. Which part of the world has above-replacement-level fertility and surplus young people? Africa. While the Pacific nations will continue to be important sources of immigrants for us in the near term, look for Nigeria and other African countries to start gaining on them over the longer term.

We have figured out how to tap into Pacific markets to access both employees and potential customers before their move to Canada. This strategy has worked well for companies that have tried it. Now, what about doing the same for African markets? Is anyone implementing the lessons from Asia to get a head start in Africa? There's a first mover's opportunity here for someone to take advantage of.

## Win the War for Public Trust

Because the composition of our population is changing, how organizations build trust with Canadians will change too. Without trust, little works in commerce, and almost nothing works in politics. Building trust isn't a question of technology; it's about connecting with the reality of people's lives. If you want to build trust in the suburbs or among Perennial women, for example, you need to know something about how these people live and what they desire. When was the last time you spoke to an older woman about her life? When was the last time you shopped in a suburban strip mall? For too many leaders of too many of Canada's most important organizations, which are mostly located in the downtowns of our big cities, I bet the answer is almost never. That will need to change if you want to win trust in the New Canada.

# Acknowledgements

This book has had a long gestation. I first started thinking about writing it in 2014. It's now January 2020. The reason it took so long is that what you are reading is not the book I originally set out to write. The original book was to be a quickly written version of a popular speech that I give to business and other audiences on the basic trends that will define Canada's future. The task seemed simple enough—put the speech between two covers and voilà, you have a book. But what I discovered as I tried to write that book was that my speech raised more questions than it answered about what is really going on in Canada. To do justice to the topic, I felt I needed to dig a lot deeper and think a lot harder than I had originally intended. The product of that additional digging and thinking is what you are now reading.

In addition to accepting that there was a need to dig and to think more, I also had to decide how I would reference the enormous amount of research I used to inform my analysis. I was determined that this would not be an academic book, weighted down with lots of footnotes, charts, and graphs. I wanted it to be a smooth, clean narrative that would be accessible to as wide an audience as possible. That's why there are no footnotes or extensive visual presentations of data. In the end, this was an easy decision to make, because almost all the data I used came from three sources: Statistics Canada, the United Nations Population Division (UNPD), and Ipsos. If I used data from another source, I've referenced it in the text.

I discovered that writing about demographic trends is frustrating, especially if the book takes as long to write as this one did. The numbers keep changing. Canada conducts a census every five years. This book took six years to write and uses data from the 2011 and 2016 censuses. The UNPD updates its numbers every two years. What's especially frustrating is that both Statistics Canada and the UNPD stagger their data releases, so the most recent data is not always available for every topic. There's a lot of data involved, and good analysis takes time. I have used the most recent data available to me at the time of writing. By the time you read this, there will be some numbers that are out of date because new data have been released. Also, in 2021, Statistics Canada will be conducting another census, so all that I've reported for 2011 and 2016 will be out of date by then.

Not to worry. The assurance I can offer is that what I have reported here will not have changed in any meaningful way. If anything, it will have accelerated in the predicted direction. My expectation is that the 2021 census will show that Canada's fertility rate has not appreciably risen, that the aging trend (along with longevity) has increased, that even more of our population growth has come from immigration, and that Canadians are continuing to congregate in the suburbs.

Another assurance I can offer is that, despite the recent politics associated with the census, the numbers that matter for my analysis have not been meaningfully affected. As you will remember, the Harper Conservatives cancelled the mandatory long-form census for

2011 and went with a voluntary methodology instead. For the record, at the time, I testified at the House of Commons that this should not have been done without running appropriate parallel tests to determine the impact of the voluntary methodology on the data. My view, both then and now, is that what the Harper government did to the census was capricious and cavalier.

I also testified, however, that while a voluntary long-form census was not ideal, the claims from critics that it was destroying Canada's statistical record were overstated. I said this for two reasons. The first is that the short-form census remained mandatory in 2011; only the long-form census became voluntary. The short form contains most of the key information for determining population trends: population counts, household composition, gender, age, marital status, and language. Second, the mandatory long-form census is not as statistically pristine as claimed by the Harper government's critics. The truth is that the mandatory long-form census isn't mandatory for all Canadians. In 2016, the long form was sent to a sample of one in five Canadian households. In 2011, the long form was sent to a third of Canadian households.

Leaving the politics aside, any statistician knows that a sample is never perfectly representative of a population. That includes the samples for both the mandatory (2016) and voluntary (2011) long-form censuses. That's why the short-form census, which is the only actual census (because it's the only form that every household was mandated to complete in both 2011 and 2016), has been used to fill in holes and adjust the results from the long-form census for both years. This is called data ascription, and it is a common technique used to compensate for missing data in any sample.

In truth, then, the 2016 long-form census was mandatory for only 20% of us. Even then, not everyone selected responded. Two percent didn't respond. And that 2% was not randomly distributed. Some specific, important groups have historically been notorious non-responders. For example, response rates from Aboriginal reserves are always well below the norm for the sample. And some respond-ers, even though it is illegal, systematically lie on the long form. For example, do you honestly believe that 20,000 Canadians practise "Jedi" as their religion?

I stand by today what I said to the House committee in 2012. The best of all worlds would be a voluntary census that Canadians feel a personal duty to respond to honestly. Maybe I'm an idealist, but I continue to believe this would give us the most accurate statistical portrayal of the country. However, the real question for this book is whether the switch from a voluntary to a mandatory long-form census impacted anything I have written here. I don't believe so. The trends I have catalogued were valid for 2011 and are confirmed again in 2016.

Leaving aside the struggles over statistics, this has been a com-plicated book to manage. There have been several stops, starts, and other difficulties along the way. All were deftly managed by my agent, John Pearce. This is my seventh book with John. I can't imagine trust-ing my writing endeavours to anyone else. In addition to John's sup-port, this book would not have been completed without continuous guidance and encouragement from my editor at HarperCollins, Jim Gifford. A special thanks to the wonderful editing team of Sue Sum-eraj and Natalie Meditsky. Their efforts were instrumental in making this a better book. While there were several times over the last six years when I thought I had met my match with this book, Jim always knew the right thing to say to get me back to my keyboard. Thanks to all of you.

My colleagues at Ipsos, especially Ipsos Public Affairs, had a big impact on this project. Not only did they challenge and improve my thinking, they were also an important source for the public opinion research that I reference. Special thanks go to Mike Colledge, Chris Martyn, Sean Simpson, and Gary Bennewies. Other Ipsos colleagues who influenced my thinking include Clifford Young, Trent Ross, Chris Jackson, Henri Wallard, and Bobby Duffy. And most importantly, Ipsos founder and CEO, Didier Truchot. Outside of Ipsos, those who influenced my thinking most include John Wright, John Ibbitson, Cal Bricker, Cole Bricker, and Joseph Bricker.

I must also thank Statistics Canada. While they have not been directly involved in this book, it would not have been possible without the excellent work of their researchers and analysts. Most of the data and trends I cite are from their reports. I hope I have done justice to their work. If not, the fault lies entirely with me.

Finally, this project would not have been possible without the love and understanding of my wife, Nina, and my daughter, Emily. Too many times, their needs have come second to my compulsion to keep writing. I didn't take time away from my day job to write this book. Instead, I stole nights, weekends, and holidays from my girls. That's why I dedicate this book to them.